How Offenders Transform Their Lives

How Offenders Transform Their Lives

Edited by

**Bonita M. Veysey, Johnna Christian
and Damian J. Martinez**

Routledge
Taylor & Francis Group

LONDON AND NEW YORK

First published by Willan Publishing 2009
This edition published by Routledge 2011
2 Park Square, Milton Park, Abingdon, Oxon OX14 4RN
711 Third Avenue, New York, NY 10017

Routledge is an imprint of the Taylor & Francis Group, an informa business

First published 2009

ISBN 978-1-84392-508-8 paperback
      978-1-84392-509-5 hardback

British Library Cataloguing-in-Publication Data

A catalogue record for this book is available from the British Library

Project managed by Deer Park Productions, Tavistock, Devon
Typeset by TW Typesetting, Plymouth, Devon

Contents

List of tables

Notes on contributors

Johnna Christian is Assistant Professor in the School of Criminal Justice at Rutgers University-Newark. She received her PhD in Criminal Justice from the University at Albany, State University of New York. In 2004 she was the National Institute of Justice W.E.B. Dubois fellow and conducted a study of family members' connections to incarcerated individuals. She is currently the Co-Principal Investigator of a research project evaluating family oriented reentry programs for juveniles. Dr Christian is also conducting a qualitative study of the process of identity transformation and recovery. She has published articles about prison visitation and the social and economic implications of family connections to prisoners. She recently co-authored a policy guide aimed at criminal justice agencies, community-based organizations, schools, and other stakeholders, with concrete strategies for addressing the needs of offenders' families in the reentry process.

M. Kay Harris is a member of the Graduate Faculty in the Department of Criminal Justice and an Affiliated Professor of Women's Studies at Temple University. She has conducted policy-oriented research on positive peer intervention and cognitive transformation, reducing jail and prison crowding, community corrections legislation, programs for women in the justice system, restorative and community justice, and judicial intervention in corrections. She teaches in the Inside-Out Prison Exchange Program and is an external member of the Steering Committee of the Lifers Public Safety Initiative at the State Correctional Institution at Graterford, PA. Previously Kay held positions with the National Council on Crime and Delinquency, the National Moratorium on Prison Construction, the American Bar Association's Resource Center on Correctional Law and Legal Services, the Attorney General of the United States, the National Advisory Commission on Criminal Justice Standards and Goals, and the federal Bureau of Prisons.

Bryn Herrschaft is a doctoral student in the School of Criminal Justice at Rutgers University-Newark. She received her bachelor's degree in psychology and sociology from New York University in 2003. Her research interests include reentry and offender change, women and the criminal justice system, prison culture, restorative justice, and gender and crime. Bryn is currently employed by the Center for Women and Work at Rutgers University-New Brunswick in the Evaluation Research Department that is currently responsible for several reentry initiatives and programs for women in the state of New Jersey.

Emma Hughes is Assistant Professor of Criminology at California State University, Fresno. She has an MPhil in Criminology from the University of Cambridge and earned her doctorate in Criminology from Birmingham City University (BCU) in the UK, where her research focused on prisoners' experiences of education. She has also worked as a lecturer at BCU, and has conducted research for British charities involved in educational and arts provision in prisons.

Russ Immarigeon, MSW, is editor of *Offender Programs Report*, *Community Corrections Report*, and *Women, Girls & Criminal Justice*, all published by the Civic Research Institute. He is also a contributing editor of *Crime Victims Report*, *Corrections Managers Report*, and *The ICCA Journal of Community Corrections*. He edited the volumes *Women and Girls in the Criminal Justice System: Policy Strategies and Program Options* (Civic Research Institute, 2006) and *Women and Girls in the Criminal Justice System, Vol. 2 Policy Strategies and Program Options* (Civic Research Institute, 2010). He also co-edited, with Shadd Maruna, the volume *After Crime and Punishment: Pathways to Offender Reintegration* (Willan Publishing, 2004). He currently serves as Town Court Justice in Hillsdale, New York.

Suzanne Kurth is Associate Professor in the Sociology Department at the University of Tennessee. She received her PhD from the University of Illinois, Chicago in 1971. Her areas of interest include social psychology, gender, sexual harassment, technological change in communications and social interaction/relationships.

Thomas P. LeBel is Assistant Professor in the Department of Criminal Justice in the University of Wisconsin-Milwaukee's Helen Bader School of Social Welfare. In 2006 he received his PhD from the School of Criminal Justice at the University at Albany, State University of New York. Tom is the author or co-author of articles and book chapters on prisoner reintegration, desistance from crime, prison reform, substance abuse treatment, and stigma. He has served as a consultant, panelist, and discussant for prisoner reentry related projects sponsored by the National Academy of Sciences-Committee on Law and Justice and the Urban

Institute. Currently, Tom is a Co-Investigator for the Supporting Jails in Providing Drug Abuse Services to Women Project, which is funded by the US Bureau of Justice Administration. The overall goal of this project is to improve motivation, access, and utilization of substance abuse services by women who are in jail and as they transition back to community living.

Damian J. Martinez is Assistant Professor in the School of Criminal Justice (with a joint appointment in the Department of Social Work) at Rutgers University-Newark. He holds a BA in sociology from the University of California at Los Angeles (UCLA), and an MA and PhD in social service administration at the University of Chicago. He has worked with high-risk and imprisoned youth and their families in a variety of settings, including the Alameda County Probation Department, Los Angeles County Probation Department, and State of Illinois Department of Corrections. In addition, Dr Martinez has been a social worker with a private foster family agency, the executive director of a non-profit youth social service agency, and the chief administrator and clinical consultant for an adult social service agency. He completed a research internship on incarcerated Hispanics in the Corrections Statistics Program at the Bureau of Justice Statistics, Office of Justice Programs, US Department of Justice. His publications and research have focused on adult incarcerated Hispanics; Latino former prisoner reentry; and informal support mechanisms in prisoner reentry and reintegration. These articles have appeared in the *Journal of Ethnicity in Criminal Justice, Columbia Human Rights Law Review, Journal of Offender Rehabilitation* and *Journal of Contemporary Ethnography*.

Shadd Maruna is Professor in Criminology at Queen's University Belfast. Previously, he had been a lecturer for four years at the University of Cambridge's Institute of Criminology, and before that was an assistant professor for three years in the School of Criminal Justice at the University at Albany, SUNY. He holds a PhD in Human Development and Social Policy from Northwestern University and his primary interest is in ex-prisoner reintegration. His first book, *Making Good: How Ex-Convicts Reform and Rebuild Their Lives* (American Psychological Association Books) was named the Outstanding Contribution to Criminology by the American Society of Criminology (ASC) in 2001. He is the co-editor of two new books with Willan Publishing on the subject of ex-prisoner coping and reintegration (*After Crime and Punishment*, 2004; *The Effects of Imprisonment*, 2005), and has recently co-authored the book *Rehabilitation* (Routledge, 2007) with Tony Ward.

Nick Mitchell has a long career working in addiction counseling and ex-prisoner reintegration work. He has also been an instructor in corrections for the School of Criminal Justice at the University at Albany, SUNY. He is the author of articles and chapters on the process of rehabilitation and desistance from crime, in journals including *Psychology, Crime and Law*. He has a Masters degree in Criminal Justice from the University at Albany.

Merry Morash is Professor at the School of Criminal Justice, Michigan State University. Her recent publications include *Gender, Crime, and Justice* (Sage, 2006), and articles on police stress and coping, domestic violence in immigrant groups, and women and girls who break the law. She is Director of the Michigan Victim Assistance Academy, which educates individuals who work with crime victims, and the Michigan Regional Community Policing Institute. Teaching areas include juvenile justice, criminological theory, and qualitative research.

Michelle Naples has over a decade of experience working in the public and private, non-profit sectors to improve services for adults and youth with mental health and substance abuse problems in the justice system. Her research interests include program evaluation, jail diversion/alternatives to incarceration, and treatment effectiveness. She holds a Masters in Public Policy and a Masters in Criminal Justice and is working towards her PhD in Criminal Justice from the University at Albany, SUNY.

Barbara Owen is a nationally-known expert in the areas of girls, women and crime, women-centered policy and women's prison culture. A Professor of Criminology at California State University, Fresno, she received her PhD in Sociology from UC Berkeley in 1984. Prior to returning to academia, Dr Owen was a Senior Researcher with the Federal Bureau of Prisons. She has provided training for the National Institute of Corrections in such areas as operational practice and agency planning for women offenders, staff sexual misconduct, women and community corrections and improving health care for women offenders. Dr Owen is the author of 20 articles and chapters, numerous technical reports and two books. She is currently working with The Moss Group on the Prison Rape Elimination Act, developing research and training pursuant to the Act and with the California Department of Corrections and Rehabilitation in their work on gender-responsive strategies for adult and juvenile female offenders.

Lois Presser is Assistant Professor of Sociology at the University of Tennessee. She holds a Bachelor's degree in Human Development and Family Studies from Cornell University, an MBA from Yale University, and a doctoral degree in Criminal Justice/Criminology from the University of Cincinnati. Prior to earning her PhD, Dr Presser worked for ten years in the criminal justice system in New York City. She worked with and on behalf of both offenders and victims of crime. Dr Presser's current research examines how offenders talk about their lives, their crimes and their experiences of justice. She has written several articles on the philosophy and practice of restorative justice. Her recent articles have appeared in *Crime & Delinquency, Justice Quarterly, Social Justice* and *Social Problems*. Currently she is developing a book that recounts narratives of moral struggle told by violent offenders.

Heather Tubman-Carbone is a doctoral student in the School of Criminal Justice at Rutgers University-Newark. She received her Masters from the London School of Economics and Political Science in Criminal Justice Policy in 2005. Her research interests are sex offender management, the role of victims in criminal justice policy, co-morbidity/co-occurring disorders, and the role of trauma. Heather is also currently employed by the Center for Women and Work at Rutgers University-New Brunswick in the Evaluation Research Department that is currently responsible for several reentry initiatives and programs for women in the state of New Jersey.

Bonita M. Veysey is Associate Professor in the School of Criminal Justice at Rutgers University-Newark. Prior to her employment at Rutgers, Dr Veysey was a senior research associate at Policy Research Associates in Delmar, New York. During that time she was the Director of the Women's Program Core and the Associate Director of the National GAINS Center and a primary researcher in the area of mental health–criminal justice systems interactions. Dr Veysey's research to date has focused on behavioral health and justice issues, including police interactions with persons with mental illnesses; mental health and substance abuse treatment in jails and prisons; diversion and treatment services for youth with behavioral health problems; and the effects of trauma. More recently, Dr Veysey has focused much of her attention on issues of recovery. Currently, she is conducting a qualitative study of transformation and recovery. She was the Co-Principal investigator of the Franklin County (MA) site of the SAMHSA-funded Women, Co-occurring Disorders and Violence Study, and was the Lead Evaluator on the CSAT-funded RECOVER Project also in Franklin County. She consults with local communities to help develop comprehensive peer-to-peer supports for people in recovery from addictions, physical and sexual abuse, and mental health problems.

Chapter 1

Identity transformation and offender change[1]

Bonita M. Veysey, Damian J. Martinez and Johnna Christian

The United States has now achieved a milestone unprecedented in its history. The recently released Pew Center on the States (2008) report estimates that 1 in 99 Americans are incarcerated in our nation's jails and prisons today. This represents over 2.3 million adults. If one considers not only those incarcerated on a given day, but also those who are admitted to prisons and jails over the course of a year, the numbers are staggering. Over 12 million Americans are booked into jails alone in any given year (Veysey, forthcoming). While 1 per cent of the population is horrific, these odds still represent a good bet to the average citizen. The non-incarcerated population may still rest assured that arrest and prison time will not intrude upon their lives. However, if one considers any time spent incarcerated, nearly 3 per cent of today's adults (1 in 37) have been incarcerated (Bonczar 2003). This 2001 statistic is expected to grow progressively worse over time. In fact, if incarceration rates remain the same, 6.6 per cent of people born in 2001 will be imprisoned at some time in their lives (Bonczar 2003).

Much of our sense of security comes from the recognition that persons arrested and sentenced to jails and prisons are not randomly selected from US society. They are disproportionately poor people, and they are largely people of color. These facts allow mainstream America to consciously and unconsciously assign them to the 'them' category, reassuring the 'us' category that we are morally superior. If there is, in fact, a 'them', then they are by necessity different from the 'us'. It should come as no surprise, then, that our investigations on offenders focus on their problems. We know that many offenders, particularly the incarcerated population, have serious health, addiction and mental health conditions. They also have poor educational and employment skills, marginal housing and often come from violent neighborhoods and dysfunctional families. They are, then, distinguishably different from the common notions of an average citizen.

This year, over 600,000 people will be released from prison (Visher and Travis 2003), and many millions will be returning to their communities from shorter stints in jails. Reentry is the current buzzword used to organize and control the panic that states and communities are now voicing. Reentry is concerned with providing released prisoners with the services and supports (and often correctional supervision) that are presumed necessary for their successful reintegration into their home communities. But reentry is not new. Reentry is after all the reason parole was created many years ago. Like the early conversation about parole, the discourse centers largely on the lamentable and often deplorable conditions in which offenders find themselves. It is a short step from the problem to the solution. Logically, if offenders have a particular set of identifiable disorders and challenges, remedying those problems should reduce criminality. However, this assumes that these problems are directly and causally related to the offender's criminal behavior – in the past and in the future. While research has demonstrated that certain pre-existing problems, such as drug addiction, are associated with criminal behavior, it is not clear that curing the addiction will result in a crime-free lifestyle. The way into criminality isn't necessarily the way out in reverse.

Correctional programming in many ways is no different from medical, psychiatric or substance abuse treatment. These formal interventions by nature are symptom-focused, and therefore, deficit-based. Ameliorate the symptom and the disease process is contained and managed, if not eliminated. Interestingly, many fields are beginning to understand the limitations of this narrow perspective, and have begun to focus more attention on the role of social contexts in which illness processes are embedded. Twenty years ago, Arthur Kleinman, MD (1988) stated that medicine plays two roles: control of disease processes and the management of the illness experience. More recently, Jack Coulehan, MD (2005) similarly stated that medicine plays both an instrumental and a symbolic role. Medicine provides direct medical interventions to produce positive health outcomes. More importantly, the diagnosis of illness and the ontological meaning of that illness are constructed in the physician/patient interaction. Coulehan goes on to say that how illness is embedded in the life narrative has important implications for recovery. Persons who believe they will recover or who have narratives that find positive meaning in the illness experience are more likely to survive life-threatening illnesses than those who don't. While it is unclear what physiological mechanisms are at work to produce this puzzling result, this same phenomenon is repeatedly observed in other disciplines, whether it is called a placebo effect, a Hawthorne effect, or is ascribed to unmeasured personal characteristics.

To this point, one of the more interesting facts cited by the European correctional evidence-based practices proponents comes from the psychotherapy literature (McNeill *et al.* 2005). A meta-analysis of this literature found that 40 per cent of 'success' was attributable to personal factors, 30 per cent to the therapeutic relationship, 15 per cent to expectancy or a placebo effect, and 15 per cent to the specific modality. Forty per cent, the person-specific attributes, are typically considered random factors. While studies included in the meta-analysis varied on the person-specific constructs measured (e.g. locus of control, self-efficacy), there is no consistent set of variables. The 'random' factors may, in fact, be systematic elements that remain unmeasured largely due to a lack of consensus regarding the importance of these variables in personal change. However, the importance of what people bring to the change endeavor cannot be underestimated.

In addition to the intangible personal resources that people bring with them the second most important factor is the human connection reflected in the therapeutic relationship. Fifteen per cent can be attributed solely to the belief that change can happen; that is, the placebo effect or expectancy factor. This leaves the remaining 15 per cent to the intervention itself. Yet in designing and implementing correctional and reentry programs, we disregard individuals' strengths, resources and desires (the 40 per cent), don't hire people who have excellent relational skills (the 30 per cent), don't believe that hope matters (the 15 per cent), and rely on the remaining 15 per cent to solve the problem. We throw away 85 per cent of the resources that could be mobilized to support formerly incarcerated persons in their efforts to become productive citizens.

Roles and identity transformation

Much of what every person does in his or her day-to-day activities is prescribed by self-perceptions of roles and the normative behaviors associated with those roles. These self-concepts and their attendant behaviors are reinforced continuously by those in the person's social networks. This is as true of a 'prisoner' role as it is for the role of 'mother'. Transformations of core identities require substantial shifts in self-understanding as well as significant effort in renegotiating interpersonal interactions. Theories developed in the 1960s and 1970s have great relevance to this topic of identity transformation: Goffman's (1963) conceptualization of stigma in particular. Symbolic interactionists and labeling theorists were interested in describing the manner in which people assume or are assigned deviant labels. While these theorists explain the pathway into negative identities, they did not explain the pathway out. In fact, Goffman (1963) suggests that once tainted, one could never regain normalcy unless the stigma could be hidden. Even so, the person was always at risk of discovery through the accidental use of interpersonal cues or being linked to someone from his or her past. Ebaugh (1988) generalized the aspects of these theories to describe all role transitions, positive and negative, and proposed a conceptual framework for role exit. While focusing on transitions in general, she acknowledges that the framework may be applied to transitions from negative to positive roles, such as addict to ex-addict, and for both voluntary and coerced exits, such as changing jobs or being arrested for the first time. The critical idea from her work is that role exit involves a period of dissatisfaction with the current role, weighing of alternative roles, a preliminary testing of a new role and the transition into the new role.

When applying these concepts to offenders, three predictable challenges to the change process emerge. First, when people make dramatic shifts in their primary identities, they may or may not be supported by their existing family and friendship networks. In order to sustain a new identity, a new network must be established. Second, available alternative roles may be limited. The number and nature of alternative roles are largely dependent on roles known to the individual, and, therefore, the breadth of possible roles may be limited due to a lack of exposure. Roles also may be limited by society's level of tolerance. We want people to stop being criminals, but we do not necessarily want them to teach in our schools or be our neighbors or bosses. Third, possessing a stigma of criminal (or addict or mentally ill person, for that matter) is a visible blemish on the fabric of the moral character. It is a small leap to form the link between immorality and lack of trustworthiness. Trustworthiness, however, is the collateral used to get a job, buy a house or babysit for a neighbor's child. Stigma discredits the individual and reduces trust. Thus, any trust extended will be minor, and the person's behavior in a new role will be highly scrutinized.

Formal justice interventions and personal change

Much of the discussion on offender change focuses on programs operated by community corrections agencies. Implicit in this is the ability to provide surveillance together with linkages to needed services. In many respects, community corrections is exactly the wrong place using the wrong people to achieve the wrong goals. Community corrections agencies (and custodial facilities as well) across the country operate under a risk and needs model. Using validated risk instruments, criminogenic needs are targeted to reduce recidivism and improve community safety. Here's the catch. Many of the criminogenic needs are related to personality structure. Humans are constantly in a state of flux, incorporating new experiences and knowledge into a largely stable set of personality traits and their attendant behaviors. All humans experience change. Every significant change is accompanied by a period of adjustment and stress. Behaviors may change, but the essence of the person persists. However, we believe that offenders must change core characteristics in order to remain crime-free. Somehow offenders are seen as essentially different and are expected to make dramatic changes not required of others who make life transitions. Maruna (2001), in *Making Good*, makes an interesting observation. Common personality characteristics that offenders exhibit, like anti-authoritarianism and risk-taking, that are directly related to criminal behavior are the very same characteristics that distinguish innovators. The challenge, therefore, is not to change personality traits (which are difficult to change in any event), but to maximize and redirect these traits to support positive roles.

Corrections professionals find themselves in the unenviable position of being both enforcer and helper. Some corrections staff persons are very good at engaging offenders in their own change process; others are abysmally poor. No standard exists for interpersonal skills, nor is there a priority placed upon hiring those with these skills. More importantly, the knowledge of how offenders remain crime-free resides within the offender community, not in the expert community. When asked, offenders can describe exactly how they changed and what they needed to sustain their change. Commonalities exist and generally reflect basic human needs: hope, people who believed in them, meaningful things to do. Rarely do the successful state that symptom control was key. Sometimes they say that treatment or programming had a positive effect, but often this had more to do with the relationship with the therapist or a specific corrections staff person than problem reduction.

The greatest criticism of corrections-based programs is that they operate under flawed assumptions, including: (1) offenders are essentially different from all other human groups; (2) reducing problems will reduce criminal behavior; (3) if services are made available, offenders will use them; and (4) services actually accomplish what they are designed to do. Even if we were able to create the perfect set of comprehensive and integrated services targeted to what former prisoners want and need, 'fixing' offenders' problems only brings them halfway back. Corrections and reentry programs may accomplish the role exit component, but do not address the role entry component. Telling someone to stop being criminal may work for a period of time, but that person needs a replacement identity, and this identity may be chosen only by the individual who is in the process of change. Only offenders can accomplish the changes necessary to become productive members of society. No matter how coercive or punitive, corrections can't do it, nor can treatment. The most these organizations can do is create the environments and conditions in which change is most likely to occur.

The importance of self-perception and life stories in the change process

This book presents a series of studies (mostly qualitative) that investigate individual identity transformation beyond offenders' criminal selves and how former or current prisoners change their lives from offender to pro-social, non-offending roles. The studies cover a broad range of topics including education, support network interactions and reciprocity, and moments of change. Through these studies, we provide evidence that engaging former and current prisoners in their own change process is more meaningful for rehabilitative and reentry measures than is using external, formal programmatic measures to 'fix' them. To a large extent the book captures the difference between the risk, needs, responsivity and the good lives models described by Ward and Maruna (2007). The former approach relies on formal interventions and expertise and emphasizes a reduction of offending behavior as the primary measure of success. The latter is concerned with building meaningful lives and changing the factors that are most problematic from the offender's perspective. Moreover, many of the contributors draw from a strengths-based perspective which 'begins with the assumption that ex-convicts are stigmatized persons, and implicitly that this stigma (and not some internal dangerousness or deficit) is at the core of what makes ex-convicts likely to reoffend' (Maruna and LeBel 2003: 97). Working from this assumption, the contributors to the book illuminate the various ways that former offenders exercise agency in resisting such stigma and creating a sense of self that promotes and sustains change.

Much of the previous work in this area draws from studies based in the United Kingdom. In response, this book emphasizes research in the United States and selectively includes studies from the United Kingdom that complement the focus. It is vital that questions of transformation and internal change be applied in the United States because the scale of incarceration is unmatched anywhere else in the world (Pew Center on the States 2008), and the history of the marginalization of racial and ethnic minorities creates structural barriers to transformation that interact with the internal mechanisms of change. Moreover, the work in this volume highlights the perspective of the men and women who are currently or formerly incarcerated. Each piece provides an empirical analysis of the interaction between current or former prisoners and innovative pro-social programs and networks, which are grounded in the most current theoretical work about individual transformation and change.

This introductory chapter introduces the reader to the primary concepts of social roles, the effects of stigma on the ability of individuals to negotiate positive roles and identities, and the challenges faced by offenders as they adjust to community life after incarceration. To give the reader a sense of the material covered and the interrelatedness of each chapter, we outline the general substance and focus of each of them. The following chapters are organized into three broad areas of concentration: the nature of identity transformation (Chapters 1 to 3), the role of programs, families and social support on the transforming self (Chapters 4 to 8), and how reformed peers use their ex-identity in service to others (Chapters 9 and 10). The book concludes with a chapter on the policy implications of these studies and ideas.

Many fields are beginning to ask similar questions about the nature of change: from illness to wellness, from addiction to recovery; from criminal to citizen. Essential to all of these discussions is the concept of identity transformation. What all of these perspectives share is: (1) the limitations of formal systems to change individuals, (2) the importance of personal identity embedded in a cultural or personal narrative, (3) a reduced emphasis on deficits, (4) the role of the social context in defining the problem and the solution, and (5) the importance of role identity in illness and wellness. What is not known are the mechanisms of identity transformation and the necessary and sufficient conditions under which transformation is possible. In Chapter 2, Christian, Veysey, Herrschaft and Tubman-Carbone explore these issues based on a study identifying shared themes and elements of transformation narratives of formerly incarcerated people and persons in other stigmatized groups.

The study of desistance from crime has come of age in recent years, and there are now several competing theories to account for the ability of long-term offenders to abstain from criminal behavior. Most prominently, recent explanations have borrowed elements from informal social control theory, differential association theory, and cognitive psychology. In Chapter 3, Maruna, LeBel, Mitchell, and Naples argue that labeling theory may be a neglected factor in understanding the desistance process. Drawing on interview data collected as part of a study of an offender reintegration program, they illustrate how the idea of the 'looking-glass self-concept' is a useful metaphor in understanding the process of rehabilitation or recovery in treatment programs.

Continuing the theme of shedding negative identities into pro-social ones, Martinez examines newly freed prisoners' reintegration into family life and the actual process of interaction between former prisoners and their family members in Chapter 4. In addition, he investigates how former prisoners and their family members renegotiate their respective roles and how such renegotiation potentially affects the (bidirectional) exchange of various forms and levels of support in both perceived and real terms. He addresses and examines these issues using primary data collected from the Evaluation Project of the Illinois Going Home Program as part of the US Department of Justice's Serious and Violent Offender Reentry Initiative. The study collected information through in-depth interviews with a sample of nine dyads of former prisoners and their corresponding family members. The findings give insight into how former prisoners return to their family members, how the roles in their relationships can be clarified, and how specific forms of support can be matched and exchanged to help ease the transition from prison to home.

In Chapter 5, Presser and Kurth consider how ex-convicts narrate themselves with multiple, active interlocutors. Data were drawn from a university class session during which James, an African-American gay man with a criminal record, told his personal story. James' narrative shifted with the discursive challenges of his interlocutors. James variably asserted and denied agency and moral reform, all the while emphasizing his cunning in triumphing over oppression. The analysis extends the understanding of the construction of narrated identities and resistance to subjugation through discourse. It also highlights the strategic, intersectional and performative nature of self-narrative.

This self-narrative is analyzed further by Hughes in Chapter 6 as she examines the role that prisoner education can play in encouraging the development of new identities among prisoners and considers the implications for post-release decision-making. The qualitative research is based on 47 interviews with prisoner-students engaged in education programs in UK prisons. The study assesses the effect that education has on the prisoners' self-perceptions, their experiences of prison, their social interactions inside and outside of the prison, and considers the effect that this can have on the development of pro-social identities such as 'student'. Her chapter explores the consequences of these new identities for post-release intentions, including the desire to continue education and to find work related to their studies. Consideration is also given to the students' previous life experiences, including exposure to education. The decision to undertake education in prison is examined in this context. For some students, as the research indicates, the decision to begin prison-based education, and the self-described benefits gained from studying, signal what can potentially be viewed as a turning point in their lives. While acknowledging the myriad factors that may disrupt their plans, education nevertheless offers the students possible scripts to follow post-release.

In Chapter 7, Owen describes the experiences of women as they negotiate an in-prison drug treatment program. Based on extensive ethnographic interviewing, these accounts detail initial resistance to such change, skepticism at the effectiveness of the program and, for some, epiphanies about the possibilities of changing identity. While other women persist in holding on to their identity of 'dope fiend', Owen also describes the change as some women come to understand the goals of the program and their acceptance of the need to change. The chapter concludes with descriptions of the women's vision for the future as they prepare to return to the free world.

Upon reentering the new free world, women released from prison and jail enter complex environments that include parole supervision, mandated and self-selected treatment, educational and work skill and placement programs, and reconnection with family, friends and intimate partners. It is within these contexts that Morash, in Chapter 8, examines the interrelatedness between parole supervision and the law-abiding, sober self in a qualitative analysis of parole officers' case notes and 50 women offenders' interviews during the year after release from jail or prison. Her investigation describes the ways that parole supervision influenced interactions that affirmed (or denied) the law-abiding, sober self. All the women had a recent history of substance abuse, and their use and addiction to drugs was largely responsible for their illegal acts. Women differed in their search for, and their acceptance of or resistance to, interactions that affirmed or disconfirmed a pro-social self. The analysis describes the styles of parole supervision that promoted the different outcomes, and the agency of women offenders to circumvent supervision of any type; that is, that supported or that contradicted the law-abiding, sober self.

In Chapter 9, Harris draws on her investigation of a transformation model of identity change developed and advanced by a group of incarcerated men, the LIFERS, Inc. Public Safety Initiative (PSI) at the State Correctional Institution at Graterford, Pennsylvania. Crafted as an alternative to professionally driven models of correctional rehabilitation, this grassroots approach aims to achieve new ways of thinking among individuals who are or have been active in street crime through positive peer intervention. The findings are drawn from structured, in-depth interviews with incarcerated men who designed, facilitated, and/or experienced the PSI transformation process. The chapter describes the model and its core values and goals. It also explores what transformation has meant to participants, according to their self-reports.

The obstacles and mechanisms through which formerly incarcerated persons transform their lives is the focus of LeBel's analysis in Chapter 10. He refers to the concept of 'identity politics', which has been used to refer to social movements that seek to alter societal conceptions of stigmatized persons. Today, formerly incarcerated persons are 'coming out' to lead and/or join advocacy groups to confront the stigma faced by prisoners and former prisoners in society. Advocacy/activism of this sort involves proactive and collective attempts on the part of stigmatized persons to change public perceptions and create a more positive identity. In his analysis, LeBel used a sample of approximately 230 formerly incarcerated persons participating in prisoner reentry programming in New York State. His chapter focuses on the development of an advocacy/activism scale in which higher scores indicate support for and/or involvement in actions to improve the public's perception and treatment of prisoners and former prisoners. The relationship between the advocacy/activism scale and measures for demographics, criminal history, perceptions of stigma, social bonds, social identity as a former prisoner, and program-related items is examined in this quantitative analysis. These analyses identify the characteristics of formerly incarcerated persons that are associated with this proactive coping orientation.

The final chapter synthesizes findings from the chapters in the volume and presents a set of policy recommendations stemming from this overview. The current approach to policy in the area of formal offender rehabilitation programs and prisoner reentry emphasizes the need to deliver services and programs that offenders will use upon release from prison. While these are crucial aspects of successful reentry, this volume has emphasized the internal mechanisms and how those are related to the innovative change efforts that the offenders experience. It is the combination of these factors – that is, the provision of basic resources necessary to live in the community upon release from prison and the acquisition of the social supports and tools needed for the identity shifts – that better explain the complex process of how offenders transform their lives beyond the criminal self.

Note

1 Some passages in this chapter are based on B. M. Veysey (2008) 'Rethinking reentry' in *The Criminologist*, 33(3): 1, 3–5, and we are grateful to the American Society of Criminology for their permission to draw on this.

References

Bonczar, T. P. (2003 *Prevalence of Imprisonment in the U.S. Population, 1974–2001*, Bureau of Justice Statistics Special Report NCJ197976. Washington, DC: U.S. Department of Justice, Office of Justice Programs.

Coulehan, J. (2005) 'Empathy and narrativity: A commentary on "Origins of healing: An evolutionary perspective of the healing process"', *Families, Systems, & Health*, 23, 261–5.

Ebaugh, H. R. F. (1988) *Becoming an Ex: The Process of Role Exit*. Chicago: University of Chicago Press.

Goffman, E. (1963) *Stigma: Note on the Management of Spoiled Identity*. Englewood Cliffs, NJ: Prentice-Hall.

Kleinman, A. (1988) *The Illness Narratives: Suffering, Healing and the Human Condition*. New York: Basic Books.

McNeill, F., Batchelor, S., Burnett, R. and Knox, J. (2005) *21st Century Social Work. Reducing Re-offending: Key Practice Skills*. Glasgow: Social Work Inspection Agency.

Maruna, S. (2001) *Making Good: How Ex-convicts Reform and Rebuild Their Lives*. Washington, DC: American Psychological Association.

Maruna, S. and LeBel, T. (2003) 'Welcome home? Examining the "Reentry Court" concept for a strengths-based perspective', *Western Criminology Review*, 4(2): 91–107.

Pew Center on the States (2008) *One in 100: Behind Bars in America 2008*. Washington, DC: The Pew Charitable Trusts.

Veysey, B. M. (forthcoming) 'Management and treatment of women diagnosed with mental illnesses in US jails', in B. L. Levin, A. K. Blanch and A. Jennings (eds) *Women's Mental Health Services: A Public Health Perspective*. Thousand Oaks, CA: Sage Publications.

Visher, C. A. and Travis, J. (2003) 'Transitions from prison to community: Understanding individual pathways'. *Annual Review of Sociology*, 29: 89–113.

Ward, T. and Maruna, S. (2007) *Rehabilitation: Beyond the Risk Paradigm*. London: Routledge.

Chapter 2

Moments of transformation: formerly incarcerated individuals' narratives of change

Johnna Christian, Bonita M. Veysey, Bryn Herrschaft and Heather Tubman-Carbone

Introduction

Conviction and imprisonment are life experiences with profound implications for an individual's future life chances (Garland 2001; Western 2006). Formerly incarcerated people face systemic barriers to their full integration into society such as laws limiting where they can live and the types of jobs they can hold (Travis 2002), as well as labeling that leads to stigma and rejection (Goffman 1963; Maruna *et al.* 2004). Research demonstrates that the likelihood of employment and marriage are diminished when a person has been incarcerated (Huebner 2005; Lopoo and Western 2005), and that social ties, particularly those to family members, may also suffer (Edin *et al.* 2004). We have reason to be particularly concerned about such consequences of imprisonment in the United States as the rate of incarceration has more than doubled in 20 years from 313 per 100,000 residents of the population incarcerated in state and federal prisons and local jails in 1985 to 750 per 100,000 residents in 2006 (Pastore and Maguire 2007). Indeed, Travis (2002) contends that the scale of imprisonment in the United States has led to the social exclusion of nearly entire classes of citizens who face invisible punishments even after their prison sentence has ended.

Despite these barriers, people do successfully rebuild their lives after a period of imprisonment, confronting a number of challenges such as histories of substance abuse, trauma and mental health problems. How such individuals describe events in their lives and what they have learned from them illuminate important questions such as how formerly incarcerated people identify problematic areas of life that need to be changed, what specifically they do in the process of change, and what they learn as a consequence of positive life changes. Moreover, once change has been made, offender narratives of reform help to understand how change is sustained and reinforced.

Traditionally, the criminal justice system has answered such questions by focusing on criminal behavior, managed through a control narrative of minimizing risk, or a support narrative centered on the needs related to criminal behavior (Maruna and LeBel 2003). Concern about the various dimensions of positive and fulfilling lives for people who have been incarcerated has been limited until recently as scholars have begun to challenge more narrow views of offending and desistance from offending (Maruna 2001; National Research Council 2008). Following a more nuanced view of desistance, simply living a crime-free life is not an adequate marker of success. Instead, formerly incarcerated individuals may have a range of desires and goals that signify a fulfilling life (Maruna and LeBel 2003).

To further explore these issues, our study centers on how meaningful change is defined by people who have been incarcerated and what they have learned from their positive experiences. We do not assume that offending behavior takes on primary salience, but want to know how incarceration is situated among a range of life events, since formerly incarcerated individuals often have other life-shaping experiences including addiction, mental illness and histories of violence (National Research Council 2008). Our study recruited participants who self-identified as having one or more of the following experiences, including addiction, psychiatric treatment, physical or sexual abuse, and incarceration. We asked them to provide a narrative account of a positive experience in their lives and what they learned from this experience. We were interested in how participants framed their primary understanding of their problems, the catalysts for change, and their status at the end of the process. In this chapter, we describe the process of positive transformation for individuals who have been incarcerated, situating the experience within the context of a larger life narrative. Through their stories, we learn how people navigate beyond the barriers to successful lives after a period of incarceration.

Previous research

The way scholars and policy-makers conceptualize the desired changes and indicators of success for people who have been incarcerated have been shaped by larger philosophical shifts in correctional philosophies (Seiter and Kadela 2003; Ward and Maruna 2007). The move from a medical model of corrections, dominant until the 1960s and focused on program provision and rehabilitation, to a more punitive era concerned primarily with incapacitation and deterrence, meant that parole agents were charged with monitoring behavior and detecting violations, rather than guiding parolees in rebuilding their lives and integrating into their families and communities (Seiter and Kadela 2003; National Research Council 2008). The outcome of this approach has been a strong emphasis on offending behavior and risk assessment/management, but scholars and policy-makers are increasingly recognizing the limitations of such an approach.

For example, in outlining the desired outcomes of prisoner reentry, the National Research Council Committee on Community Supervision and Desistance from Crime stated,

> one can think of completely successful reentry [from prison to the community] as a person's having a place to live, a job, not committing crimes, and otherwise being a fully integrated member of a community. At the other end of the continuum, one can think of homelessness, unemployment, and the violation of the terms of parole or the commission of new crimes as characteristic of failed reentry. (National Research Council 2008: 14)

Further, the committee suggested that one limitation of the term recidivism is that it 'implies a simple 0 or 1 outcome: either a person is returned to prison or not; yet desistance from criminal behavior, like cessation of smoking or drug use or even dieting, may involve several attempts over time' (National Research Council 2008: 15). These statements recognize that making life changes after a period of incarceration is in fact a process, and that the desired outcomes are not easily compartmentalized and vary substantially from person to person. The committee's statements also reinforce a change among criminal justice professionals who, like those in the treatment fields, are advocating strengths-based approaches to prisoner reentry (Maruna and LeBel 2003).

Other scholars have explored what types of life changes are needed for formerly incarcerated persons to be successful, and how specifically people go about making them. On this point, Giordano et al. (2002) contrasted their cognitive analysis of desistance with Sampson and Laub's (1993) social control model. The former centers on cognitive shifts related to openness to change, the availability of 'hooks for change', the development of a new self, and a shift in perspectives about a former deviant lifestyle. In examining gender differences in the desistance process, Giordano et al. (2002) found more similarities than differences in men's and women's narrative accounts, with the most prominent hooks for change centered on formal organizations such as prison and treatment or religion and intimate relationships with children or marital partners.

In the shift from desistance-centered research to investigations based upon personal strengths, agency and cognitive transformations, life narratives have taken an important and prominent role largely because change is complex and highly individualistic and narratives are an especially powerful vehicle for understanding movement from one societal status to another (Ebaugh 1988; Gadd and Farrall 2004; Maruna 2001; Singer 2004; Vaughan 2007). In explaining why they centered their analysis on the concept of 'hooks for change', Giordano *et al.* (2002: 1000) offer the following:

> [W]e wish to emphasize the actor's own role in latching onto opportunities presented by the broader environment. Second, we recognize that actors' accounts within a narrative or life history will not access the full array of influences that literally produced successful changes. Instead, like novels, situation comedies, or grant proposals, narratives (here, narratives of change) have hooks – shorthand ways to describe what seems essential from the communicator's point of view.

This excerpt describes several important points we wish to explore further in the present research, including the capacity for formerly incarcerated people to exercise agency in the process of life change and the role of narratives in uncovering the nature and form of such change.

Methodology

The methodology builds upon a study conducted by Professor Noreen Graf, University of Texas-Pan American. In the '100 Words/100 Women' study, participants were recruited using snowball sampling via e-mail transmission. The goal was to collect 100 words related to sexual abuse from 100 women around the country. Participants were asked 'to write 100 words about your experiences with sexual abuse victimization. It will be up to you to decide what is most important to write about, such as how you feel, or what happened to you in the past, or what is happening currently.' This basic methodology was adapted to examine change experiences for people with a multitude of stigmatized experiences, including incarceration. We were interested in the ways incarceration intersected with other life experiences and how people conceptualized positive life changes in relation to these experiences.

Sampling frame

Individuals from four stigmatized (and often overlapping) groups (i.e. mentally ill, addict/alcoholic, victim/survivor, criminal) were identified through existing lists of experts, including meeting participants in

15

Substance Abuse and Mental Health Services Administration (SAMHSA) (i.e. federally sponsored) meetings. SAMHSA's commitment to substantial involvement of persons with lived experience guarantees that a significant proportion of attendees at some point in their lives have struggled with one or more of these problems. Because they also have achieved great stature in the field, they are likely to have successfully overcome or successfully manage their identified problem. These lists reflect participants in the Center for Mental Health Services (CMHS) Recovery Summit, the Center for Substance Abuse Treatment (CSAT) Recovery Summit, and the Dare to Vision Conference focused on persons with histories of physical and /or sexual abuse.[1]

Recruitment[2]

A request for participation was sent to 406 individuals via e-mail (CMHS=63, CSAT=112, Dare to Vision=221). The e-mail invitation briefly described the project and some research protections. It also included a link to the web-based survey. The introduction embedded in the survey fully explained human subjects protections and response to the web-based survey constituted consent.

Data collection

The study asked two open-ended questions: (1) 'Please describe an experience that changed your life in a positive way', and (2) 'How did this influence your later life?' The survey also included a checklist of all four identities that might apply and minimal demographic information (e.g. gender, race/ethnicity and age). The open-ended questions were purposefully vague. The questions were asked in a general way so as not to focus the participants' attention on the stigmatized role and allow them to highlight the most salient life events.

Moments of transformation study

The following sections present the demographic characteristics of the participants and the self-identified group membership distributions.

Participants

Thirty-seven individuals responded to the survey. This represents an unknown percentage of possible participants. Of the 406 persons who were sent the invitation, approximately 50 per cent or 203 persons were estimated to be eligible. This is based on the estimate that 50 per cent of attendees of the SAMHSA-sponsored meetings were invited because of their expertise based in lived experience. Therefore, 37 participants would

Table 2.1 Characteristics of all and formerly incarcerated participants

Variable	All (n=37) %	FI (n=8) % (n)
Demographics		
% Female	77.1	62.5 (5)
Age group		
% 20s	5.7	0
% 30s	8.6	12.5 (1)
% 40s	37.1	37.5 (3)
% 50s	37.1	25.0 (2)
% 60s	11.4	25.0 (2)
Racial/ethnic identity		
% African-American/Other Black	14.3	37.5 (3)
% Asian	5.7	0
% Caucasian	60.0	25.0 (2)
% Hispanic	5.7	12.5 (1)
% Native American/Pacific Islander	0	12.5 (1)
% Mixed	8.6	12.5 (1)
% Other	5.8	0
Experiences		
% Addiction	65.7	87.5 (7)
% Psychiatric treatment	62.9	75.0 (6)
% Physical and/or sexual abuse	62.9	50.0 (4)
% Incarceration	22.9	100.0 (8)
Number of life experiences		
% One only	31.4	0
% Two	34.3	37.5 (3)
% Three	22.9	12.5 (1)
% All four	11.4	50.0 (4)

reflect a minimum of 18.2 per cent response rate; small, but not inconsistent with other surveys of this nature. Of the total participants, eight people had been incarcerated.

Table 2.1 presents the sample characteristics for all participants as well as those for the persons who acknowledged being incarcerated. In the full sample, most of the participants (77 per cent) were female. Age was grouped into decades. Six per cent of participants were in their twenties, 9 per cent in their thirties, 37 per cent in their forties, 37 per cent in their fifties and 11 per cent in their sixties. Sixty per cent identified as Caucasian, 14 per cent as African-American, 6 per cent Hispanic, 6 per cent Asian and 9 per cent as being of mixed race/ethnicity. An additional 6 per cent stated 'other'.

Of the total participants, 66 per cent acknowledged having an addiction, 63 per cent had noted psychiatric treatment, 63 per cent had acknowledged having been physically and/or sexually abused, and 23 per cent indicated incarceration was among their experiences. Thirty-one per cent identified with only one category, while 11 per cent acknowledged having experiences across all four categories.

Table 2.1 also presents the sample characteristics for the formerly incarcerated participants. Similar to the full sample, over half of the formerly incarcerated participants were female. Half of these participants were 50 years of age or older. The most notable difference between the full sample and the formerly incarcerated sample was the percentage of non-Caucasian participants. Only two of the eight were Caucasian, with three African-Americans and the others identifying as Hispanic, Native American, and mixed race/ethnicity.

Of the formerly incarcerated participants, seven of the eight acknowledged having an addiction, six noted psychiatric treatment, and four acknowledged having been physically and/or sexually abused. Similar to the full sample, when one problem is present it is not unusual for others to be as well. Half of the formerly incarcerated participants identified with all four experiential categories. It is here where gender differences emerge. Each of the three men noted only one problem status in addition to incarceration, while four of the five women noted all three additional statuses (and the remaining woman noted two).

Theme development

The study explores, through participants' personal narratives of transformation, both why and how formerly incarcerated people changed their lives in a positive way, and what they learned from the experience. More specifically, it investigates how people framed their identities, whether their primary identities were implicitly or explicitly tied to the different life experiences (addiction, psychiatric treatment, survivor/victim of physical or sexual abuse, incarceration) selected in closed-ended portions of the survey, and how their understanding of their problems shaped their approaches to change.

The following description of the theme development was derived from the full study (see Veysey and Christian, under review). Narratives are comprised of content and structure. The narrative content contains themes that are shared across participants, as well as unique and nuanced particulars. The structure of the narratives follows the general pattern of: (1) I was here, (2) I had this problem, (3) this event/experience occurred that changed or resolved the problem, and (4) I am now here as a result.

To analyze the structure of the narratives, a coding scheme was developed that followed the basic logic of the story, including (1) presentation of initial identity, (2) identification of the problem, (3) description of the transformative event, and (4) presentation of the emergent self. These stages of the narrative encompass important dynamics in the change process. Codes were assigned to ensure categories were not imposed where they were neither stated nor clearly inferred. The specific words and ways people described the events of change, as well as the life events preceding change, were central to the analysis.

The coding was conducted by the two lead evaluators independently and then compared. In the event of a disagreement, the narrative was reviewed together to refine the coding scheme. All narratives were then reviewed and coded a final time. The four stages/categories are described below.

Presentation of initial identity
Initial identity referred to how participants described themselves before the positive event that transformed their lives. While the closed-ended survey questions at the conclusion of the survey allowed participants to identify previous life experiences, the written narratives allowed them to describe transformative experiences outside these boundaries and, thus, identify the aspects of their lives that were most salient to them. For example, one woman began her narrative with, 'After years of drinking and using drugs, I entered a TC (therapeutic community) only to relapse after being clean for 30 months.' Her story and, therefore, her identity are couched within the confines of an addiction-recovery narrative. Other life experiences may be mentioned to provide detail or context to the narrative, but they do not change the centrality of the addiction-recovery narrative or of the individual's presentation of self.

Identification of the problem
The participants' understanding of the problem (that was resolved in the course of the narrative) was also coded. In most cases, the initial identity and the problem is linked. In some cases the two variables differed. For example, one participant began, 'I was a teenaged runaway. I got into prostitution . . .' She began her narrative here, but the change revolved around her addiction and how she was finally able to become clean and sober. Thus, among the many identities she could have claimed, the addict identity was the problematic one and the one that was the focus of the transformation. Participants' understanding of their problem was coded into eight general categories, including the four target statuses of interest.

Moments of transformation
What we call the 'moment' of transformation encompasses many possible elements. The moment of transformation is the central focus of this study. There is an assumption that when individuals provide a narrative, no piece of information is superfluous. In reviewing this part of the narrative, in addition to content, other elements appeared regularly, including (1) whether the transformation was tied to a specific event or was a process,

(2) whether the catalyst for change came from within the individual or from an external source, and (3) whether the change involved a description in how the person thinks about the self, the problem or the context differently (that is, describes a cognitive shift).

Presentation of the emergent self

Finally, how participants' described who they had become and what they were doing as a result was analyzed, meaning how they conceptualized their lives after their transformation. Here the analysis centered on whether the participants' end status or self was related to their initial identity and understanding of their problem, or was unrelated. The codes assigned to end status were advocate/employee in the field, person in recovery, survivor, well/healthy, and various citizen roles.

Transformation narratives of formerly incarcerated individuals

Table 2.2 presents coding summaries of the eight formerly incarcerated people.

As an example, the first entry is a white man in his fifties. He checked that he had been incarcerated and had been diagnosed with a psychiatric disorder. His narrative follows:

> I was unemployed, diagnosed with mental illness after a suicide attempt, and had been convicted of theft, partially related to the untreated mental illness. Hope for any future was lost until I was finally offered a part-time job working 6 'til 10 each evening as a janitor. For most 40 year old men with a Masters degree this may not seem like much, but it got me out of the pattern of smoking, drinking coffee, pacing the floor and feeling desperate. I was able to begin looking for jobs more related to my background and education, while feeling that there was always a job to fall back on, and promotional opportunities within the cleaning company.

The coded narrative runs as follows. Restating the narrative, the story runs, 'I was unemployed (primary identity), I had a mental illness and had been arrested due to my mental illness (secondary and tertiary identities). Employment is central to who I am ("40 year old man with a Masters degree") and the biggest problem and focus of transformation for me is work.' This man was overqualified for this job, yet at the same time he recognized that this was the first step toward a 'good life'. It helped with time and negative feelings. He was then free to look for work better suited to him. Getting part-time work was an event, external to this man. He did not change his cognitive structure (that is, he did not note a cognitive shift in his perception of himself) to assume an employee identity (end identity).

Table 2.2 Moments of transformation

| Life experiences | | | | Demographics | | | | Moments of transformation | | | |
MH	SA	Abuse	Sex	Age	Ethn	InitID	Problem	Event	Locus	CogSh	EndID
X			M	50s	White	Unemployed Mentally ill	Unemployed Mental illness Convict	Event	External	N	Citizen
	X		M	60s	AfrAm	Sex addict Addict	Addict Criminal	Event	External	N	Recovery Advocate
	X	X	M	60s	Hisp	Addict	Addict	Event	External	Unclr	Advocate
X	X	X	F	40s	AfrAm	Addict	Addict	Process	Internal	Y	Recovery Citizen Advocate
X	X	X	F	40s	AfrAm	Addict	Addict	Mixed	External	Unclr	Advocate Recovery
	X	X	F	50s	Mixed	Unspecified Runaway Prostitute Addict	Self-esteem Addict Criminal	Process	External	Y	Undefined
	X	X	F	40s	Mixed	Addict		Event	Mixed	N	Recovery Advocate
X	X		F	30s	White	Addict	Family history Addict	Process	Mixed	N	Advocate

As stated, the formerly incarcerated participants in this sample had a number of life experiences in addition to incarceration, including psychiatric treatment, physical and/or sexual abuse, and addiction. Seven of the eight participants checked the addiction box and six of these made an explicit statement in their narrative accounts that this was their primary problem. One participant described being a mental health consumer, and the other's initial identity was unspecified. The participants' understanding of the problem was matched to initial identities, but they also highlight the role of other life experiences. Most notably, incarceration is most often presented as a consequence of other life experiences, and, in fact, three people did not even make reference to this experience within their narratives. For half of the participants, change began with a specific event, and for half it was a longer process. For five, the catalyst was primarily external, while for one it was internal and for two it was a combination of both. The end status for six of the participants was being an advocate or employed in a field related to addiction or mental health. One participant focused on her role as a healthy person and another emphasized the citizen role of being employed.

Narratives of transformations and change

One participant, an African-American woman in her forties, who identified all four experiences, stated:

> I am a recovering addict of 16 years now, however I have experienced physical, sexual, verbal, emotional abuse since a little girl; some I remember and some I don't. I have been to jail because of my substance abuse and went to treatment for two and a half years in order to not go to prison. I am now on anxiety meds, anti-depression meds for my mental health, but I think all of these factors played a part in who I am now.

By starting the narrative with the statement 'I am a recovering addict' she gives primacy to this life experience, but it is clearly not the only significant factor in her life. She says explicitly that her time incarcerated was related to her substance abuse, and indicates she is taking medication for anxiety and depression. She also describes being abused since childhood.

In describing the positive experience in her life, she says, 'I play a big part in women's lives that live now like I used to live, to help make a difference in someone else's life. Of course I work in the field of substance abuse and have had the privilege to also work in the field of HIV/AIDS prevention.' Change, therefore, unfolded as a process with a number of steps including being in a treatment program, receiving medication, and giving back to others with similar life circumstances. While change was initiated by the external event of potential incarceration, this participant also underwent internal shifts as illustrated by the following: 'I am still clean and sober. I want to go to school, which I never thought I was smart enough to do. I need education to back up my experience. I still have fear, but I am no longer stuck in my fear.' This narrative illustrates that incarceration is one of many life experiences, but is not central. In this case, as in the others represented in this sample, formerly incarcerated people focus on changing behaviors other than criminality.

Another participant, a woman in her forties of mixed race/ethnicity with a primary identity of addict, also described incarceration as one factor among many life experiences and also made positive life changes in a series of steps. She tells the following story:

> I was a teenaged runaway. I entered a life of prostitution through manipulation of a pimp . . . I began to drink and do cocaine with a woman I met while still working in the sex industry. I eventually started doing heroin. I ended up with paranoia from using cocaine and with the help from my family entered a detox . . . I entered more than 20 detoxes over the courses of treatments. I changed the behavior of working in the sex industry, but could not remain abstinent from using drugs. I did six months in jail for assault and battery with a motor vehicle. Upon release I returned to my family and got a 'straight job'. I did eventually stop using substances. I entered detoxes, halfway houses, therapeutic communities, and a sober house (each of these treatments is meant to be plural). I eventually began working in the office of the sober house as an administrative assistant and women's housing coordinator. I learned of a position as a case manager at a detox, applied, and worked there for two years. I currently work as an outreach and engagement worker, working with homeless families living in shelters. I work in the areas of mental health, substance abuse, and trauma.

This participant's narrative illustrates the peaks and valleys of the change process, especially when addiction is involved, and the high potential for derailment along the way. Moreover, her change was motivated by a combination of internal and external events. Getting a 'straight job' was a significant turning point, but working in the field of substance abuse treatment was even more relevant.

Another participant, a white woman in her thirties with an initial identity of addict, also underwent change as a process, but was primarily driven by an external factor. She described a family history of addiction, stating:

> I am a child of an addict. My mom was addicted to pain pills from when I was 8 until I was 12. She is still in recovery to this day, and I am 37. You would think I would not go down that road, but I did. I

have used every drug known to man, except I did not use intra-
venously. I especially got into trouble with alcohol and heroin. I
managed to go to jail for my fourth DWI (driving while intoxicated)
and 'got better' only to pick up a heroin habit when I was 30.

In further describing why and how she changed, she said, speaking of her
drug use:

I had to ask myself why would I continue to do these things to myself
and my children. I know exactly how that felt, but that did not deter
my addictions. I am now six years clean, and on maintenance
methadone. I am graduating in May with my degree in Chemical
Dependency Counseling, and I have just been accepted into a very
expensive and well-known college. I am also working an internship
and a part-time job for my first internship. I am able to help people
where I could not help myself. This may not be a perfect story, and
I pray each day that addiction passes right past my children and my
children's children, but for now, all I can do is go to work, go to
school, go to my clinic – which I am reducing my dose each week,
and go to meetings.

Recognition that her use was harming her children and perpetuating the
cycle of addiction in her family led to different decisions about her life and
resulted in getting clean and finding activities that have meaning,
including the pursuit of education and working in a job that involves
helping others with the same problems she had experienced herself.

For some participants, change was not the result of a long process, but
began with a specific event. For one Puerto Rican man in his sixties, the
change began with the external event of finding a recovery group that
matched his own values and beliefs. Not only did the alternative sobriety
group lead to his own transformation, but he started to advocate for
others who might benefit from a similar experience:

After countless years addicted to cocaine, heroin and alcohol, after
many treatments, therapeutic communities, methadone maintenance
and endless 12-step meetings, I was introduced to my first alternative
sobriety group, Secular Organizations for Sobriety. It was at my first
meeting that I had my 'Ahaa' experience.

Despite years of trying different treatment options, it was the specific
event of attendance at this meeting that was the catalyst for change for
this participant. He continues:

I have become an advocate for SOS and alternative sobriety groups
in general. Attempting to influence professionals to include in their

treatment plans information on all the alternatives so clients are well informed and have choices in their quest for quality sobriety. I think it unethical to do otherwise.

Interestingly, this man never presented any information regarding incarceration or criminal activity in his narrative. His journey focused solely on his problems with addiction and his end identity, like so many others, revolves around advocating in the field.

Another respondent who experienced change through an external event stated he experienced a 'lifelong sexual addiction' in addition to alcoholism. This African-American man in his sixties spoke in detail about prior criminal activity, which included rape and aggravated kidnapping, and 14 years with alternating periods of being on parole or incarcerated. In describing the event that led to change, he offered the following:

After entering a hospital for the 'umpteenth' time for detox from my alcohol use, I was 'divinely' freed from the obsession/compulsion need for alcohol. Just like that. And to my surprise, a short time later, I was also freed from the compulsion to rape. Then came the freedom from cigarettes. I was moved to tears, happy tears. I can remember shouting at the time, 'Free at last, free at last, thank God Almighty, free at last.'

He concludes:

I returned to school . . . and became certified as an alcohol and other drug abuse counselor, entered [university] and earned a Bachelors in Business Management, then proceeded to earn a Masters in Community/Family Counseling from [university]. I am presently an Associate Clinical Director at a well-known community mental health agency. I have been married (for the third time) for nine years.

An African-American woman in her forties who experienced change as a specific event explained that: 'It took the near death experience of myself . . . and the death of my only son. I had continued to use crack cocaine and booze to escape reality for another 30 months to realize that I could recover.' This event was the start of an internally based cognitive shift that led to further changes. She explained the results of her transformation:

Today I have been clean eight years, own a home, [am a] single proud parent of a graduate, and work as an addiction counselor for a non-profit whose mission is to serve underprivileged women of color who smoke crack cocaine. Today, along with therapy and twelve-step programs, my life is golden.

25

Like others, this participant does not link her problems to criminal behavior but to substance abuse. Moreover, the key transformation for her is the ability to give back to others, stating her life has been influenced by 'the ideal of helping others, because someone helped me'.

One Native and African-American woman in her fifties was less specific about the nature of her problems, stating, 'The most positive experience was getting involved in the holistic healing arena. This includes meditation, eating the right foods, getting some exercise, and last, but by no means least, changing my thought pattern from negative to positive.' She also stated: 'This still influences my life. I am a holistic practitioner because this is what has brought me into balance and healing. I have been able to heal much quicker, I believe more thoroughly, and with more substance than with traditional therapy.' For her, change was a process that involved education about different approaches to wellness and a cognitive shift to positive thinking. Her change was also reinforced by her perception of continued benefits and her belief that holistic healing produced better results than traditional therapies would have.

Discussion and conclusion

Our research provides a description of significant life experiences of formerly incarcerated people and how they describe the process of changing their lives. Notably, incarceration was but one of many experiences which included addiction, histories of abuse and psychiatric treatment. These overlapping experiences show the importance of individuals' points of view and the necessity for those who are the focus of change to define for themselves the most salient problems and most troubling statuses or identities. While the findings from our study cannot be generalized, and this cross-sectional analysis does not tell us how long change is sustained, we offer several important points that might inform future research in the area.

In analyzing these narratives, we find that the focus of change in fact has little to do with criminal behavior, but rather a multitude of other life experiences. Addiction was a prominent aspect of our participants' lives, and for many of them incarceration was a manifestation of problems with substance abuse. While the criminal justice system has long acknowledged the prevalence of addictions among incarcerated populations, finding ways to address this specific need has been particularly challenging. For one thing, it is addiction as a contributor to offending that is usually the primary concern, whereas our participants highlight the ways that addiction impacted on the general quality of their lives including relationships with children and their personal well-being. For the two participants who did not have experience with addiction, change still did not center on offending, but rather on finding meaningful employment and practicing holistic healing.

In terms of the other aspects of transformation (i.e. process/event, internal/external locus of control and cognitive shifts), no consistent patterns emerged. People described various ways of coming to a good place in their lives. This suggests that there is no single pathway through the role transformation process; and no cookie-cutter approach can address the many problems and/or make maximum use of the individual strengths and resiliencies that formerly incarcerated people bring with them.

The findings challenge reentry and desistance researchers' focus on former offenders' material needs to the neglect of some of the less tangible resources that are necessary tools for change. Our research does not deny the importance of other resources; for example, recent evaluation studies of the Serious and Violent Offender Reentry Initiative (SVORI) found that the most common needs for those coming out of prison are education, financial assistance, obtaining a driver's license, job training and employment (Visher and Lattimore 2008). Instead, we propose that these needs are the minimal level of resources necessary for success and help provide the foundation for change. The narratives of change for formerly incarcerated people point to the crucial role of personal agency in creating fulfilling lives and sustaining necessary changes.

These findings also challenge traditional criminal justice system approaches to desistance that center on offending behavior and the personal deficits and needs believed to be associated with such behavior (Maruna and LeBel 2003). In missing the most important aspects of change, as identified by the people with particular lived experiences, the system may target behaviors that are not central to the individual and with minimal personal impact. Since offending behavior is not the most salient feature of our participants' lives, the markers of success should perhaps instead focus on meaningful employment, appropriate treatment, and finding ways to give back to others.

Creating roles and activities that help sustain life changes was a crucial part of the process for our participants. Sustaining change was facilitated by taking on the role of giving back to others, particularly to those experiencing similar difficulties that the participants themselves had overcome. LeBel (this volume) finds that an advocate role can be an important part of personal transformation for people who have been incarcerated. Indeed, of the eight formerly incarcerated participants in our study, six became advocates or were in some way employed in fields related to addiction or mental health. In giving back, people may serve the dual function of helping others, and in helping others reinforce a new identity as a changed person (Maruna *et al.* 2003).

Finally, incarceration is a byproduct; a passive status imposed on persons through a legal procedural process. Respondents commonly acknowledge arrest and incarceration in their narratives. They acknowledge poor choices in their pasts, but the poor choice is not the choice to be a criminal – that is, to intentionally commit a crime – but to use drugs or otherwise be in a situation that places them at risk of being arrested. It may be that the process of becoming a criminal is in fact largely a legal process that is not assumed into the dominant identity. While the non-criminal public believes and acts as if this is the sole master status, those who possess this status resist identifying with it. Instead, they provide explanations of how and why they were involved in criminal behavior while claiming other problematic identities. Much like formerly incarcerated people, corrections specialists and policy-makers alike must transform their thinking and practices, understanding how people shed negative identities and assume pro-social ones, to achieve greater and more lasting success in their work with former prisoners.

Notes

1 Lists specifically for formerly incarcerated persons were difficult to find. Contacts with the NuLeadership Policy Group, a public policy think tank founded and staffed by formerly and currently incarcerated people, were initially promising, but did not generate lists to contact potential participants. However, we ended up with nearly 25 per cent of our sample being formerly incarcerated.
2 This study meets the federal standards for research involving human subjects (IRB Protocol 06-322M, Moments of Transformation Study, approved 24 April 2006).

References

Ebaugh, H. R. F. (1988) *Becoming an Ex: The Process of Role Exit*. Chicago: University of Chicago Press.

Edin, K. Nelson, T. J. and Paranal, R. (2004) 'Fatherhood and incarceration as potential turning points in the criminal careers of unskilled men', in M. Patillo, D. Weiman and B. Western (eds) *Imprisoning America: The Social Effects of Mass Incarceration*. New York: Russell Sage Foundation.

Gadd, D. and Farrall, S. (2004) 'Criminal careers, desistance, and subjectivity: Interpreting men's narratives of change', *Theoretical Criminology*, 8(2): 123–56.

Garland, D. (2001) 'The meaning of mass imprisonment', *Punishment and Society*, 3: 5–7.

Giordano, P. C., Cernkovich, S. A. and Rudolph, J. L. (2002) 'Gender, crime and desistance: Toward a theory of cognitive transformation', *American Journal of Sociology*, 107(4): 990–1064.

Goffman, E. (1963) *Stigma: Notes on the Management of Spoiled Identity*. New York: Simon & Schuster.

Huebner, B. M. (2005) 'The effect of incarceration on marriage and work over the life course', *Justice Quarterly*, 22(3): 281–303.

Lopoo, L. M. and Western, B. (2005) 'Incarceration and the formation and stability of marital unions', *Journal of Marriage and Family*, 67: 721–34.

Maruna, S. (2001) *Making Good: How Ex-Convicts Reform and Rebuild their Lives*. Washington, DC: American Psychological Association.

Maruna, S. and LeBel, T. P. (2003) 'Welcome home? Examining the "Reentry Court" concept from a strengths-based perspective', *Western Criminology Review*, 4(2): 91–107.

Maruna, S., LeBel, T. P., Mitchell, N. and Naples, M. (2004) 'Pygmalion in the reintegration process: Desistance from crime through the looking glass', *Psychology, Crime and Law*, 10: 271–81.

National Research Council (2008) *Parole, Desistance from Crime, and Community Integration*. Committee on Community Supervision and Desistance from Crime. Committee on Law and Justice, Division of Behavioral and Social Sciences and Education. Washington, DC: The National Academies Press.

Pastore, A. L. and Maguire, K. (eds) (2007) *Sourcebook of Criminal Justice Statistics Online*. Available at: *www.alban.edu/sourcebook/* (accessed 31 July 2007).

Sampson, R. J. and Laub, J. H. (1993) *Crime in the Making: Pathways and Turning Points Through Life*. Cambridge, MA: Harvard University Press.

Seiter, R. P. and Kadela, K. R. (2003) 'Prisoner reentry: What works, what does not, and what is promising', *Crime and Delinquency*, 49(3): 360–88.

Singer, J. A. (2004) 'Narrative identity and making meaning across the adult lifespan: An introduction', *Journal of Personality*, 72(3): 437–60.

Travis, J. (2002) 'Invisible punishment: An instrument of social exclusion', in M. Mauer and M. Chesney-Lind (eds) *Invisible Punishment: The Collateral Consequences of Mass Imprisonment*. New York: The Free Press.

Vaughan, B. (2007) 'The internal narrative of desistance', *British Journal of Criminology*, 17: 390–404.

Veysey, B. M. and Christian, J. (under review) Moments of transformation: Narratives of recovery and identity change. *Japanese Journal of Sociological Criminology*.

Visher, C. A. and Travis, J. (2003) 'Transitions from prison to community: Understanding individual pathways', *Annual Review of Sociology*, 29: 89–113.

Visher, C. A. and Lattimore, P. (2008) 'Major study examines prisoners and their reentry needs', Research brief. Washington, DC: The Urban Institute.

Ward, T. and Maruna, S. (2007) *Rehabilitation: Beyond the Risk Paradigm*. London: Routledge.

Western, B. (2006) *Punishment and Inequality in America*. New York: Russell Sage Foundation.

Chapter 3

Looking-glass identity transformation: Pygmalion and Golem in the rehabilitation process[1]

Shadd Maruna, Thomas P. LeBel, Michelle Naples and Nick Mitchell

The mere existence of this book on the subject of 'identity transformation' in criminology represents a huge leap forward for the discipline. Almost everyone knows someone who has experienced a dramatic metamorphosis in their lives and is now a 'new' person from who they were. Indeed, these radical changes in behavior, thought, beliefs, and sense of self – sometimes referred to as 'quantum change' in psychology (see Miller and C'deBaca 1994) – are a staple among published autobiographies (for a powerful recent example, see Carr 2008). Yet, remarkably, the academic literature on criminology has been mostly silent on this subject until now.

Of course, the closely related subject of 'desistance from crime' has become extremely popular in academic research over the past 20 years (for reviews, see Laub and Sampson 2001; Maruna *et al.* 2004; Kazemian 2007). Desistance, however, is a behavioral concept. To 'cease and desist' means to stop offending and to abstain from committing further offending behavior. A change in behavior that is as extreme as this presumably does involve a personal transformation of some sort, but not necessarily (see, e.g. the argument in Laub and Sampson 2003). In general, criminologists have been eager to study desistance, but wary of the idea of personal transformation. The difference is that whereas desistance is tangible and measurable (at least in theory[2]), identity change is anything but. One can 'prove' that someone has not offended – or at least that they have not gotten caught – but this is not proof that a person has 'changed'. Perhaps, they are still 'criminal' underneath and are just pretending to conform temporarily – to mislead a gullible researcher or secure a book contract for a redemption memoir. It is impossible to know for certain.

This problem is irksome for researchers like ourselves who are interested in identity transformation, but it is positively infuriating for the formerly incarcerated, who often want to make the case that they have permanently 'changed', 'reformed' or become 'new' people (Harris 2005). Yet, it is far easier to establish oneself as deviant than it is to establish one's credentials as a reformed person. In what is referred to as the 'negativity bias' (Skowronski and Carlston 1989), a single deviant event or episode can be enough to stigmatize a person indefinitely as an 'offender' or 'felon'. At the same time, a hundred *non*-deviant acts may not be enough to earn someone the recognition of non-deviant. As Lofland (1969: 210) writes, 'Long years of truly exemplary conformity or even hyperconformity and stellar service to society may be required' before the stigma of having been an 'offender' can be lifted. As such, even the 'lowest risk' former prisoner is likely to be treated with considerable suspicion and fear (LeBel 2008). Since employers, agents of social control and other community members have little confidence in their own ability to discern between legitimate and illegitimate claims to personal reform, the safest option is to interpret any claim to going straight as 'phony, feigning, unbelievable or implausible' (Lofland 1969: 210). To do otherwise would be to 'open oneself to the perceived possibility of being hurt, taken in, suckered, abused, put down or in some other way being made to seem a less-than-competent player of the social game' (Lofland 1969: 212).

Unfortunately, this skepticism toward former prisoners' claims to reformation might exacerbate their lack of success after prison (i.e. contribute to high recidivism rates) by feeding in to a self-fulfilling prophecy of sorts. If everyone around a person treats him like he is a danger and a threat, he may eventually internalize this view himself and fulfill the prediction by returning to criminal behavior. This, of course, is a central premise of labeling theory (Lemert 1951; Becker 1963), or what is referred to as the 'Golem effect' in psychology: low expectations of a person typically lead to poor outcomes (Babad *et al.* 1982). Indeed, there is an extensive literature on the role of stigma and labeling in the lives of ex-prisoners (for a comprehensive review see LeBel 2008). In this chapter, however, we will also focus on a different use of labeling theory, introducing another self-fulfilling prophecy that is the opposite of the Golem effect. In the so-called 'Pygmalian effect', the *high* expectations of others lead to greater self-belief (and subsequent performance) in an individual (Rosenthal and Jacobson 1992). We argue that personal transformation (or 'recovery' in the highly related arena of addiction treatment) also contains a looking-glass element. People start to believe that they can successfully change their lives when those around them start to believe they can. In other words, rehabilitation (or recovery) is a construct that is negotiated through interaction between an individual and significant others (Shover 1996: 144). Not only must a person accept conventional society in order to go straight, but conventional society must accept that person has changed as well (Meisenhelder 1982).

In what follows, we briefly review the evidence in favor of both Golem and Pygmalion effects in the process of desisting from and persisting in crime. Next, we will provide an empirical illustration of how this identity negotiation process might work in practice, drawing on interview data from a study of an ex-prisoner reintegration program. We conclude that the labeling theory metaphor of the looking-glass self-concept (especially as reformulated by Gecas and Schwalbe 1983, and others) could supplement and complement existing understandings of the transformation process in criminology.

Labeling, persistence and desistance

Golem effects on desistance

Although criminologists do not typically use the term, 'Golem effects' themselves are well known in criminology. A half century ago, Edwin Lemert (1948: 27) introduced considerable clarity into the debate on the origins of deviance by differentiating between two 'sharply polarized or even categorical phases' in this developmental process: primary deviation and secondary deviation. Primary deviation involved the initial flirtation and experimentation with deviant behaviors. Secondary deviation, on the other hand, is deviance that becomes 'incorporated as part of the 'me' of the individual' (Lemert 1951: 76). Lemert's argument was that 'criminal careers are fashioned in the time of personal identity' and that 'to deviate over time is to assume a self-understanding consistent with the behavior' (C. C. Lemert 2000: 5).

Primary deviation, according to Lemert (1948) can arise out of a variety of 'causes'. In the case of alcoholism, for instance, Lemert suggests these triggers might include the death of loved ones, exposure to death in battle, the strain of business competition, family role ambivalence, inferiority feelings and the like (reflecting the Freudian tenor of the times, Lemert also lists 'nipple fixation'). Secondary deviation, on the other hand, could be said to take place when the person begins to employ his or her deviant behavior, or a role based upon it, 'as a means of defense, attack, or adjustment to the overt and covert problems created by the societal reaction to it' (Lemert 1951: 76). In other words, 'A person who began to drink heavily because of anxieties over his [or her] professional competence now drinks heavily because of the failures due to his drinking and corresponding sense of guilt and introjected self-definitions' (1951: 28).

This two-pronged understanding of deviance allowed Lemert (1951: 75) to avoid 'the fallacy of confusing original causes with effective causes'. Freed from what he saw as a 'burdensome' debate around initial etiology, Lemert focused on why some primary deviants underwent a symbolic reorganization at the level of their self-identity and others did not. Lemert's story for how this process works is, of course, his most enduring legacy to criminology. Lemert and subsequent labeling theorists argued that second-ary deviance was largely a product of societal reaction. Drawing on the symbolic interactionist notion of the 'looking-glass self-concept,' the theory suggests that a stigmatized individual will come to view himself based upon what he believes other people think he is. 'The escalation to secondary deviance rests heavily on the subjective effects of being labeled; that is, the labeling experience serves to recast individuals *in their own eyes* as well as in the eyes of others' (Paternoster and Iovanni 1989: 378).

Labeling theory came under considerable attack in the 1970s (see especially Gove 1975), although much of this criticism was probably unfair (see Petrunik 1980). In fact, theorists like Sampson and Laub (1997) and Braithwaite (1989) have argued convincingly in favor of resuscitating labeling theory in the cause of understanding criminal persistence. Sampson and Laub (1997) argue that persistent offending may not necessarily be attributable to permanent traits of individuals, but could also be explained by a process of 'cumulative continuity' whereby future opportunities to lead a conventional life are 'knifed off' as a consequence of choices made in adolescence. They argue that deviant behavior might be seen as a kind of 'chimera' (Patterson 1993), 'mortgaging one's future' (Nagin and Paternoster 1991) by blocking opportunities for achieving success in employment, education, and even in marriage. Braithwaite (1989) argues that when society's reaction to deviants is to stigmatize, segregate and exclude, such persons are left with limited opportunity for achieving self-respect and affiliation in the mainstream – but are wel-comed among subcultural groups of similarly stigmatized outcasts. In this light, the vicious circle of persistent offending makes perfect sense.

The empirical evidence for this sort of Golem effect is impressive. In a study of 95,919 men and women who were either adjudicated or had adjudication withheld, Chiricos and colleagues (2007) found that those who were formally labeled were significantly more likely to recidivate within two years than those who were not. Similar findings have emerged in longitudinal cohort studies (see, e.g. Bernburg *et al.* 2006; Farrington 1977). Interestingly, Bernburg and colleagues (2006) found that the process worked in much the same way as theorized by Braithwaite – intervention by the juvenile justice system predicted involvement with deviant gangs, which then led to increased offending. LeBel and colleagues (2008) also found that individual perceptions of being stigmatized are an important mediating mechanism in the labeling process. Research participants who reported feeling stigmatized and excluded in a prison-based interview were more likely to be reconvicted and reimprisoned in a ten-year follow-up study, even after controlling for the number of social problems an individual experienced after release. In the sample, only two out of the 40 (5 per cent) participants who felt stigmatized were not reconvicted of a crime versus 24 per cent (21/86) of participants who did not perceive stigma against them.

Desisting from crime is a difficult process, especially for those who are deeply entrenched in criminal networks and living in disadvantaged circumstances. Successfully changing one's life in such circumstances requires a tremendous amount of self-belief, and this is made highly difficult, if not impossible, when everyone around him or her believes they are likely to fail. Anecdotal evidence from ex-prisoner biographies suggests that many former prisoners who perceive that opportunities are blocked develop a sense of hopelessness and despair. The formerly incarcerated writer Nathan McCall (1994: 234), for instance, writes: 'Every time I filled out an application and ran across that section about felony convictions, it made me feel sick inside. I felt like getting up and walking out on the spot. What was the use? I knew what they were going to do.' Although McCall eventually changed his life, it is easy to understand how a majority of ex-prisoners end up returning to crime and incarceration (Langan and Levin 2002).

Pygmalion effects

Nonetheless, there may be a role of labeling effects on the process of desistance from crime as well as in persistence. For instance, there may be (at least) two distinguishable phases in the desistance process – primary and secondary desistance – parallel to Lemert's formulation of deviance. Primary desistance would take the term desistance at its most basic and literal level, to refer to any lull or crime-free gap in the course of a criminal career (see West 1961; Piquero 2004). Because every deviant experiences a countless number of such pauses in the course of a criminal career, primary desistance would not be a matter of much theoretical interest. The focus of desistance research, instead, would be on secondary desistance: the movement from the behavior of non-offending to the assumption of the role or identity of a 'changed person' (in other words, the subject matter of this book). In secondary desistance, crime not only stops, but 'existing roles become disrupted' and a 'reorganization based upon a new role or roles will occur' (Lemert 1951: 76; see also Ebaugh 1988 for a discussion of 'role exit'). Indeed, recent research (Giordano *et al.* 2002; Maruna 2001; Shover 1996) provides compelling evidence that long-term desistance does involve identifiable and measurable changes at the level of personal identity or the 'me' of the individual.

As in Lemert's formulation, this reorganization at the level of self-concept might be attributable to a 'looking-glass' process of societal reaction. Essentially, if almost every person engaged in patterns of criminality experiences a break or lull during an 'offending career' (primary desistance), perhaps those who are labeled as 'rehabilitated' during such a lull are more likely than those who are not to move on to secondary desistance. That is, desistance may be best facilitated when the desisting person's change in behavior is recognized by others and reflected back to him in a 'delabeling process' (Trice and Roman 1970).

Meisenhelder (1977: 329) describes the 'delabeling process' as the 'certification' stage of desistance, and suggests this is often formalized in a social ritual. This might take the shape of a 'status elevation ceremony' that could 'serve publicly and formally to announce, sell and spread the fact of the Actor's new kind of being' (Lofland 1969: 227). In such rituals, 'Some recognized member(s) of the conventional community must publicly announce and certify that the offender has changed and that he is now to be considered essentially noncriminal' (Meisenhelder 1977: 329).

As with the 'degradation ceremony' (Garfinkel 1956) through which wrongdoers are stigmatized, this delabeling would be most effective when directed not at specific acts, but to the whole character of the person in question (Braithwaite and Braithwaite 2001: 16).

> So when a child shows a kindness to his sister, better to say 'you are a kind brother' than 'that was a kind thing you did' . . . praise that is tied to specific acts risks counter productivity if it is seen as an extrinsic reward, if it nurtures a calculative approach to performances that cannot be constantly monitored . . . Praising virtues of the person rather than just their acts . . . nourishes a positive identity.

According to Makkai and Braithwaite (1993: 74), such praise can have 'cognitive effects on individuals through nurturing law-abiding identities, building cognitive commitments to try harder, encouraging individuals who face adversity not to give up . . . and nurturing belief in oneself'.

Finally, delabeling might be most potent when coming from 'on high', particularly official sources like treatment professionals or teachers, rather than from family members or friends – where such acceptance can be taken for granted (Wexler 2001). In particular, if the delabeling were to be endorsed and supported by the same social control establishment involved in the 'status degradation' process of conviction and sentencing (e.g. judges or peer juries), this public redemption might carry considerable social and psychological weight for participants and observers (for development of this idea see Maruna and Lebel 2003; Travis 2005).

There is only scattered evidence in support of this sort of Pygmalion effect in the behavioral reform process (see especially Maruna 2001). For instance, in a now famous experiment, Leake and King (1977) informed treatment professionals that they had developed a scientific test to determine who among a group of patients were most likely to be

35

successful in recovering from alcoholism. In reality, no such test had been developed. The patients identified as 'most likely to succeed' were picked purely at random. Still, the clients who were assigned this optimistic prophecy were far more likely to give up drinking than members of the control group. Apparently, they believed in their own ability to achieve sobriety because the professionals around them seemed to believe it so well (see also Miller 1998).

Outside of criminological research, hundreds of different studies have found confirmation for the idea that one person's expectations for the behavior of another can actually impact the other person's behavior. Meta-analyses of studies conducted both inside and outside the research laboratory suggest an average effect size correlation (r) of over .30 in studies of interpersonal expectancy effects (Rosenthal 2002; Kierein and Gold 2000). In the most famous example, Rosenthal and Jacobson (1992) found that teacher expectancies of student performance were strongly predictive of student performance on standardized tests, and that manipulating these educator biases and beliefs could lead to substantial improvements in student outcomes (see also Miller *et al.* 1975). A nursing home study demonstrated that raising caretakers' expectations for residents' health outcomes led to a significant reduction in levels of depression among residents (Learman *et al.* 1990). Similar Pygmalion effects and expectancy-linked outcomes have been found in courtroom studies, business schools, and numerous different workplaces (e.g. Babad *et al.* 1982; Eden 1984; McNatt 2000; Reynolds 2007; see Rosenthal 2002 for a review).

Whether the same processes could be called into play in the rehabilitation process is, of course, a different matter and an open question. Performance on standardized tests or even in a factory setting is far different from criminal recidivism, as the latter is arguably impacted by a wider variety of influences. Still, the argument that a process of labeling and label negotiation takes place in the typical reentry program appears less open to question, as is demonstrated below.

Negotiating reform: a case study

Unfortunately, we present no original data to either confirm or disconfirm the role of labeling theory in the desistance process below. What follows is not an empirical examination of the role of identity change on recidivism (for that, see LeBel *et al.* 2008). Still, we hope to ground the rest of this chapter in qualitative data collected as part of an evaluation study of Peter Young's Housing Industry and Treatment (or PYHIT) program for ex-prisoners in New York State. These findings are intended to provide some illustration of the potential role for Pygmalion effects in the development of a 'changed' or 'transformed' identity.

As the name suggests, PYHIT is based on what is called a 'three-legged stool' model of aftercare – providing housing assistance, addiction counseling, and job training to those coming out of prison. Perhaps the most innovative aspect of the program is its ownership and operation of a variety of commercial services, including several hotels, restaurants and retail outlets across the state. All these operations are managed and staffed primarily by program participants and graduates as part of a 'strengths-based' (Maruna and LeBel 2003) treatment regime.

Before we could evaluate whether such a large-scale and complex enterprise 'worked' or didn't 'work', we decided we first had to ask what it was that the organization itself was hoping to accomplish. As such, the first phase of our research involved eleven months of focus groups, observations and one-on-one interviews with PYHIT management, treatment counselors, job training staff, clients, and successful program graduates.[3] During this exploratory pilot research, we questioned all of the key participants regarding their working definitions of 'success' in the reintegration process. Obviously, we did not use the academic word 'desistance' in these conversations. Instead, we wanted to know how they (clients and counselors) understood the process of personal transformation (sometimes called 'recovery' or 'rehabilitation'). We also probed all of the groups on the basic question of 'how the rehabilitation *process* works' or in other words how ex-prisoners desist from crime. Their responses indicate a delicate process of identity negotiation between counselors and clients in constructing this 'transformation'.

How counselors view success

Counselor	. . . I'm just disappointed in you.
Client	That's bullshit, you know I'm not using.
Counselor	You're not using, but you're not recovering either. You're not working at your recovery.
Client	What do you mean? What am I doing that is not 'in recovery'?
Counselor	You just don't get it.
Client	See what I mean? You're good at finding fault, but you don't have any answers. You do that. You criticize, but you don't have anything to teach me.
Counselor	The way you behave, the way you think, that isn't recovery.
Client	I don't use drugs. I don't hang around no dealers. I don't go out drinking . . .
Counselor	You're abstinent, but that is only half of it. That's abstaining, not recovery.
Client	OK, then what *do* I need to do? You tell me.

(*Maruna, fieldnotes*, 8 July 2000)

To our frustration, we found that, like social scientists, neither the clients nor the counselors we interviewed had an agreed-upon standard for defining 'recovery' or determining whether a person has 'rehabilitated' or 'reformed'. Most agreed that, like pornography, 'You'll know it when you see it.' Yet, when we asked them to provide specific signs (either internal or external of what rehabilitation looks like), both clients and counselors had difficulty addressing the question.

Counselor   We don't know if they're ready [to make it in the free world on their own as a 'straight' person]. You don't know how ready they are necessarily. 'Cause I've seen them say, 'I'm ready', and they appear like that, and I have seen some say they're ready and they're 'full of it'. And, I have seen some say they are not ready and they do well.

Counselor   I don't think you can really ever tell. Sometimes there are things you can look for. Like, the person's demeanor changes, they walk, talk and breathe different . . . But you can't really tell.

Client   You can notice change to an extent, but you can't predict if a person is going to succeed or not until they get out there.

In fact, counselors in the program (almost all of whom are themselves recovering persons) seemed to strongly resist the idea that they were even in the business of assessing the legitimacy of client change or desistance.

Counselor   It's real hard for anybody, not only here, any program, to say who's gonna make it. That's not my decision. We're not that good at this crap for us to say [who will succeed]. It would be unfair to say that about somebody. The reason I say this is because that's what people told us: 'You're not going to make it.'

All of the staff stated emphatically that everyone is given a chance to change and that they do not label anyone as non-redeemable before giving them the opportunity to 'get with the program'. Likewise, they were not ready to declare any client as 100 per cent 'cured' or a 'sure bet' for success:

Counselor   I've seen people with 10–12 years clean [go back to using drugs]. So I don't put that expectation on anybody that they're gonna stay clean.

That said, counselors still admitted that part of their work was to recognize signs of change and transformation when they saw them. The most often-repeated response was that successful recovery/transformation was about more than mere abstinence from drug use and crime.

Counselor   The first place that they're going to have to stop at is no longer using [drugs]. Once they do that they can address the fact that you were stealing from your mother at 4 a.m. and you now owe her an apology or at the very least showing her that you can be a productive, responsible individual. So now you start dealing with responsibility for some of your actions and part of doing that is realizing that what you were doing was wrong ... So you begin to feel bad about some of the things you did and begin to want to repair the damage. At some point you realize that you've got values, that this is not a place that you really wanted to be – at a point you are homeless, unemployed, extremely strained family relations, you've got no viable employable skills, you once had a goal ... at the very least to help people, and you're way off the mark.

Several staff members talked about the 'dry drunk' phenomenon whereby individuals had overcome their substance abuse problems but still suffered from patterns of 'criminal thinking' or other characteristics associated with addiction and deviance:

Counselor   Because you're not using the drugs, the attitudes and behaviors can still be there. You pick up other things to substitute. Complaining all the time. Some people think that the world owes them, that they don't owe nothing back ... What you put in is what you get out. Some people are not willing to put in nothing and get something in return. That's impossible. You're not doing the work.

The typing of clients

The PYHIT counselors we interviewed spontaneously identified four basic 'types' of clients at the reintegration program:

- The Resisters

- The Wallflowers

- The Fakers

- The Buy-ins

Interestingly, although this represents an 'indigenous typology' (Patten 1980) that seemed to be used by counselors at the PYHIT program, similar typologies have appeared in two recent works on rehabilitation theory (Jones 2002; Battjes *et al.* 2003).

39

In this typology, *Resisters*, of course, are the rebels who reject the program's structure and orientation. Prochaska and DiClemente (1992) would label these individuals 'precontemplators', and they can probably be found in every treatment program. According to the counselors, there is little hope of getting through to someone in this stage of the change process.

Counselor   If a person is resistant to the change, that is a good indicator that not much is gonna happen. They're just fighting the process the whole, every inch of the way. And you usually see that particular person fighting that, whatever venue he is in. He is just gonna fight this whole thing 'til the bitter end.

Counselor   See you gotta really watch the ones that are not engaged with people, that are still out there, living by themselves, keeping secrets, nobody knows where they are. Like 'I go to meetings'. Well, which meetings do you go to? 'Well, where nobody goes.' You know he's lying . . . That's classic stuff, ya know, I never see you in meetings. 'Well, I go where nobody goes.'

Wallflowers, on the other hand, might appear to be 'resisters', but in fact they might simply be 'buy-ins' (or 'fakers') in waiting. Probably in Prochaska and DiClemente's 'contemplation' stage, these are individuals who 'sit back', listen, learn and observe, but are not ready to take on leadership roles in the program.

Counselor   And I think that is what our job is – to watch that guy, not where is he sitting, but why is he sitting there? Ya know, don't label everybody the same, sitting back like disinterested, ya know, just sort of apathetic, just sort of ambivalent, that's not always being uncooperative. *See if you label him/her that you're in trouble.* He may just be like frightened, . . . being a wallflower is not necessarily a bad thing, everybody doesn't get out on the dance floor. Some people succeed very well in life without ever doing the dance, just sort of watching people dance, that's OK.

Counselor   Ahh, [some clients] just need time. At one time when I came through, I wouldn't say anything to anybody. I would just look, look at you, see what you're about, ya know. And then, eventually, after time and time and time, you finally say 'OK, now it's my turn to say something.'

This process of not labeling clients until they've had a chance to become more engaged (on their own) in the program is, of course, at the heart of the Alcoholics Anonymous philosophy that encourages people to 'keep coming back' because eventually the program will get them.

The real difficulty is discerning the 'faker' from the 'buy-in', and this delicate discrimination in essence becomes the process of certification or negotiating recovery in a treatment program. A *faker* is someone who appears on the surface to go along with a treatment regimen, but is only 'gaming'.

Counselor	They get to the faking stage. A lot of our clients are used to complying, they are complying because they want to stay, they want to have a roof over their head, they want to have meals, they want to get off the street for a while.
Counselor	From my own personal experience, you can tell, I think fairly clearly, when someone is gaming you, even if it takes a little while. Even if it's subtle . . . And it's a game to them. But normally, I think that you can see it in their behavior. If somebody sounds perfect after 30 days clean, something is wrong. If somebody is talking a pretty good game after 30 days, nothing in their life is wrong . . . sometimes it's just subtle things.
Counselor	One of the ways I feel clients try to game me is they give me what I want to hear . . . Gives me surface information. Distracts me from what's really bothering them inside, what we call core issues, paints an illusion.

Importantly, the authenticity of reform and the discovery of insincerity (i.e. fakers) is not only determined in treatment sessions and official program activities that often take up only a fraction of the clients' time and occur in somewhat contrived settings (see Prochaska and DiClemente 1992). Instead, the staff's determination of insincerity often takes place in more real-life settings through the observation of clients during their 'down-time' in the residential program, and by watching their daily interactions with peers and non-program persons such as customers, family and friends. In effect, staff believe strongly that fakers will eventually expose themselves.

Counselor	He is a major crack player, and if you don't know what I mean by that, he looks for every scam that he can get, you know he looks for every way out and not taking responsibility for who he is and his addiction. As far as I can tell from the interactions and conversations I have had with his counselors, umm, treatment is a joke and it is not taken seriously. He creeps around the house, he creeps around where he lives and he is always on the sly, he is always, this is a guy you've got to watch. It's a shame.

Counselor When I asked him to do something, he was all about 'What do I get out of it?' He would do a great job at it, but there was always something behind it . . . he did it because it allowed him to stay here. It allowed him three hots and a cot, and he did it with a smile on his face, but deep down inside he only did it with a smile on his face so that you didn't give him any flack about it.

Buy-ins, on the other hand, are essentially the ones deemed most 'redeemable' by counseling staff. The terms 'buy-in' or 'consumer buy' were used exclusively by the job-training staff at PYHIT, but similar concepts could be found in our interviews with treatment staff.

Counselor I know from my own experience when I was ready to change, that's when I bought in to whatever was in front of me . . . That is what I call consumer buying . . .

The definition of a buy-in is someone who engages with the program in complete sincerity:

Counselor They're more voluntary in their heart. There are some guys in there that are here because of parole and probation, but I think in their heart, they're voluntarily doing this and they're okay with that.

PYHIT staff frequently referred to this as doing the 'right things for the right reasons':

Counselor And I think what we try to talk about, in terms of recovery, once we put down the drug, is behaviors and consequences, you know, do the right thing for the right reason, usually the right thing happens.

Counselor If you see an individual make it through the treatment process, maybe sometimes display defiance, and resistance, but sticks around long enough to develop the understanding that it's better to do the right thing because it's the right thing to do and not because I don't want to go to jail.

Counselors say they look for four main characteristics when deciding whether someone is truly 'buying' into the program:

- Compliance/conformity

- Disclosure

- Going the extra mile

- Signs of role modeling

While the first criterion might seem the most basic, conformity was also the one mentioned most frequently among counselors as a prerequisite for certification and the assignment of additional responsibility.

Counselor   Takes direction, takes guidance. Takes direction from his church members . . . Takes direction from his counselor, takes direction from the director, takes direction from the cooking or kitchen staff . . . Never hear anything negative.

Counselor   And we can see in fact, how has the addiction impacted those skills, do you still have those skills, can you take guidance and supervision, can you get along with your co-workers, can you show up on time, can you be consistent, can you put in a good day's effort. And those are the things that we'd be looking at in that process.

Conformity alone, however, is not enough to be relabeled as a successfully recovered individual. Clients are expected to 'open up' or share one's self with the program participants and counselors. A failure to do so was often used as a criterion for one's being deemed a 'faker'.

Counselor   We do see changes, people start to take responsibility for their actions. That's one that we could see when they're here. They start talking about personal issues.

Counselor   And then she mentioned about childhood trauma issues. Over time, they learn how to suppress, but they resurface. You don't deal with them, they come back up. Trigger something. Somebody says something, you hear a voice, it triggers these core issues from deep down inside. These things need to be addressed, they need to be disclosed.

Next, clients are expected by program staff to 'go the extra mile' in their new roles.

Counselor   At times you're asked to volunteer, and when I see somebody do that without blinking an eye, like I was just in the back on the dock with David, there is a kid that was just coming through the kitchen . . . David said, 'I need you to help me', and without hesitation, he grabbed the other piece of the wood and he was helping David. And things like that are just like indicators that this guy's looking to do something, ya know, do the right thing for the right reason.

Counselor   Where a guy can come in here and regardless of how long he has been here, you can still ask him to do something and he will still do it with the same tone that he did it when he was thirsty for this . . . They still continue to give when they don't have to.

Frequently, this 'extra mile' involves 'giving something back' through a sort of informal restitution process – not so much directly to one's victims or long-suffering family members, but to the community at large:

Counselor   Also, when a person is here, one of the ways, and there are many ways you can gauge success, is if you see that they . . . repair some of the damage.
Counselor   The guy is involved, and the guy gives back. He receives but he also gives back and that is the difference, you know.

Finally, probably the most interesting finding of our interviews is that one rule of thumb that counselors (themselves mostly recovering addicts) used to discern a 'buy-in' from a 'faker' was whether the client reminded the counselor of him or herself, and thought the way that she or he thought. That is, implicit in the idea that 'they are who we were' is the presumption that 'they need to get to where we are at'. Counselors look for aspects of 'themselves' in the clients and assign significance to the strategies and philosophies that they themselves have utilized in their own recovery processes. The more the client appears to be a mirror image of the counselor role model, the more likely the counselor will see potential for success.

In summary, then, the counselor's working typology might be understood as involving two dimensions (see Table 3.1): engagement in the program and sincerity of interest in reform. Whereas the first is the easiest to measure objectively as a behavior (see Hiller *et al.* 2002 and Knight *et al.* 2000 for a discussion of treatment engagement), the second, which can be viewed more as 'having the right attitude', seems to be the more crucial dimension in terms of expected outcome. In addition to being the clients expected to make it in the real world, it is the buy-ins that are held up to the public as 'success stories' to indicate that the treatment program works.

Table 3.1 Dimensions in the client typology

	Engaged	Not engaged
Sincerity	Buy-ins	Wallflowers
Insincerity	Fakers	Resisters

It is important to note that counselors viewed these as dynamic categories, in theory, and stressed that it was common for a person to begin in one group then move toward another.

Counselor The ability to change, that could change at any given time. You know some people come in and they are resistant. Then once they get some type of information and they see that other people are doing great that came through the program, things change.

Counselor I like to give the guys the benefit of the doubt and in the beginning you know how things are, you know their goals are different but once they get towards the end they start changing their minds.

Therefore, hope is held out that 'wallflowers' may develop the 'right attitude', and therefore might be 'buy-ins' in waiting.

Clients' views on success: recovery in the looking glass

While complementary in many ways, this professional definition of recovery or success differs in some ways from the definition that emerged from our discussions with clients in the program (see also Laudet 2007). Like the counselors, clients of the treatment program had great difficulty in articulating or delimiting precisely what recovery meant or how they would know it if they found it. Ironically, we found that while clients often looked to counselors to know when the recovery was complete, the counselors often told clients to look within themselves.

Client You'll just know [when you are recovered]. It comes to you when you're ready. Like I was [asking the staff], 'How do I know I'm ready to walk out these doors? How do I know when my program's over?' They're like, 'You'll know deep in your heart, when the time's ready. God will give you that signal in your heart.' Now, I'm ready to leave the program, but I wasn't two months ago. And I – you just know deep in your heart, you'll know when you're ready.

Client I'm almost through with the program, so I've been like . . . I've been talking to my counselors. I've been saying, ya know, 'I think it's time for me to move on. I've been already to three treatments and I'm still here, ya know.' Right now, I'm qualified to work. I got my physical strength back. I can think creatively, ya know, and I'm ready to move on. But umm, as they say, it's not time yet. 'It's not your time yet. Your time will come, you won't know when your time's gonna come, but it will come.'

In these examples, 'readiness' is clearly a complicated negotiation between clients and counselors. Clients are told that the change has to happen from within themselves, yet client self-declarations of 'being ready' alone are not enough to qualify as evidence of success. Knowing this well, individuals who are trying to go straight become preoccupied with formally establishing the authenticity of their reform (see also Weinberg 1996).

As a result, most individuals cling to the few hard and tangible measures of success available to them. For instance, clients made numerous references to concrete achievements and milestones (graduation ceremonies, job promotions) when describing their change.

Client   I have achieved a whole lot of things in the six months that I was in this program . . . I got my diploma, my high school diploma, something that I thought I would never get. Umm, I go to meetings, I'm connected, I do service work . . . And yesterday I went and umm, something I thought I would never do, I went and registered for college yesterday, ya know . . . I know that I've changed . . . I have some direction . . . I accomplished a whole lot of things in six months that I never did in 20 years, and that's deep.

Moreover, client descriptions of desistance in our study were constantly interspersed with testimonies from 'respectable' others:

Client   The director from the house that I am at, she can't believe the way I've changed.
Client   I was talking to my mother the other day, ya know, and she used to tell me every time we talked I always talked about stuff that was insubstantial or inconsequential, didn't have any substance to it or anything . . . And when we talk today, it has meaning to it [she said] . . . She was so happy . . . You know my whole family sees that.

Indeed, although understood as an internal change, desistance was often described by treatment clients by referring to its external manifestations or, more specifically, the reflections of self the person perceives. A 'looking-glass self-concept' seems to be clearly at work in the following definitions of rehabilitation, for instance:

Client   I like the way people look at me, they trust me. They know I can do things without having to worry about me. Things like that, having a sense of being trusted really turns me on.
Client   The way I present myself and *the shine I have about me*. I mean that's the greatest gift right there. Why do I want to give that back up, ya know?

Client   Even the judge when I went back to court a week ago, he just noticed the 180 degrees.

Until the clients recognize that others recognize *them* as 'success stories', they appear to not quite believe it themselves. This makes perfect sense, of course, as only a few years ago all of the clients had been officially and publicly stigmatized as 'junkies' and 'criminals' by social control authorities. Clients seem to use pro-social labels from other authorities to override these previous deviant labels.

Quite often, the authorities called upon to certify individual reform in this way were the counselors, clinicians and staff of the PYHIT program, who have the most contact with the recovering persons. This recognition of change usually came in the form of assigning the client additional power or responsibility within the treatment program. In a Therapeutic Community (TC) setting, clients who 'prove themselves' are promoted to the position of expeditor, coordinator, or administrator of programming. Even in less rigorously structured reintegration settings, like the PYHIT program, clients who 'do well' are often put in charge of running meetings, assigned supervisory positions within the various industries, or asked to assist newer clients in various program activities.

As such, when we asked clients how they defined 'rehabilitation' in their personal lives, they often described this as a process of being trusted with additional responsibility over others – which they defined as power and authority.

Client   I've come through this program, I graduated this program, and now I am a staff member here at this hotel. Umm, I have responsibilities every day. *I oversee people*, which is something new. I always had to report to people. I never had *anybody underneath* me, ya know, which is something new. But I am *learning how to take responsibility*.

Client   I just got four job offers in the hotel industry that I have to mull over. I never got that before. I always get menial jobs like gas station attendant or delivering flowers or what have you. Ya know, dairy clerk in grocery store, ya know I've always known I'm better than that but I never pushed myself.

Clients believed in their recovery when others showed that they believed in them.

Although these findings suggest a strong role for a social process of negotiation in the development of a reformed identity, the data also point up an important limitation to the looking-glass metaphor when thinking about rehabilitation. Our findings seem to suggest that treatment clients are active participants and not passive victims of the labeling process. The PYHIT clients we interviewed emphasized the *intrinsic* motivation underlying their change – they were not doing it just for the external recognition. They had learned to enjoy and appreciate pro-social behaviors and were no longer just driven by external contingencies (Kelman 1958).

Client [I realized] I could do something well, which I never thought I could, ya know. Umm, I found out the culinary really worked for me. I enjoy it. Something I would like to do for the rest of my life. It's not like a job that I am stuck with and I have to do it . . . you know what I am saying. This is something that I enjoy very much and want to improve on.

They described finding some sort of 'calling' – be it parenthood, an occupation or a hobby – through which they find meaning and purpose outside of crime (see Sennett 2003). In particular, PYHIT clients described a new-found ability to find satisfaction in altruistic, other-centered behavior – quite diametrically opposed to the types of behavior that led the person to prison in the first place (see also LeBel 2007; Maruna *et al.* 2003).

Client I gotta give back what's been freely given to me. And uh, being nice to people is a big change for me, ya know, 'cause ahh, I was the type that had a serious attitude. Now that attitude is gone, I worked on it until I got rid of it.
Client All I want is a beautiful job, and if it's helping people, serving people, doing whatever I have to do for it, I'm willing to do it. I gotta give back what God has given me and he's given me my life back so I could help others.

These experiences of 'giving back' then lead to increased feelings of personal self-worth and self-esteem.

Client You start to love yourself. When you do drugs you are killing yourself. You have to learn to like yourself.
Client It's self-acceptance with me, umm . . . I feel good about myself; I love myself today, getting back to the self-acceptance piece. See a lot of people, we all tried to make everybody happy but ourselves, we all ran to medicate our feelings, most addicts do. See that's what, everybody that is sitting at this table has the same thing in common.

Discussion: redemption through the looking glass

Interviews with clients and counselors at PYHIT revealed the delicate negotiations that take place in the rehabilitation process whereby counselors look for signs of change within the clients, and clients look for signs of change from counselors. We argue that success, at some level, is dependent upon these mutual reflections. Indeed, many of the counselors who work for the PYHIT program understood this process intuitively and talked about the demonstration of trust as a means of encouraging self-change.

Counselor   My philosophy is pretty simple: show them that you believe in them, and they believe in themselves.

When a PYHIT client seems both sincere and engaged in the program, he or she is often rewarded with something like a 'certification ceremony' or a 'redemption ritual' (Maruna 2001):

Counselor   I had a client who said to me I have 30 days clean. He has never had that in his life. That is tremendous, because he's not in our housing, we're not monitoring him. He walks almost two miles to come here to the clinic on his own. You understand what I'm saying to you? That's a step. With that individual I would say to him congratulations, we would clap and we would be happy. To this point he has achieved a milestone. It's like achieving his GED, gee whiz. That's how important it is to the guy. And [we have to] acknowledge that.

Likewise, an understanding of Golem/labeling effects was incorporated in the program's disciplinary process, which seemed to take the form of a reintegrative shaming model (Braithwaite 1989). According to one counselor:

Counselor   [Rule violators] are treated as someone who has made a mistake; and therefore we treat them with some dignity. Example: Rather than saying your actions are bad, we'd say that we believe that the offender is capable of acting correctly.

The simple idea, of course, is that if the counselor shows belief in a client's ability to change, the client will too.

At the same time, we are inclined to agree with the many modifiers of the looking-glass self-concept notion (e.g. Felson 1993) that the traditional societal reaction account assigns an overly submissive and reactive role to the labeled individual. In our interviews, we found that both clients and counselors emphasized the role of change 'from within' (i.e. changes in the individual's intrinsic motivations and core beliefs) as well as external factors like societal reactions. Former prisoners need to be morally and socially reintegrated, but they also have to feel that this reintegration has been justified by their own efforts to 'make good' and redress past crimes.

As such, of the many reformulations of the notion of the 'looking-glass self', we prefer Gecas and Schwalbe's (1983: 79) argument that: 'Human beings derive a sense of self not only from the reflected appraisals of others, but also from the consequences and products of behavior that are attributed to the self as an agent in the environment.' By emphasizing that self-conceptions are built on the experience of 'self as a causal agent' as well as the reactions of others, this is a more 'active self' than the passive image offered by the looking-glass metaphor (1983: 79). It also seems to better fit our own data in which clients spoke passionately not so much about the labels others assigned to them, but what they did to earn those labels.

Bazemore (1998: 768) calls this a process of 'earned redemption' and in a sense ours is a theory of redemption rather than desistance. The difference between the two terms is subtle but important. Desistance is a behavioral term referring to the absence of criminal behavior after a pattern of offending behavior. Redemption, on the other hand, is always in the eyes of some beholder, and involves forgiveness and the appreciation of a person's contributions and accomplishments. One interviewee memorably told us: 'I know I've redeemed myself in the eyes of my little girls – they know how hard I've worked to make it up to them for all those years I was away. That's what matters' (see also Carr 2008). This change in others' view of a person is at the heart of the looking-glass process. What is interesting is that so often, the 'eyes' involved are those of young people – children or grandchildren, the next generation – rather than of one's superiors:

Client I got a 16-year-old son. I went and got my son about three weeks ago. He's proud of his father today. See, I can be a role model today. I sat down and explained to him I'm going to college at 34 years old.

Client 2 Something I can tell my grandchildren when they grow up a little bigger, because right now, they babies ya know. They don't really know what life's all about . . . What they do know, their grandpa is in a program. He's trying to make his life better. That's all they know, but when they get bigger I can explain to them, these are the things that happened to me. These are the things that I don't want to happen to you. Ya know and it's beautiful, this is an experience that I never had in my life and now I have it.

Finally, we should emphasize that our argument is not that desistance is 'all about' labeling. The important role of informal social control (Sampson and Laub 1993) and differential association (Warr 2002) in the desistance process has received considerable empirical support. Our argument is that an additional, under-researched aspect of maintaining successful desistance from crime might involve the negotiation of a reformed identity through a process of pro-social labeling. Without some concrete external recognition of their reform (i.e. some 'certification'), many individuals might not be able to maintain the difficult process of 'recovery' and desistance.

Notes

1 Some parts of this paper previously appeared in the article: S. Maruna, T. LeBel, N. Mitchell and M. Naples (2004) 'Pygmalion in the reintegration process: desistance from crime through the looking glass', *Psychology, Crime and Law*, 10(3): 271–81. Used with permission from the Taylor and Francis Group of Routledge Publishing.

2 In practice, operationalizing desistance has not been at all straightforward. Since even the highest rate offender surely takes a rest between committing crimes, researchers have struggled with how exactly to distinguish 'real' desistance from these predictable lulls between offences (see esp. Bushway *et al.* 2001). What looks like desistance at time X, might appear like a mere lull from the vantage point of time Y. As Farrington (1986: 201) warns, 'Even a five-year or ten-year crime-free period is no guarantee that offending has terminated.'

3 While we present these data in terms of 'counselors' and 'clients', these artificial labels break down in actual practice. The treatment program we looked at borrows much of its structure from the TC and self-help model of treatment. Therefore, clients often act as counselors for one another in a peer-support structure. Similarly, almost all of the counselors we spoke to (with two exceptions) were themselves recovering persons, some of whom had been through the treatment program we are evaluating. Some of these so-called 'wounded healers' spoke of 'rehabilitation' in terms of their own experiences, rather than their work as practitioners.

References

Babad, E., Inbar, J. and Rosenthal, R. (1982) 'Pygmalion, Galatea, and the Golem: Investigations of biased and unbiased teachers', *Journal of Education Psychology*, 74: 459–74.

Battjes, R. J., Sears, E. A., Katz, E. C., Kinlock, T. W. and Gordon, M. (2003) 'Evaluation of a group-based outpatient adolescent substance abuse treatment program', in S. J. Stevens and A. R. Morral (eds) *Adolescent Substance Abuse in the United States: Exemplary Models from a National Evaluation Study*. Binghamton, NY: Haworth Press.

Bazemore, G. (1998) 'Restorative justice and earned redemption', *American Behavioral Scientist*, 41(6): 768–813.

Becker, H. (1963) *Outsiders*. New York: Free Press.

Bernburg, J. G., Krohn, M. D. and Rivera, C. J. (2006) 'Official labelling, criminal embeddedness, and subsequent delinquency: A longitudinal test of labelling theory', *Journal of Research in Crime and Delinquency*, 43(1): 67–88.

Braithwaite, J. (1989) *Crime, Shame and Reintegration*. Cambridge, UK: Cambridge University Press.

Braithwaite, J. and Braithwaite, V. (2001) 'Part One', in E. Ahmed, N. Harris, J. Braithwaite and V. Braithwaite (eds) *Shame Management Through Reintegration*. Cambridge, UK: University of Cambridge Press.

Bushway, S. D., Piquero, A., Broidy, L., Cauffman, E. and Mazerolle, P. (2001) 'An empirical framework for studying desistance as a process', *Criminology*, 39: 491–515.

Carr, D. (2008) *The Night of the Gun*. New York: Simon & Schuster.

Chiricos, T., Barrick, K. and Bales, W. (2007) 'The labelling of convicted felons and its consequences for recidivism', *Criminology*, 45(3): 547–81.

Ebaugh, H. R. (1988) *Becoming an Ex: The Process of Role Exit*. Chicago: University of Chicago Press.

Eden, D. (1984) 'Self-fulfilling prophecy as a management tool: Harnessing Pygmalion', *Academy of Management Review*, 9(1): 64–73.

Farrington, D. P. (1977) 'The effects of public labelling', *British Journal of Criminology*, 17: 112–25.

Farrington, D. P. (1986) 'Age and crime', in N. Morris and M. Tonry (eds) *Crime and Justice*, Vol. 7. Chicago: Chicago University Press.

Felson, R. B. (1993) 'The (somewhat) social self: How others affect self-appraisals', in J. M. Suls (ed.) *The Self in Social Perspective: Psychological Perspectives on the Self*, Vol. 4. Hillsdale, NJ, England: Lawrence Erlbaum Associates.

Garfinkel, H. (1956) 'Conditions of successful degradation ceremonies', *American Journal of Sociology*, 61: 420–4.

Gecas, V. and Schwalbe, M. L. (1983) 'Beyond the looking-glass self: Social structure and efficacy-based self-esteem', *Social Psychology Quarterly*, 46(2): 77–88.

Gendreau, P., Cullen, F. T. and Bonta, J. (1994) 'Intensive rehabilitation supervision: The next generation in community corrections?', *Federal Probation*, 58: 173–84.

Giordano, P. C., Cernkovich, S. A. and Rudolph, J. L. (2002) 'Gender, crime and desistance: Toward a theory of cognitive transformation', *American Journal of Sociology*, 107: 990–1064.

Gove, W. (1975) 'The labeling perspective: An overview', in W. Gove (ed.) *The Labeling of Deviance: Evaluating a Perspective*. Beverly Hills, CA: Sage.

Harris, M. K. (2005) 'In search of common ground: The importance of theoretical orientations in criminology and criminal justice'. *Criminology and Public Policy*, 4: 311–28.

Hiller, M. L., Knight, K., Leukefeld, C., and Simpson, D. D. (2002) 'Motivation as a predictor of therapeutic engagement in mandated residential substance abuse treatment', *Criminal Justice and Behavior*, 29(1): 56–75.

Jones, L. (2002) 'An individual case formulation approach to the assessment of motivation', in M. McMurran (ed.) *Motivating Offenders to Change: A Guide to Enhancing Engagement in Therapy*. Chichester: Wiley & Sons.

Kazemian, L. (2007) 'Desistance from crime: Theoretical, empirical, methodological, and policy considerations', *Journal of Contemporary Criminal Justice*, 23, 5–27.

Kelman, H. C. (1958) 'Compliance, identification and internalization: Three processes of opinion change', *Journal of Conflict Resolution*, 2: 51–60.

Kierein, N. M. and Gold, M. A. (2000). 'Pygmalion in work organizations: A meta-analysis', *Journal of Organizational Behavior*, 21: 913–28.

Knight, K., Hiller, M. L., Broome, K. M. and Simpson, D. D. (2000) 'Legal pressure, treatment readiness, and engagement in long-term residential treatment', *Journal of Offender Rehabilitation*, 31: 101–15.

Langan, P. A. and Levin, D. J. (2002) *Recidivism of Prisoners Released in 1994* (NCJ 193427). Washington, DC: U.S. Department of Justice, Bureau of Justice Statistics.

Laub, J. and Sampson, R. J. (2001) 'Understanding desistance from crime', *Crime and Justice: A Review of Research*, 28: 1–70.

Laub, J. and Sampson, R. J. (2003) *Shared Beginnings, Divergent Lives*. Cambridge, MA: Harvard.

Laudet, A. B. (2007) 'What does recovery mean to you? Lessons from the recovery experience for research and practice', *Journal of Substance Abuse Treatment*, 33: 243–56.

Leake, G. J. and King, A. S. (1977) 'Effect of counselor expectations on alcoholic recovery', *Alcohol Health and Research World*, 1(3): 16–22.

Learman, L. A., Avrorn, J., Everitt, D. E. and Rosenthal, R. (1990) 'Pygmalion in the nursing home: The effects of caregiver expectations on patient outcomes', *Journal of the American Geriatrics Society*, 38, 797–803.

LeBel, T. P. (2007) 'An examination of the impact of formerly incarcerated persons helping others', *Journal of Offender Rehabilitation*, 46(1/2): 1–24.

LeBel, T. P. (2008) 'Perceptions of and responses to stigma', *Sociology Compass*, 2: 409–32.

LeBel, T. P., Burnett, R., Maruna, S. and Bushway, S. (2008) 'The "chicken and egg" of subjective and social factors in desistance from crime', *European Journal of Criminology*, 5(2): 130–58.

Lemert, C. C. (2000) 'Whatever happened to the criminal? Edwin Lemert's societal reaction', in C. C. Lemert and M. F. Winter (eds) *Crime and Deviance: Essays and Innovations of Edwin M. Lemert*. Lanham, MD: Rowman and Littlefield.

Lemert, E. M. (1948) 'Some aspects of a general theory of sociopathic behavior', *Proceedings of the Pacific Sociological Society. Research Studies, State College of Washington*, 16: 23–9.

Lemert, E. M. (1951) *Social Pathology: Systematic Approaches to the Study of Sociopathic Behavior*. New York: McGraw-Hill.

Lofland, J. (1969) *Deviance and Identity*. Englewood Cliffs, NJ: Prentice-Hall.

Makkai, T. and Braithwaite, J. (1993) 'Praise, pride and corporate compliance', *International Journal of the Sociology of Law*, 21: 73–91.

Maruna, S. (2001) *Making Good: How Ex-convicts Reform and Rebuild their Lives*. Washington, DC: American Psychological Association.

Maruna, S. and LeBel, T. P. (2003) 'Welcome home?: Examining the reentry court concept from a strengths-based perspective', *Western Criminology Review*, 4(2): 91–107.

Maruna, S., Immarigeon, R. and LeBel, T. (2004) 'Ex-offender reintegration: Theory and practice', in S. Maruna and R. Immarigeon (eds) *After Crime and Punishment: Pathways to Ex-Offender Reintegration*. Cullompton: Willan.

Maruna, S., LeBel, T. P. and Lanier, C. (2003) 'Generativity behind bars: Some "redemptive truth" about prison society', in E. de St Aubin, D. McAdams and

53

T. Kim (eds) *The Generative Society: Caring for Future Generations*. Washington, DC: American Psychological Association.

McCall, N. (1994) *Makes Me Wanna Holler: A Young Black Man in America*. New York: Vintage Books.

McNatt, D. B. (2000) 'Ancient Pygmalion joins contemporary management: A meta-analysis of the result', *Journal of Applied Psychology*, 85(2): 314–22.

Meisenhelder, T. (1977) 'An exploratory study of exiting from criminal careers', *Criminology*, 15: 319–34.

Meisenhelder, T. (1982) 'Becoming normal: Certification as a stage in exiting from crime', *Deviant Behavior: An Interdisciplinary Journal*, 3: 137–53.

Miller, R. L., Brickman, P. and Bolen, D. (1975) 'Attribution versus persuasion as a means of modifying behavior', *Journal of Personality and Social Psychology*, 31: 430–41.

Miller, W. R. (1998) 'Why do people change addictive behavior?', *Addiction*, 93, 163–72.

Miller, W. R. and J. C'deBaca (1994) 'Quantum change: Toward a psychology of transformation', in T. Heatherton and J. Weinberger (eds) *Can Personality Change?* Washington, DC: American Psychological Association Books.

Nagin, D. S. and Paternoster, R. (1991) 'On the relationship of past and future participation in delinquency', *Criminology*, 29: 163–90.

Paternoster, R. and Iovanni, L. (1989) 'The labeling perspective and delinquency: An elaboration of the theory and an assessment of the evidence', *Justice Quarterly*, 6: 359–94.

Patten, M. Q. (1980) *Qualitative Evaluation Methods*. Beverly Hills, CA: Sage.

Patterson, G. R. (1993) 'Orderly change in a stable world: The antisocial trait as chimera', *Journal of Consulting and Clinical Psychology*, 61: 911–19.

Petrunik, M. (1980) 'The rise and fall of "labelling theory": The construction and destruction of a sociological strawman', *Canadian Journal of Sociology*, 5: 213–33.

Piquero, A. R. (2004) 'Somewhere between persistence and desistance: The intermittency of criminal careers', in S. Maruna and R. Immarigeon (eds) *After Crime and Punishment*. Cullompton, UK: Willan Publishing.

Prochaska, J. O. and DiClemente, C. C. (1992) 'Stages of change in the modification of problem behavior', in M. Hersen, R. Eisler and P. M. Miller (eds) *Progress in Behavior Modification*, Vol. 28. Sycamore, IL: Sycamore.

Reynolds, D. R. (2007) 'Restraining Golem and harnessing Pygmalion in the classroom: A laboratory study of managerial expectations and task design', *Academy of Management Learning and Education*, 6(4): 475–83.

Rosenthal, R. (2002) 'Covert communication in classrooms, clinics, courtrooms, and cubicles', *American Psychologist*, 57, 839–49.

Rosenthal, R. and Jacobson, L. (1992) *Pygmalion in the Classroom*, expanded edn. New York: Irvington.

Sampson, R. J. and Laub, J. (1993) *Crime in the Making*. Cambridge, MA: Harvard.

Sampson, R. J. and Laub, J. (1997) 'A life-course theory of cumulative disadvantage and the stability of delinquency', in T. P. Thornberry (ed.) *Developmental Theories of Crime and Delinquency*. New Brunswick, NJ: Transaction Publishers.

Sennett, R. (2003) *Respect in a World of Inequality*. New York: Norton.

Shover, N. (1996) *Great Pretenders: Pursuits and Careers of Persistent Thieves*. Boulder, CO: Westview Press.

Skowronski, J. J. and Carlston, D. E. (1989) 'Negativity and extremity biases in impression formation: A review of explanations', *Psychological Bulletin*, 105: 131–42.

Travis, J. (2005) *But They All Come Back: Facing the Challenges of Prisoner Reentry.* Washington, DC: The Urban Institute Press.

Trice, H. M. and Roman, P. M. (1970) 'Delabeling, relabeling and Alcoholics Anonymous', *Social Problems*, 17: 538–46.

Warr, M. (2002) *Companions in Crime.* Cambridge, UK: Cambridge University Press.

Weinberg, D. (1996) 'The enactment and appraisal of authenticity in a skid row therapeutic community', *Symbolic Interaction*, 19: 137–62.

West, D. J. (1961) 'Interludes of honesty in the careers of persistent thieves', unpublished paper.

West, D. J. (1963) *The Habitual Prisoner.* London: Macmillan.

Wexler, D. B. (2001) 'Robes and rehabilitation: How judges can help offenders "make good"', *Court Review*, 38: 18–23.

Chapter 4

Former prisoners, their family members, and the transformative potential of support

Damian J. Martinez

When individuals are released from prison, they often reenter social environments and relationships that have the potential to be disruptive to their success (Petersilia 2003; Travis 2004; Visher and Travis 2003). Also, the research evidence shows that most individuals who are released from prison interact and/or reside with their family members at some point in time after their release (La Vigne *et al.* 2004; Naser and Visher 2006; Nelson *et al.* 1999; Nurse 2002; O'Brien 2001). Within these relationships, a major context in which formerly incarcerated people navigate and lessen the desire to engage in criminal activities is their perception and management of those interactions with their families (Naser and Visher 2006). Somewhat perplexing, however, is that scholarly evidence on investigating these interactions is scant, specifically the perceived availability and exchange of social support among former prisoners and their family members when the former return to family relationships (see Martinez and Christian, 2009). Although research on interactions deemed and defined as socially supportive is relatively new and lacks robust tests of its applicability and impact, a more recent meta-analysis of its merit concluded: 'Indeed an inverse relationship between measures of social support/altruism and crime was consistently observed across empirical studies' (Pratt and Cullen 2005: 428–9).

Therefore, because the way in which former prisoners and family members perceive and exchange social support and their underlying rationale for doing so have been understudied, this chapter responds to these issues. Specifically, it investigates the process of exchanging support in the context of seven dyadic relationships – 14 research participants –

among former prisoners and select, supportive family members. Data were collected from the Evaluation Project of the Illinois Going Home Program.

The findings reveal that former prisoners and select family members perceive and rely on the availability of social support and they exchange support across various dimensions that have the potential to increase the quality of the relationship. Further, engaging in the relationship in a supportive fashion allows former prisoners and their family members alike to interpret the support they provide as exerting meaningful control over their contributions – a major life purpose – and encouraging future positive contributions to the relationship that have the potential to transform their criminal perspectives, identities, and behaviors.

Research design

The specific intent of this study was to understand how, and in what ways, interactions among family members and former prisoners were perceived as being supportive. This method allowed me to elicit the responses (perspectives) reported by former prisoners and family members about their intent for social support exchanges, and to explore the underlying meaning of those exchanges. In so doing, this study posed, and provided responses to, the following research questions: How do former prisoners and their family members perceive social support? How might those perceptions contribute to desisting from crime?

Epistemologically, the knowledge generated from this study came from in-depth interviews and from a social constructivist approach, particularly because the family members and former prisoners constructed their social reality through their perceptions and the context of the situation and interaction. This emic and social constructivist (epistemological) approach takes a position in line with Schwandt's (1994) argument that to understand the complex lived reality of individuals, we must approach it from the perspective of those who live it and construct its meaning.

Sample and sampling method

This study used purposive sampling from a convenience group (the Illinois Going Home Program[1] Evaluation Project[2]), selected via criterion sampling. Because I had research questions guiding the study of a specific topic – former prisoners' reentry into family relationships – purposeful selection of former prisoners and their family members, and adherence to certain program criteria, were required. Purposive sampling can 'establish particular comparisons to illuminate the reasons for [similarities and] differences between settings or individuals' (Maxwell 1996: 71–2); here, it allowed me to analyze the similarities in the information reported among the dyads.

The sample consisted of seven dyads: seven former prisoners and seven corresponding family members. Family members who were to be interviewed were selected by the former prisoner, and the former prisoner defined who family members were. Because most (94 per cent) of the released prisoners who return to North Lawndale are African-American (La Vigne and Mamalian 2003), the sample was primarily African-American and reflected the community's racial makeup, except for one dyad that was of Mexican origin. The former prisoners were Raymond, Jose, Arnold, Chris, Devon, Henry and Johnny. The family members were Raymond's aunt, Jose's sister, Arnold's aunt, Chris's mother, Devon's aunt, Henry's brother and Johnny's mother.[3]

Data collection

Individuals included in the sample (former prisoners and family members) were interviewed using a focused, semi-structured interview guide. Eligible research participants were referred by a case manager affiliated with the Illinois Going Home Program. Cross-sectional interviews were conducted in the North Lawndale community and at a local university. Interviews were tape-recorded because taping preserves the participants' actual words, the sense of which paraphrasing might miss; helps to improve interview techniques; and assures participants of a record to verify what actually was said and that the interviewer has not changed the content when reporting (Maxwell 1996; Seidman 1998).

Coding and data analysis

The coding scheme used was important because, 'Coding is analysis. To review a set of field notes, transcribed or synthesized, and to dissect them meaningfully, while keeping the relations between the parts intact, is the stuff of analysis' (Miles and Huberman 1994: 56). Codes are essentially labels that are used to categorize portions of the participants' words; the codes I used were not meant to describe their words but, rather, the meanings the participants attached to those words. I attempted to find patterns and also to describe and interpret participants' words through themes. I did not want to create a content-specific coding scheme; instead, I wanted to create one that would allow an examination of general domains that could be developed inductively as more participants were interviewed and that operated on both the *etic* (general) and the *emic* (close to the participants) levels (Miles and Huberman 1994; Stake 1995).

During analysis of the data, I began to draw some conclusions by noting patterns and making contrasts and comparisons (see Miles and Huberman 1994). I identified themes by analyzing the participants' discussion and meaning of interactions of support to determine if they believed that support would be provided.

Social support exchanges: examining perceptions

Perceived support in interpersonal relationships is widely accepted to serve as a resistance and protective factor in reducing a wide range of psychological and life stressors, as well as having buffering effects for physical illnesses (Wills and Shinar 2000). In fact, 'the data suggest that whether or not one actually receives support is less important for health and adjustment than one's beliefs about its availability' (Cohen *et al.* 2000: 7). Thus, clearly there is great power in individuals' beliefs that support would be provided if needed because it contributes to, if not creates, a sense of mutuality and interdependence.

Although the social psychological and social epidemiological research literature provides a substantial body of evidence on the impacts of social support among the general population, these concepts have been less explored among populations impacted by the criminal justice system – namely, those released from incarceration facilities. There is a large and burgeoning knowledge base examining prisoner reentry (Bushway *et al.* 2007; Petersilia 2003; Thompson 2008; Travis 2004, 2005; Travis and Visher 2005; Visher and Travis 2003), but even with a majority of former prisoners returning to family relationships, the actual perceptions of former prisoners and their role in the (re)adjustment and (re)integration process with select family members is unexplored.

Therefore, and to explore this function, this chapter and the study on which it is based analyzed former prisoners and their family members' perceptions of the exchange of social support. That is, the former prisoners and family members discussed the tangible and intangible resources that were available if needed, and this revealed their positive perceptions of support existence and occurrences. Further, the interviews clearly showed that, despite any reported obligations or lack of resources, they still wanted to provide support to one another and they ensured a commitment to the relationship, which has transformative power. When former prisoners rely on their positive perceptions of select family members' support, and family members do the same, this contributes to a stable social base that has the potential to allow former prisoners to shift their self-perceived identity from that of criminal to the non-offending social role and attending responsibilities to that of support provider.

Perceptions of providing social support

The information provided in this chapter is derived from former prisoners and family members who reported that they believed others would provide support to them. A variety of contextual, explanatory and background factors influence this process; however, this study did not investigate those factors, as it is uncertain if individuals might have provided social support in the past because it was not necessary or it had not yet been requested. What this chapter does do is to offer some data and analysis to support the claim that former prisoners and their families perceived that social support would be given if needed, and that such perceptions/interpretations serve as a motivator and encouragement to continue on a positive path to avoid engaging in behaviors that might jeopardize their exchange of support, as this process can potentially influence their internal identity shift.

The individuals interviewed perceived that social support would be available if needed, and they based those perceptions particularly on past exchanges of support. That is, they believed that if a former prisoner or family member needed something in the future, the other person would be willing to provide it. They did not mention whether they actually had the resources to deliver on their promises; rather, the focus was on the intent, not the actual support promised or provided. For example, the aunt of former prisoner Raymond, commented:

> I mean, if he needs money, he hasn't asked me for it. He may ask me for a few dollars or something like that, and that's probably to get him some cigarettes or money in his pocket, but other than that I don't ask him for none 'cause right now he doesn't really have it and I don't think I would ask for it 'cause he is my nephew. If it is something that he needs, he will ask me for it.

Because of their supportive relationships, if former prisoners needed something, their family members were available to assist them. They had an understanding that family members would provide, but not ask for, support because former prisoners did not have the tangible resources necessary to assist family members. Financial (instrumental) resources were available, and such envisioned exchange of those resources served as emotional supports.

Raymond's aunt, too, emphasized the closeness of that relationship, and she provided a brief historical account of some of the reasons. With the relationship came certain expectations for both Raymond and his aunt. On this topic, she explained:

> If it is something that he needs, he will ask me for it. I never really asked him what he is expecting from me. He just appreciates the fact that I am getting his sisters. Two of them are not biologically my nieces, but I am going to get them anyway 'cause I don't want them separated and he always telling me that he appreciates the fact that I am doing that and he is going to do whatever he can to help me. Like I said, he appreciates that I am doing it. Like I said, he always telling me that he appreciates that I am doing it, you know, telling me they teenagers. He knows it's gonna be hard. Auntie, and I say, well, I

been a girl before, I can raise a girl better than I can raise a boy, and he says so, just the fact they gonna be four of them, it gonna be hard so I'm gonna help you the best I can.

This notion of indirect support gave family members a sense of purpose. They were willing to be accessible and available for former prisoners' requests regarding any number of things, even if the support they received in turn was moral support (appreciation of what was being done). Not only were family members willing to help, but also they were willing to help family members other than the former prisoners, which translated into helping the former prisoners, albeit indirectly. This means that former prisoners knew support was being provided to people they cared about. This can lead to former prisoners' supporting others; it is inspirational and motivational.

Another example comes from Jose, who discussed the availability of social support from his sister. He commented: 'Well, [my sister] would probably talk to me to see if I am having problems with my girlfriend. If I am having problems with my girl ... I would go to her and talk.' Although this instance of social support could be interpreted as purely emotional support, it also could be an example of purely informational support. The exchange of support in this context can be interpreted in many additional, different ways. It constitutes emotional support because Jose would turn to his sister for her caring and acceptance and believes that she would be his emotional confidante. It also constitutes informational support, because she might provide information about what to do; and it is about validation, in that she could provide her brother Jose with feedback about the appropriateness of his behaviors.

The perception that someone would help regardless of whatever additional responsibilities that individual had supports the claim that those interviewed did not necessarily view their relationships as entailing negative obligations, although increased interaction poses additional possibilities for negative interactions (Cohen *et al.* 2000). None of the former prisoners or family members described interacting or establishing relationships with each other as a burden, nor did they indicate that they wanted to limit interactions with each other. Arnold provided a particularly poignant example.

As far as financially, she knows I'm used to having money so she knows by me not being employed she tries to help me out. You know, give me money. But I be turning it down because I know she got kids. I be telling her, you got kids, you ain't got to give me no money. I'm gonna get through it. She's very supportive. She's very supportive. Anything I do, even if ... she might not agree with it, even if it was good or bad, she's been supportive.

Impacts of receiving and providing support

This commentary powerfully demonstrates that former prisoners are not individuals who make haphazard or unreasonable requests for support. Instead, they show a thoughtful understanding of how that support could impact the giver. Although some research evidence indicates that family expectations are overbearing and can lead or contribute to former prisoners engaging in further criminal acts (Breese *et al.* 2000), what is revealed here is quite the opposite: former prisoners are not actually a drain on, or struggling with, family members and their expectations.

On this point, the interviews support O'Brien's (2001) conclusion that former prisoners should be encouraged to build from, and improve upon, their existing relationships (e.g. increase frequency of contact and support exchanges) even when such a relationship was tenuous. (In O'Brien's study, the women conveyed that working through the conflict contributed to an overall positive sense of well-being. Through the interviews, she concluded that healthy relationships (with family and others) were vital to ensuring that the former prisoners grew emotionally and dissociated themselves from previous troubles.)

The brother of former prisoner Chris also discussed the multidimensional, interrelated aspects of social support exchanges and commented on the same issue that Arnold did. Chris's brother admitted that he received elements of support from Chris:

> We talk every day – well, almost every day. [As for support, how] could he be supportive to me? Nah, he don't support me with no money, [but] he encourage me to get into barber school, like that, and that's it. No, not really [I don't give him money]. I wouldn't want to deny him like that, but more than likely he know if I had it or not, but if I had it, I give it to him.

Along with a perception that support would be provided, there is, once again, the acknowledgement that support often is not requested from someone who might be harmed by providing such support. Former prisoners often wanted family members to succeed in their own endeavors; knowing that the latter had a specific goal served as an incentive for former prisoners to lead productive lives because they were connected in pursuing shared goals. Former prisoners and family members frequently interacted with each other and frequently were encouraging to each other.

Also, family members believe that accepting support from former prisoners could jeopardize whatever path they might want to pursue. Family members did not want to overwhelm former prisoners with requests for help because they thought it might prevent the former prisoners from achieving their goals. Nevertheless, former prisoners were available and willing to give family members whatever support they needed.

Even when former prisoners noted the lack of support they received and implied that they might be reluctant to provide support, they still expressed having the *desire* to support their family members. Only one released prisoner, Devon, commented on the limited aspects of social support and mentioned that he did not give or get any emotional support. 'No, none at all (*laugh*) . . . If [my family] needed my support, I would give it to them in the fullest, but after that I am gone.'

The seeming contradiction in this statement – that he does not give his family support but would give it to them if they needed it – reveals that even in supportive relationships there can be some reluctance to provide support because willingness to support reflects and is influenced by how much support the person thinks he has received from his family in the past. Even when former prisoners had not experienced an overabundance of positive social support exchanges, they were dedicated to providing something. This shows that former prisoners and their family members are invested in helping each other despite obstacles, problems, or moments of reluctance. Devon elaborated on this issue:

> Well, if I would need her, she knows I am trying to do better for myself, and if I needed her, she would come through for me, but if she know I am on the same bullshit as when I got locked up, she would say the hell with me, so there ain't too much I can ask for. [As for now,] I go over there, talk to her for a while. Tell her how it is with the Going Home Program I am in.

Promotion of non-criminal behavior

There also was the perception and implicit notion that family members would not support former prisoners who continued on the same pre-incarceration path. Former prisoners viewed this condition as showing that their family members' purpose was to ensure and promote their non-criminal well-being.

Perceiving that someone would be available to provide support was a constant theme identifiable throughout the experiences of the former prisoners and family members interviewed; this theme carried the underlying meaning that the former prisoners were being encouraged to pursue non-criminal paths. The categories of social support identified in the literature – emotional, instrumental, informational, companionship, and validation – are frequently intertwined (Rook and Underwood 2000), as evidenced by the data previously analyzed.

Former prisoners often discussed how 'close' they were to certain family members, and reported instances of how they defined that closeness. An example of the closeness of their relationships and the perception that social support would be exchanged concerns Arnold, who discussed his relationship with his sister:

I can go to my sister and she can come to me with anything, anything. Ain't nothing we'd never . . . Like I said, we was closest of anybody. Of all my brothers, we was the closest. We ain't never . . . We had a situation when she wouldn't even talk to my mother, but she'd come talk to me. Not my father or anybody, but she'd come talk to me about it. I was the same way with her . . . [My relationship with her,] it means a lot. It means a whole lot.

The telling of life stories is not easily compartmentalized. A combination of various support types exist and operate even within the same instance. Here, what was revealed was that social support exchanges operated in ways so that former prisoners and family members both perceived that support existed. Further, the commentaries provided by former prisoners showed that they perceived that their family members would be emotionally supportive, would provide validation and companionship, and that both parties would provide such support to each other.

The idea of losing someone who is incarcerated can translate into concern upon release. Knowing of the possibility that someone could be reincarcerated when there is a strong bond weighs heavily on the emotions of people who rely on the relationship with the former prisoner. For the family member of former prisoner Henry, the relationship has special meaning.

Oh, man. I wouldn't even know what to do if I lost my brother. That's like the only person that really I can count on in the family. If I got it, he got it. If he got it, I got it. So that's really the main person that I can call on in my life, you know, because we just been through too much. Man, that's my right-hand man in life. I'd go crazy if something really happened to my brother because that's the only person that I can run to if I have problems that I can depend on. So if I lose him there's just really not no reason for me living if my brother was to die. What's my purpose really then? There wouldn't be no use for me. I'd just be over with.

Because these individuals knew and relied on the perception that they would 'be there' for each other, the loss of the other person (figuratively or literally) was potentially devastating to their emotional well-being and could alter their desire to pursue and remain in supportive relationships. Counting on another person to be present in one's life, and acknowledging the importance of supportive relationships, showed that the perceived exchange of support in these close relationships resulted in, and was influenced by, mutual caring.

Findings

My findings show that part of the mutual exchange of social support occurs as a way to motivate and encourage the former prisoners to excel. The thematic pieces indicated that by assisting a former prisoner, family members felt encouraged and were willing to help the former prisoner (directly or indirectly). The story in which I was interested was how former prisoners and their referred family members exchanged support, and I wanted to understand what purpose those interactions served. In addition, I asked how that purpose might impact both the former prisoner and the family member. My conclusion is that family members felt encouraged and motivated to help the former prisoners to pursue positive aspects of their lives. Nevertheless, even the best-functioning families have difficulties and face tremendous hardship. To better understand the dynamics of these relationships, I had to elicit insights about former prisoners' lives and their relationships with family members and understand the dynamics of social support.

Families in this study were, for the most part, resource-poor families that were subject to many additional demands. My data cannot speak directly to the resource deficiencies of these families; however, this study does provide a basis for the claim that they and former prisoners provided meaningful support in a mutual way that served as motivation and encouragement to the former prisoners to pursue non-criminal paths; and that advantages accrued not only to those who received the support but also to those who provided the support. Ultimately, the kinds of support that former prisoners access, and the challenges inherent in that support, may help them succeed.

The themes that arose throughout the analysis reveal that *perceptions* of support – the belief that someone would be there if needed – have the potential for transformation; that is, perceptions possibly can motivate and encourage positive behavior and improvement in the dyadic relationship. Simply, former prisoners and family members believed that social support, in its various, interlocking manifestations, would be given if requested. The analysis also showed that individuals perceived aspects of their relationships as being supportive in a variety of ways. From Raymond's aunt's commentary on the perceived availability of instrumental (financial) assistance as emotionally supportive, to Chris's brother's discussion of acts that could be interpreted as emotional and validation support, the interviews elucidated how instances of interaction and their supportive nature are intertwined. Former prisoners' family members perceived that former prisoners would be generally supportive.

Discussion and conclusions

Analysis of the data shows the importance of social support to former prisoners and their families. The data presented herein reveal that perceptions of being supported motivate and encourage non-criminal behavior and that the same act of support can serve multiple functions (e.g. receipt of instrumental support may also feel validating). Further, the recognition that individuals believed that support would be exchanged is evidence of a base of strengths to work from in providing families and former prisoners with mechanisms to encourage abstinence from (or a decrease in) criminal behavior. In addition, not only are there advantages to the person who is receiving the support, but also there are advantages – namely, feeling that one has purpose and a role, a value in the family – to those who are givers of the support; this is important even if the support does not contribute to the end of their criminal behaviors. These exchanges, and the underlying meaning and rationale for these exchanges, ideally would offer an alternative identity for former prisoners, an alternative to the 'criminal' identity and the associated purpose of that identity.

Specific social support exchanges among former prisoners and family members illustrate that family members and former prisoners alike benefit from the social support exchange process. This finding clearly is indicated by former prisoners being encouraged to contribute positively to their relationships. For family members, providing support gives meaning to their lives, in that their purpose is to ensure that the former prisoners do not return to their previous situations. These social support exchanges illustrate the complex nature of support, as the exchanges can be perceived and defined in more than one way, and the meaning one attributes to that support may vary; it reaffirms the family connection.

Gouldner's (1960) seminal article on the topic of reciprocity provides a useful analytical tool to clarify the underlying rationale of social support exchanges in the context of former prisoners' family relationships. In his treatment of the norm of reciprocity, he wrote that there are 'two interrelated, minimal demands: (1) people should help those who have helped them, and (2) people should not injure those who have helped them' (Gouldner 1960: 171). He elaborated, arguing that 'motivation for reciprocity stems not only from the sheer gratification which Alter receives from Ego but also from Alter's internalization of a specific norm of reciprocity which morally obliges him to give benefits to those from whom he has received them' (1960: 174).

In this sense, family members of former prisoners would help former prisoners if they could. Family members would assist former prisoners if they were truly in a bind, and vice versa, and both parties to the relationship had the perception that they were willing to help, and would help, if called upon. This illustrates that the exchange of social support does, in some ways, create buy-in (a norm of reciprocity), with the family member becoming dedicated to the relationship with the former prisoner despite his past criminality.

Moreover, it should be highlighted that former prisoners and family members in this study did not merely intend to exchange resources because they felt obligated, but, rather, because there was a moral justification for doing so (Uehara 1995); that is, they thought it was the right thing to do. More specifically, Gouldner (1960) (as cited in Uehara 1995) explained that gratification is present when receiving tangible or intangible goods *and* that the moral obligation encourages – and, I speculate, motivates – both parties to return any benefits received. On this note, with respect to the norm of reciprocity, Uehara adds that individuals tend to 'strive to meet reciprocity obligations and avoid "overbenefiting" from their socially supportive relationships' (1995: 488).

Knowing that former prisoners would seek out family members with whom to consult about their other relationships shows that the family member–former prisoner dyadic relationship validates and encourages improvement in other non-family relationships, which also can improve the former prisoners' social and mental well-being. Further, former prisoners' belief that family members would help in relationships is evidence that families want to help, and that former prisoners believe that their support is available. Such willingness to help shows that the support provided can make a difference in the future behavior of former prisoners and in their relationships with their family members (La Vigne *et al.* 2004; Naser and Visher 2006); it means that neither would not want to put the other in a position where they had to request help (e.g. incarceration) or 'overbenefit' from the exchange (Uehara 1995).

These findings also validate and build on the existing research evidence on post-release former prisoner–family member relationships. Family support mechanisms are important elements that contribute to the successful reentry of former prisoners to society. Specifically, exchanging – both giving and receiving – emotional support can reduce the prevalence of post-release depression and improve familial relationships (Ekland-Olson *et al.* 1983). Self-defined support among select family members is a predictor of former prisoners' success (Nelson *et al.* 1999). Further, in familial relationships that are supportive but occasionally experience conflict, working through conflict contributes to overall healthy relationships for former prisoners (O'Brien 2001). These studies resonate with the findings in this chapter.

The findings indicate that former prisoners and family members want to provide social support despite the many obligations of each. They perceive that social support is available if needed; and they exchange support in an effort to improve their relationship, encourage and motivate former prisoners to desist from crime, and provide a purpose for family

67

members to help in ways that allow them to exert control over their contributions. Further, they showed a great deal of empathy, as well as great need, in the ways they asked for, and interpreted receiving, support. Ultimately, it is healing and helpful for the former prisoners in this study to feel that they have a purpose and role in their families, if for no other reason than for their own well-being.

Implications

By understanding the multitudinal and multilayered aspects of social support – the underlying meaning associated with support exchange and its reciprocal nature – and the various outcomes that former prisoners and family members are experiencing, practitioners can begin to conceptualize interventions that encourage the incorporation of supportive family members. This chapter provides criminal justice practitioners with some evidence that families should be included in the development of prisoner reentry programs. Specifically, supportive individuals (family members and others) should be identified and included; family and community resources and deficits should be analyzed so the programs will respond effectively; and efforts should be targeted to increase the provision of whatever productive social support is available. The systems currently in place do not necessarily include family members and their existing support capacities in programs that assist released prisoners.

Regardless of the potentially stressful socio-economic and community conditions to which former prisoners return upon release, some former prisoners believe they have 'free will' (Maruna 2001). Further, self-defined family support is the strongest predictor of individual success (Nelson *et al.* 1999). As former prisoners are likely to return to their families (Fishman 1986; Nelson *et al.* 1999; Nurse 2002; O'Brien 2001), and because such return is nearly inevitable, we should encourage family members to emphasize former prisoners' strengths. In particular, when working with individuals released from prison, clinicians and criminal justice practitioners must focus on former prisoners *and* family members in the treatment context. The idea that released prisoners should be the primary focus of interventions leads treatment providers, criminal justice agencies, and policy advocates down the wrong road because it excludes individuals who can contribute significantly to the transformation of former prisoners.

Moreover, interventions should be directed to what the families and former prisoners can offer, and build on the unique strengths of their relationships. Mechanisms for changing former prisoners' notions about their non-criminal selves, ranging from using verbal affirmations in support of a former prisoner's ability to participating in support of skills improvement, must be explored.

In addition, although therapeutic interventions, desistance-focused policies, and resource-based supports are in some respects helpful in curbing criminal behaviors, these often operate from a deficit-based approach (Ward and Maruna 2007). Former prisoners do have risks, but concentrating merely on decreasing those risks leaves a vacuum as to what actually should be done – such as using their skills to complete tasks, reinforcing positive cognitive shifts in their identity, and maneuvering through institutional and programmatic obstacles.

In line with the Good Lives Model rehabilitation theory and one of the phases of the good-lives-oriented case formulation treatment plan, it is recommended that '[we] identify the individuals' particular strengths, positive experiences, and life experiences' (Ward and Maruna 2007: 136). Therefore, there is some legitimacy and transformative power in investigating how former prisoners and family members, particularly in this study, rely on and use their strengths, however they are self-defined. Former prisoners and family members understood their various needs and did not ask for or try to provide more than was possible.

Criminal justice practitioners and policy-makers also must recognize that informal social support arrangement and interactions often serve as comfort mechanisms that alter the social control aspect of criminal justice policy (Cullen *et al.* 1999). Family members and former prisoners can have difficulty directly confronting former prisoners' obstacles and their deficits, as doing so would complicate their relationships and make them focus on risks. Therefore, we need to use what former prisoners and their family members have to offer, both at their immediate disposal, which can strengthen their bonds, and in the future, such as opportunities to offer solid, meaningful, practical suggestions on how to improve certain aspects of their lives.

Undoubtedly, increasing the various types and amounts of resources is an important task; however, if we understand the various dimensions of family support, we can use the existing support capacity in families in combination with the former prisoners' capacity to give support. Such suggestions neither place a burden on families nor absolve the state from its responsibilities; programs should engage supportive family members and identify factors that harm the family and the former prisoners' relationships.

Former prisoners and select family members can support each other in productive ways. This social support must be considered in any treatment or intervention. Fundamentally, formal programs are limited in what they can offer, as the policy and programmatic response to facilitating reentry is often instrumental and program-based (counseling, connecting to employment, and so forth), and lacks the family support dynamics outlined here that are important to this population. Although the roles and behaviors examined herein may not contribute to the end of former prisoners' criminal behaviors, this discussion, I hope, will offer an alternative to the 'criminal' identity and the associated purpose of that identity.

Notes

1 This is a comprehensive program designed to assist individuals released from Illinois prisons by leveraging existing services in the community.
2 This evaluation project sampled males released from the Illinois Department of Corrections Westside Adult Transition Center, a minimum-security residential transition center where individuals were required to participate in non-institutional employment, education, life skills training, and/or community service, as well as institutional responsibilities, for a minimum of 35 hours per week (Safer Foundation 2002).
3 The names used here are pseudonyms to protect the confidentiality of the research participants.

References

Breese, J. R., Ra'el, K. and Grant, G. K. (2000) 'No place like home: A qualitative investigation of social support and its effects on recidivism', *Sociological Practice*, 2(1): 1–21.

Bushway, S., Stoll, M. A. and Weiman, D. F. (eds) (2007) *Barriers to Reentry? The Labor Market for Released Prisoners in Post-industrial America*. New York: Russell Sage Foundation.

Cohen, S., Gottlieb, B. H. and Underwood, L. G. (2000) 'Social relationships and health', in S. Cohen, L. G. Underwood and B. H. Gottlieb (eds) *Social Support Measurement and Intervention: A Guide for Health and Social Scientists*. New York: Oxford University Press.

Cullen, F. T., Wright, J. P. and Chamlin, M. B. (1999) 'Social support and social reform: A progressive crime control agenda', *Crime & Delinquency*, 45(2): 188–207.

Ekland-Olson, S., Supanic, M., Campbell, J. and Lenihan, K. J. (1983) 'Postrelease depression and the importance of familial support', *Criminology*, 21(2): 253–75.

Fishman, L. T. (1986) 'Repeating the cycle of hard living and crime: Wives' accommodations to husbands' parole performance', *Federal Probation*, 50(1): 44–54.

Gouldner, A. Q. (1960) 'The norm of reciprocity: A preliminary statement', *American Sociological Review*, 25(2): 161–78.

La Vigne, N. G. and Mamalian, C. A. (with Travis, J. and Visher, C.) (2003) *A Portrait of Prisoner Reentry in Illinois*. Washington, DC: Urban Institute.

La Vigne, N. G., Visher, C. and Castro, J. (2004) *Chicago Prisoners' Experiences Returning Home*. Washington, DC: Urban Institute.

Martinez, D. J. and Christian, J. (2009) 'The familial relationships of former prisoners: Examining the link between residence and informal support mechanisms', *Journal of Contemporary Ethnography*, 38(2): 201–24.

Maruna, S. (2001) *Making Good: How Ex-convicts Reform and Rebuild their Lives*. Washington, DC: American Psychological Association.

Maxwell, J. A. (1996) 'Qualitative research design: An interactive approach', in L. Bickman and D. J. Rog (eds) *Applied Social Research Methods Series*, vol. 4. Thousand Oaks, CA: Sage Publications.

Miles, M. B. and Huberman, A. M. (1994) *Qualitative Data Analysis: An Expanded Sourcebook*. Thousand Oaks, CA: Sage Publications.

Naser, R. L. and Visher, C. A. (2006) 'Family members' experiences with incarceration and reentry', *Western Criminology Review*, 7(2): 20–31.

Nelson, M., Deess, P. and Allen, C. (1999) *The First Month Out: Post-incarceration Experiences in New York City*. New York: Vera Institute of Justice.

Nurse, A. M. (2002) *Fatherhood Arrested: Parenting From Within the Juvenile Justice System*. Nashville, TN: Vanderbilt University Press.

O'Brien, P. (2001) *Making it in the 'Free World': Women in Transition from Prison*. New York: State University of New York Press.

Petersilia, J. (2003) *When Prisoners Come Home: Parole and Prisoner Reentry*. Oxford, UK: Oxford University Press.

Pratt, T. C. and Cullen, F. T. (2005) 'Assessing macro-level predictors and theories of crime: A meta-analysis', in M. Tonry (ed.) *Crime and Justice: A Review of Research*. Chicago: University of Chicago Press.

Rook, K. S. and Underwood, L. G. (2000) 'Social support measurement and interventions: Comments and future directions', in S. Cohen, L. G. Underwood and B. H. Gottlieb (eds) *Social Support Measurement and Intervention: A Guide for Health and Social Scientists*. Oxford, UK: Oxford University Press.

Safer Foundation (2002) *Adult Transition Centers* [Online]. Available at: *www.safer-fnd.org/atc.html* (22 February 2004).

Schwandt, T. A. (1994) 'Constructivist, interpretivist approaches to human inquiry', in N. K. Denzin and Y. S. Lincoln (eds) *Handbook of Qualitative Research*. London: Sage Publications.

Seidman, I. (1998) *Interviewing as Qualitative Research: A Guide for Researchers in Education and the Social Sciences*. New York: Teachers College Press.

Stake, R. (1995) *The Art of Case Study Research*. Thousand Oaks, CA: Sage Publications.

Thompson, A. (2008) *Releasing Prisoners, Redeeming Communities: Reentry, Race, and Politics*. New York: New York University Press.

Travis, J. (2004) 'Reentry and reintegration: New perspectives on the challenges of mass incarceration', in M. Pattillo, D. Weiman and B. Western (eds) *Imprisoning America: The Social Effects of Mass Incarceration*. New York: Russell Sage Foundation.

Travis, J. (2005) *But They All Come Back: Facing the Challenges of Prisoner Reentry*. Washington, DC: Urban Institute Press.

Travis, J. and Visher, C. (eds) (2005) *Prisoner Reentry and Crime in America*. New York: Cambridge University Press.

Uehara, E. (1995) 'Reciprocity reconsidered: Gouldner's moral norm of reciprocity and social support', *Journal of Social Personal Relationships*, 12(4): 483–502.

Visher, C. and Travis, J. (2003) 'Transitions from prison to community: Understanding individual pathways', *Annual Review of Sociology*, 29, 89–113.

Ward, T. and Maruna, S. (2007) *Rehabilitation*. New York: Routledge.

Wills, T. A. and Shinar, O. (2000) 'Measuring perceived and received social support', in S. Cohen, L. G. Underwood and B. H. Gottlieb (eds) *Social Support Measurement and Intervention: A Guide for Health and Social Scientists*. Oxford, UK: Oxford University Press.

Chapter 5

'I got a quick tongue': negotiating ex-convict identity in mixed company

Lois Presser and Suzanne Kurth

According to the sociological tradition known as symbolic interactionism, individuals construct their identities as they weigh other people's attitudes toward them (Cooley 1902; Mead 1934). That process occurs within social interactions, which are, specifically, communicative exchanges. In our view, it follows that identity *transformation* is likewise shaped by and within social interactions. This chapter on negotiating an ex-convict identity 'in mixed company' investigates that transformative process. We examine the ways in which James,[1] an ex-convict, presented himself to multiple co-conversationalists by telling his life story. James' co-conversationalists (or interlocutors, as we shall call them) were students in a college course on restorative justice. Our overarching research questions are: How do ex-offenders identify themselves to multiple, active interlocutors? Do they assimilate or resist contributions and challenges to their identity claims?

Research is available on hearings, such as trials, where persons vested with formal authority interrogate people's claims about why they acted as they did. Such research is primarily focused on one-on-one exchanges, particularly between an agent of law and either a defendant or a witness (e.g. Matoesian 1993; Molotch and Boden 1985). However, *multiple* others call ex-offenders to account for their actions within many treatment and restorative justice settings. Studies that encompass the voices of multiple challengers are rare, so that we scarcely know what the individual offender 'does' with all of them.

One line of sociological research investigates the control exercised over the expressed identities of ex-convicts, often within groups (Fox 1999;

McKendy 2006; Waldram 2007). For example, Waldram (2007) studied a prison-based sex offender treatment program based on a cognitive behavioral model. Inmates were asked to tell 'their' stories, but staff imposed pre-established notions of each person's true story, based on the treatment model, the inmate's official record of crimes, and notions about the characteristics of true stories. 'All any inmate can safely add is new insight, but only if that insight is compatible with the principles of cognitive behavior therapy and existing forensic psychological knowledge of the typical lives, motivations and thought patterns of sexual offenders (2007: 165). Waldram and others depict ex-convicts as highly constrained by programmatic discourses of who they are. Relatively little attention has been paid to ex-convicts' resistance to such constraints, in clinical settings or elsewhere (cf. Fox 1999).

Understanding resistance is crucial for a sociology that stresses human agency and creativity. It is also enormously useful for a program of rehabilitation. Resistance to the controlling aspect of rehabilitative interventions is a sort of engagement in the change project. The ways in which participants resist can and should inform interventions. Specifically, treatment ought to heed what participants mean when they say that we 'have them wrong'. Ex-offenders, like all people, have wisdom about who they are and what they need in order to do better and live better lives (Ward and Maruna 2007). In negotiating his ex-convict identity, James insisted upon self-knowledge, first and foremost. He also alleged both self-reform and cunning – to the point of describing recent undiscovered crimes. Our analysis of James' identity work suggests to us that interventions with ex-offenders must respect, if not totally support, their vantage on their lives.

To begin to examine how an individual negotiates and renegotiates his or her identity within a multi-person setting, the researcher must attend closely to statements made by all participants. Because of the need for analysis of the talk of several persons, we focused on one man we call James, engaging with others. Data on James are drawn from a larger study of convicted men.

The larger study, for which 27 men were interviewed, was designed to illuminate the stories that ex-offenders tell about themselves (Presser 2008). All of the men in the larger study claimed moral decency in the present. At two extremes, the men either claimed that they had always been decent, or claimed that they were basically decent but had faltered at some point and were subsequently reformed. James draws on both storylines – that which stresses moral stability (a 'stability narrative') and that which stresses moral reform (a 'reform narrative'). The narrative that contains both storylines – which was used by the majority of men in the larger study – is termed an 'elastic narrative'.

Other scholars find selective deployment of storylines to be typical of narrators. Patricia O'Connor (2000) explains that 'speakers are simultaneously presenting and re-presenting selves on several planes of discourse' (p. 154). We see James as working hard to arrive at a self that both he and others might view favorably. James presented a self that had both new and old elements; his challenge was to express both and to quell various situated protests concerning his claims of transformation. In fact, James used the questions and input of his audience to construct a desired self. Before tracking that accomplishment, we review scholarly work on self-narratives and the often unrecognized role that they play in the lives of ex-offenders.

Identities, narratives and offenders

Grounding our view of James' dynamic and discursive identity transformation is an understanding that identities are best understood as running stories of the self. This 'storied' conceptualization of identity is nicely captured in philosopher Paul Ricoeur's (1985: 214) observation that 'we recognize ourselves in the stories that we tell about ourselves'. Although anticipated by sociologists, most famously George Herbert Mead (1934) and Erving Goffman (1959), who located the self in symbolic interaction, the notion of narrated identities owes a good deal to psychology and communication studies as well. Narrative helps the narrator in the basic task of establishing self-continuity in the face of multiple, dynamic and contradictory experiences (Lecky 1945; Erikson 1956; Kerby 1991). McAdams (1999: 486) explains: 'By scripting one's life in such a way that different characters or subselves take on different roles and attributes, the "I" is able to express the multiplicity of selfhood within a single story of the self.' Relatedly, narrative helps us to present our preferred selves – those that are most valued – to other people.

Hence, storytelling should be especially important for ex-offenders. First, mainstream society rewards those who can establish that their crime does not reflect who they 'really' are. Narrative allows offenders to portray *good* selves either by denying responsibility for wrongdoing or by recasting wrongdoing in a good light (Scott and Lyman 1968). Actually, though, in telling her/his story, the ex-offender has already distanced her/himself from the person whose actions are being described – the 'protagonist' (Bruner 1990). Narrative itself creates that distance. Linde (1993: 123) explains that the activity of narrating 'allows the narrator to stand apart from and comment on the actions of the protagonist'. Second, narrative is a particularly effective vehicle for giving reasons (Stone 1982; Linde 1993; Tilly 2006), which are expected if not demanded of those who have violated norms and laws. Specifically, the plot of one's narrative at least potentially complicates and contextualizes one's actions. Finally, narrative allows offenders to put the past behind them and make promises about the future. The act of explaining why, notes Tilly, 'connects people with each other even when observers might find the reasons flimsy, contrived, or fantastic' (2006: 10). The mere fact of telling one's story humanizes the speaker.

Scholars consider storytelling among ex-offenders as potentially transformative *and* potentially oppressive. Restorative justice proponents view the exchange of stories as healing (Sullivan and Tifft 2001), yet others view the discourse of restorative justice as a new measure of controlling the socially marginalized (Arrigo and Schehr 1998). So-called twelve-step programs encourage self-described addicts to share rather scripted stories with one another (Denzin 1987; O'Reilly 1997; Swora 2002), but the tale of redemption can nonetheless provide a template for a desisting identity (Maruna 2001). In correctional treatment programs based on highly regarded cognitive models, facilitators monitor and edit ex-offenders' stories, urging speakers to adopt certain discourses about why they offended and how they might avoid re-offending (Fox 1999; Waldram 2007). In short, for ex-offenders, telling one's story promises a new start even as it invites a new sort of surveillance.

Research methods

For the larger study of narrative identities of ex-convicts, the first author conducted in-depth interviews with twenty-seven (27) men (Presser 2008). The men were referred by social service organizations working with convicts and ex-convicts in Ohio, New York and Pennsylvania. Most had been convicted of serious violent crimes and/or had had multiple encounters with criminal justice agencies. The interviews were tape-recorded. Presser (2008) used some standard prompts, designed to stimulate talk of how the men perceived themselves, their lives, and their offending behavior. However, for the most part the interviews were unstructured. Also, the interviewer avoided posing challenges to the interviewees' stories.

Presser (2008) interviewed the majority of the research participants one on one. Only James engaged with a *group* of people. James spoke to a small undergraduate class on restorative justice at a large, Midwestern university. Seven students attended class the day that James came to speak. With the basic purpose of humanizing so-called offenders, the instructor (the first author) planned a guest presentation. James was a resident of a halfway house for men recently released from prison. An associate of the instructor – a caseworker who had worked at the halfway house prior to James' arrival – facilitated contact with James. The caseworker extended an invitation to come to speak about his experiences as one who has committed a crime and been to prison. James agreed.

James is an African-American male and was in his late thirties at the time of the presentation. In addition to the seven students, he faced the instructor (a white female in her mid-thirties) and the caseworker, who sat in for the day (an Asian male in his mid-thirties).[2] The class session ran nearly two hours and was wholly dedicated to James' talk. It was tape-recorded with appropriate human subjects approval. Recordings were transcribed and then analyzed with the help of N5 (text analysis) software. The software helped us to take note of patterns across and within narratives, and later to retrieve them to discern the contexts for, and particulars of, these patterns. We used it to create reports on what each man said and what common things the men said. Repeated runs through the data led to two dominant themes across *all* of the narratives: one's *moral trajectory* and *heroic struggle*. Concerning the theme of moral trajectory, two archetypical self-claims within narratives were identified: that of moral *reform* (one has returned to goodness) and that of moral *stability* (one has always been good). The majority of research participants told *elastic* narratives, which stressed both moral stability and reform. Of course, many other themes were identified in the data. Specific themes in James' narrative included sexual identity, religion and defiance.

Finally, the interaction between research participant and interlocutor(s) was analyzed with the use of memos that read as running summaries of (1) how the man's story was unfolding and (2) what was going on between us. In this analysis involving James and his interlocutors, we draw on both the reports of what James said and our memo of his interaction with others.

Analysis

James told an elastic narrative: that is, one incorporating statements of both moral reform and moral constancy. In his story, he is one who has triumphed over adversity when others failed, and changed into a better person. He insisted at all times on a preferred self that is strong and shrewd, defiant of those who attack him on the basis of his non-heterosexual identity. In the classroom, James' interlocutors posed particular challenges to his identity claims. Some were especially critical of his claims of reform. From the memo of interaction, we determined that James used questions and comments to tell his story: they were not irrelevant to the story. In this story he is essentially special and resilient – a person to be admired. As such, he resisted feedback that would position him as a typical ex-offender, whether a now-good one or an evidently bad one. His resistance showcased the very qualities he talked up – cunning and strength.

Our analysis roughly follows the chronology of the classroom session. James began by launching a strong, somewhat scripted self-critique. In no time he changed the focus of his narrative to the self as expert (knower) and champion (over potential domination or insult). He emphasized his 'quick tongue' – his cunning – in stories and through storytelling performance. Most complex was James' claim to have abandoned his past propensity toward crime, though not all offending. The students challenged James on the consistency of this last claim. The process of claiming and modifying 'who he is' was a situated accomplishment, one of responding to what others said and asked, though not without abrupt digressions in order to recount favorite anecdotes. Our findings are organized by two overarching themes in James' narrative, which we call (1) knowledge, self-knowledge and triumph over adversity; and (2) being bad, good and resilient.

Knowledge, self-knowledge and triumph

The role of storyteller is a resource for managing what the story will be 'about', and James' story is to a large extent about challenges and triumph. The instructor briefly introduces James as a person recently released from prison and living in a halfway house. She then asks James to talk about whatever he wants to talk about. He begins with a strong critique of self for past offending, but soon turns to how he has overcome adversity:

> My name is James Smith. I'm 39. Uh, I'm a seven-time convicted felon. Spent ten years of my life in (prison) due to my stupidity. An' uh, you wanna know – the side of – what goes on, on the other side of the gate? What goes on out there? Whatever you all are goin' to school for, what you're majoring in – as far as criminal justice – is totally different when you lookin' at it from my perspective. (*Chuckle*) Ya know, so. Roll officers or whatever. And the officers, is totally different bein' supervised by them. And it's rough. Living inside of a penitentiary is not a joke. And it's totally different from what you see on television. It's a 100 per cent different from that.

Thus, James offers a strong, if vague and somewhat rehearsed, indictment of self ('due to my stupidity'). He juxtaposes that indictment with insider knowledge of what the prison system is like and presents himself as a successful survivor of the system:

> What they have to offer there is limited. But it's, you know, you do the time, you don't let the time do you. Like they say, ya know. You go up there, and you got to do it. Ya know. Some people go up there and they lose their minds. I lost my mother when I was up there, ya know. And I stayed strong.

James' strength in prison is highlighted by the loss of control he attributes to others in the same setting.

James describes his criminal history: drug use led to shoplifting, credit card fraud and motor vehicle theft. Possession of cocaine landed him in prison the first time, but James is quick to state that that first, six-month prison stay was easy: 'It was like *college*.' A few years later, James was caught shoplifting, which led to a new, lengthier prison sentence. He served two years of this prison sentence by the time he was released on parole. His parole was revoked when he was caught on a new shoplifting charge. After a rather matter-of-fact review of his record, James returns to self-critical speech:

> I can't blame – everything I did on my parents. 'Cause I grew up with a mother and father. Some people say, 'Well, I didn't have a father.' I did. And it, ya know, to this day, my mother still an' my father still is like 'I don't know what's wrong with you.' I said, 'Well maybe I'm just a bad seed.' Ya know. Every time I start somethin', I don't complete it. Ya know. But if I can start some trouble, I can start some – and – ya know – I can start that and finish that. But the – what comes with it is always jail time.

The message seems to be that James knows himself, including his propensity to get in trouble, better than others. James' professed self-awareness means that he is aware, too, of what his rehabilitation requires. He points out that he chose to be in the halfway house: 'I wasn't sent there by no parole officer.' Sending a message of reform, he adds: 'And I've been there a couple of weeks and I feel it's gonna work for me.'

Before ceding the floor, James tries to engage his audience by recalling participation in 'a group like this' while in prison where *others* were disavowing their offender status. James takes a hardline attitude with those who would deny they did wrong, recalling his stance: 'You *supposed* to be here because you *are* here! Ya know. You committed the crime, you here.' Thus does James align himself with his would-be critics in the classroom. He is critical of convicts including himself, and he is knowledgeable about the criminal justice system – indeed, more knowledgeable than the audience. In comparison with other convicts, he excels at 'doing time'. James deploys in-group/out-group distinctions – with local and extra-local referents – to establish a multifaceted superiority (Jenkins 2004; Tajfel 1981).

Invoking the identity of homosexual further allows James to establish himself as one who holds his own in the face of would-be victimizers. James adds the challenge of being gay to the refrain that prison is difficult but he has done the time with relative ease: 'I'm gay, right? And, it was rough for me in there. But – I stood up my own ground.' James strives to be known as one who has faced *and* met challenges uniquely well. James stresses his unique ability to defeat would-be oppressors when the instructor asks him about experiences of bias in prison:

I	When you said it was rough for you – as a gay man, what did you mean? What was rough?
James	You have the homopho – uh, homophobics.
I	But people, but you said you weren't raped but people like harassing you?
James	They tried, but see I got a quick tongue, so.

James also describes his clever, discursive resistance to familial demands that he embrace heterosexuality:

> And my mother – my mother said 'I want all my sons to give me a grandson.' I told her I'd buy her a set of Cabbage Patch dolls. (*Class laughter; he laughs*) . . . And she said 'No. I want a baby.' I said, 'Well I guess you're too old to be havin' 'em, don't you think?'

James' cunning defiance is also made plain in a follow-up story of taking a girl to the senior prom, only to slip away to a gay bar. He is no victim of other people's expectations. His family, he concludes, has accepted his homosexuality. When Benita, the older of the two very vocal female students, asks for more detail on how they came to accept him as gay, he sharply responds: 'I can care if they did or not (*laugh*)!' James shifts the focus to his self-presentation as a gay adult:

> I'm not one of those 'run out and just you-see-me-all-here' fags. I might be dressin' it, like 'you a fag'. Why? 'Cause I dress different?' You know. That's how I was in prison.

Talk of defiance concerning his sexuality prompts James to talk about defiance in prison more generally – this time concerning autonomy in prison and frequent rule violations, as James proclaims:

> Tennis shoes, kept 'em. Sweatsuits, kep' 'em. Ya know. Didn't want for nothin' . . . An' uh, I went through – I was up there smokin' marijuana – often: like *crazy*. Nobody knew I was smokin'.

James was sometimes sanctioned for his violations. He was once placed in segregation – 'the hole'. He implies that it was rough there, but he does not remain focused on the experience. In response to the caseworker's question, 'When you were in the hole, what kind of food did they serve you?' he replies nonchalantly that he chose not to eat. Again, he is in control.

Denial, and particularly denial of desire for what may be withheld from him as an ex-convict, was another way that James asserted invincibility. For example, Benita launched a line of questioning about the employment difficulties James might face as a hairdresser, the vocation he has chosen for himself. He denies such difficulties, as when he responds to Benita's question of whether salons check on one's criminal record:

> N – no – no, no, no, no, no. They – you go by your – your – your style and ability. You know, word of mouth. See, I used to work for two salons. I worked at one for nine years.

He describes his past experience at hair salons, then a particular job offer on the horizon:

> And, uh, I ran into a girl that used to work at Nora's and she's saying [to] me, she wants me to come work for – with her. And, I told her I'm just gonna enjoy the summer (*laugh*) and then I'm gonna go back to work.

James implies an easy road to employment thanks to a resilient self.

After an interlude, Benita and Nicky, the two active female students, continue with the theme of obstacles. Benita is oriented toward solutions. She proposes an alternative approach for ex-convicts faced with hiring discrimination: 'Well, what if, when you get out, since it's hard for felons to get a job, couldn't you get your own business?' Nicky joins this conversation as a challenger – one who interrogates James' story.

James	You know – they – you can go through bar – you can go through barber school in prison.
Benita	Can you get your – uh – business?
James	Yeah.
Benita	Is it hard for you to get a loan? I didn't think so (*unclear*).
Nicky	Have you applied for a loan?
James	I don't want my own salon (*laugh*).

The students confront James with an awareness of the problems facing ex-convicts, thus challenging his prior claims of expertise and choice. James rejects the implication of vulnerability – specifically, that he wants what he cannot and does not have. Thus he (supposedly) insulates himself from encounter with barriers to reentry.

Being bad, good and resilient

'Badness' is phenomenologically rewarding: it is fun and exciting. James recalls being bad to showcase his resilience in the face of would-be subordination. The students do not necessarily appreciate his tales of being bad post-release, and so James straddles the line between good and bad. He alternates between discourses. His responses to students' comments and questions help him to construct his story of resilience, which integrates the two discourses.

Many religions, and Christianity in particular, provide resources – literally, verbal codes – for claiming reform and redemption. Benita asks James if he has 'done any repenting'. James states: 'And like most people do, I gave myself back to *Christ*.' Hearing, too, of his frequent prayers, she approves by remarking, 'You're serious.' The instructor enters the dialogue by asking James if he thinks others' religious conversion while incarcerated is genuine. Thus does religious involvement provide a vehicle for, once again, claiming to be uniquely resilient.

I	James, do you think a lot of, um, prisoners feel – they become born-again. You think a lot of that is genuine?
James	Some of it is. But m – majority of it isn't. I done seen – some – turn – and lose their mind. But then, a lot of times, that's what's gonna happen to 'em anyway, 'cause it's already been planned.
I	Hmm.
James	That's why I take – take 'em one day at a time, and make the best of it. In or out.
I	Mm-hmm.
James	See, I was a comedian.

James here compares himself with both false converts and those who do not 'do time' well. He uses the rhetoric of twelve-step programs ('take 'em one day at a time') to construct himself as one who has survived by his wits. James returns to his preferred self-presentation as sometimes bad and always clever. He changes the subject, back to his autonomy and cleverness in prison:

> In prison, everybody's schedule basically was around you get up and the m – lights come on every morning at 6. And you didn't – like – you got to be out your bed and made up at 8 . . . And I was one of the ones like 'I'm gettin' up when I *feel* like it.' 'Nah, you gonna get up, have that bed made by 8.' But I slowed up. 'Smith, you acting up.' 'No, not yet.' But I wasn't no problem. Ya know. I have a magnetic personality. (*Laugh*)

Evidently, James has only a little to say about his religious faith. Judging from how quickly he moves away from the topic of prayer, we surmise that James does not use religion for its connotation of goodness. Rather, it presents just another resource for negotiating his preferred persona as strong and clever. On the basis of redemption and, again, autonomy, James differs from – he is better than – other convicts. Being admired for who he wishes to be is important to James.

James rejected being positioned as a victim, but he has some interest in others' positioning him as good and reformed. These are qualities generally called for among ex-offenders prior to acceptance 'back' into mainstream society. Whereas James had initially presented himself as reformed, toward the end of the session he shares that he has shoplifted recently, enthusiastically relating his ability to outwit:

James   But uh, I've peeled a few licks since – I've been here – ya know – in Old Navy. I killed them twice . . . They – I got them twice too. Now – (*Loud laughter from students*)
Nicky   Since you – since you've been out?
James   Since I've been out!

The recent crime account stirs Benita and Nicky to challenge James' perspective on his actions. The students, especially Nicky, pose questions in order to elicit cognitive re-evaluation from James.

James   Yeah, I want to do some summer gifts.
Nicky   Well, why don't you think you have – *I have to buy it* –
James   Yeah!
Nicky   – and I feel like you –
James   I should buy it, right?
Nicky   Right! And I have my own –
James   But I know I was *stealing*. (*Loud laughter from class*)
Nicky   I have to –
James   Duh!
Nicky   It's not right.
James   But see –
Nicky   It's not right!
James   But now, I understand that. I understand that.
Nicky   It's not right though!
James   It's not right. It's – it – you absolutely right. But, now, I can buy it. Now I'm in the same – like you are.

Note that the dialectical construction of good self and bad other, which Moss and Faux (2006) detected in college students' talk, was here introduced by Nicky ('*I* have to buy it'). Nicky's assertions about the wrongness of James' thinking cease once he claims that he now shares her moral perspective. In learning theory terms, she has reinforced his declaration to that effect. Elaborating, James reverts to a story of reform:

James   Well, see, I'm not – this is what I *used* to be. Where I am now, I'm, I didn't learn how to be passive. But, I still got a whole lotta aggression in me, but I learned to.
Greg   Being in prison. (*mumble*) I'm pretty sure it does make you more aggressive.
James   I was aggressive before I went there.

Referring to the aggression 'in' him, James uses the rhetoric of individual pathology as part of his reform claim: as current correctional treatment logic goes, he has gained control over such immutable pathology (Fox, 1999). Yet, James is quick to reject Greg's suggestion that *prison* caused his aggressive tendencies – that it shaped him. Instead, he was tough going into prison: he is his own bad *or* good person.

Nicky proposes that he learned to control his aggression in prison due to the consequences – prison, again, affected him, and he rejects her proposal as well, switching identities.

Nicky	Because you knew that if you acted out of that, then –
James	No. (*defiant tone*)
Nicky	– then the odds were against you?
James	No. The odds were against me for goin' in there being gay.

James follows with an expression of outrage about daily insults on the outside on account of his homosexuality. In a defiant monologue, he spurns those who abuse him in this way, but his words might also be construed as intended for his confronter, Nicky:

James	Yeah, you know, you gonna get in my face and try to – give me all this da-da-da-da. And, I'm like 'I don't even *know* you. I don't even know you *exist* before I even came here.' And the same things I faced in there, I face out here. I can be standin' in the bus stop, somebody – don't even know me and got –

While relating experiences of insult and harassment, now on the basis of both race and sexuality,[3] James reports on his quick comebacks:

James	Little girl asked me – pullin' on me in the store. So I – had my Walkman on, I turned it to take it down; I say 'Yeah?' I say 'What's wrong?' She said, uh, 'Are you African?' And I went 'Angawa!' And she jumped back. I said 'No.' (*Laughter from students*) You know, kids. And I'm on the bus stop one day. A little girl said 'You're a fag!' (*sing-song voice*) And I looked at her, said, 'Is your mama a fag?'
Nicky	But do you think that –?
James	But – but then I said it was wrong. It was wrong.

James' story of lashing out at a child meets with Nicky's disapproval, and he switches presentations – tendering a repentant self once more.

The discourses may be contradictory on their face, but we believe they form a deep structure – the defiant ex-convict story. The James who gave himself 'back to Christ' and the one who has 'peeled a few licks' since his prison release comprise one complex individual who will not be pegged by any one way of thinking and talking about who he is. In making divergent claims to goodness and badness, sometimes audaciously, to two different interlocutors, James may be seen as enacting defiance.

Conclusions

Offenders face incentives – such as reduced sanctions, both formal and informal – for alleging a lack of control over past misconduct. Their responsibility is attenuated; according to conventional legal culture, they should receive mitigated (or no) sanctions for the misconduct. A corollary of this claim is that one has regained control since the offense. Maruna (2001) found such a narrative – that of agency recovered – to be associated with desistance from offending. Yet, ex-offenders, as well as others with stigmatized and subordinated identities, might rather be seen as persons who have *consistently* maintained control, so as to profess deep self-mastery. Although James alleged personal reform ('this is what I *used* to be'), he also insisted on cunning and resilience as most central to all that he was and is – skilled shoplifter; gay man; competent hairdresser; someone who does time well and in fact succeeds in various contexts; and verbal master. He was a verbal master in the tales he told, and in the telling of them. James used the divergent questions and assertions of his interlocutors to be contradictory and thus wily. Jenkins, paraphrasing anthropologist Fredrik Barth, states: 'It is not enough to claim an ethnic identity, one must be able satisfactorily to perform it, to actualise it' (2004: 98–9). James performed a verbally resilient and complex self.

The fact of multiple interlocutors presents special challenges, such as by posing potentially discrepant expectations. The group with multiple interlocutors presents in miniature the conflicting expectations that people experience in everyday life. As Hecht *et al.* argue: 'The establishment and maintenance of identity are problematic due to the competing forces in society that push and pull individuals toward a variety of identities' (2003: 66). These pushes and pulls can be witnessed in a single encounter. But multiple interlocutors might also serve as a resource, as it was for James in our study. Switching identities – that is, being inconsistent – can be a technique for constructing a defiant self.

The study provides insights for programs to promote change among ex-offenders. Our finding that James cherished his 'bad' self insofar as it reflects his creativity and autonomy, should give pause to those who would 'correct' all that ex-offenders think and say. Currently, the dominant, cognition-oriented interventions for ex-offenders discourage creative deliberation about one's past offending. For example, Fox (1999) found that inmates who resisted the rhetoric of their cognitive treatment were seen as evidencing criminogenic pathology. We urge a rather thoroughgoing reconceptualization of resistance not as pathological but rather as a show of strength, and defiance not as an obstacle but rather as an indicator of the will to independence. We may not be able to remove all the barriers to change for ex-convicts, but we can appreciate this: if change means continued subjugation, they may want no part of it. To help ex-offenders with identity transformation that facilitates reintegration, we must begin with *their* preferred identity, not those we prefer for them.

Had the goal of the session been rehabilitation, its facilitator might have invited James to reflect on and to discriminate between others' expectations – those that are unjust (e.g. that he be heterosexual) and those that are just (e.g. that he not steal). In the exchanges we observed, James threw out the baby with the bathwater. That is, his resistance to social control was nearly complete. Programs that help ex-offenders such as James to recognize some but not all forms of control and some but not all constraints on 'being oneself' as positive, for self and for others, may promote true reintegration rather than blanket resistance.

Notes

1 With the exception of the instructor (the first author), only pseudonyms are used.
2 Race, gender and age specifics are relevant to some of the dynamics of storytelling and aid our identification of speakers. Four of the students were African-American: two males and two females. The three other students were white: a male and two females. The students whose probes we highlight, due to their active involvement in the discussion, are one African-American male, referred to as Greg; an African-American female in her twenties referred to as Nicky; an African-American female in her forties referred to as Benita; and the white male, referred to as Tom.
3 Perhaps the fact that so many of his interlocutors were also African-American made race less salient as an anchor for 'doing difference better'.

References

Arrigo, B. A. and Schehr, R. C. (1998) 'Restoring justice for juveniles: A critical analysis of victim-offender mediation', *Justice Quarterly*, 15(4): 629–66.
Atkinson, P. and Silverman, D. (1997) 'Kundera's *Immortality*: The interview society and the invention of the self', *Qualitative Inquiry*, 3(3): 304–25.
Bruner, J. (1990). *Acts of Meaning*. Cambridge, MA: Harvard University Press.
Cooley, C. H. (1902) *Human Nature and the Social Order*. New York: Scribner's.
Denzin, N. K. (1987) *The Alcoholic Self*. Newbury Park, CA: Sage.
Erikson, E. H. (1956) 'The Problem of Ego Identity', *Journal of the American Psychoanalytic Association*, 4: 56–121.
Fox, K. J. (1999) 'Changing violent minds: Discursive correction and resistance in the cognitive treatment of violent offenders in prison', *Social Problems*, 46(1): 88–103.

Goffman, E. (1959) *The Presentation of Self in Everyday Life*. Garden City, NY: Doubleday.

Hecht, M. L., Jackson, R. L. and Ribeau, S. A. (2003) *African American Communication: Exploring Identity and Culture*, 2nd edn. Mahwah, NJ: Erlbaum.

Jenkins, R. (2004) *Social Identity*, 2nd edn. London: Routledge.

Kerby, A. P. (1991) *Narrative and the Self*. Bloomington, IN: Indiana University Press.

Lecky, P. (1945) *Self-Consistency: A Theory of Personality*. New York: Island Press.

Linde, C. (1993) *Life Stories: The Creation of Coherence*. New York: Oxford University Press.

Maruna, S. (2001) *Making Good: How Ex-Convicts Reform and Rebuild Their Lives*. Washington, DC: American Psychological Association.

Matoesian, G. M. (1993) *Reproducing Rape: Domination Through Talk in the Courtroom*. Chicago: University of Chicago Press.

McAdams, D. P. (1999) 'Personal narratives and the life story', in *Handbook of Personality: Theory and Research*, 2nd edn. New York: Guilford.

McKendy, J. P. (2006) '"I'm very careful about that": Narrative and agency of men in prison', *Discourse and Society*, 17(4): 473–502.

Mead, G. H. (1934) *Mind, Self and Society from the Standpoint of a Social Behaviorist*. Chicago: University of Chicago Press.

Molotch, H. L. and Boden, D. (1985) 'Talking social structure: Discourse, domination and the Watergate hearings', *American Sociological Review*, 50(3): 273–88.

Moss, K. and Faux, W. V. (2006) 'The enactment of cultural identity in student conversations on intercultural topics', *The Howard Journal of Communications*, 17: 21–37.

O'Connor, P. E. (2000) *Speaking of Crime: Narratives of Prisoners*. Lincoln, NE: University of Nebraska Press.

O'Reilly, E. B. (1997) *Sobering Tales: Narratives of Alcoholism and Recovery*. Amherst, MA: University of Massachusetts Press.

Presser, L. (2008) *Been a Heavy Life: Stories of Violent Men*. Urbana, IL: University of Illinois Press.

Ricoeur, P. (1985) 'History as narrative and practice', trans. Robert Lechner, *Philosophy Today* (Fall).

Scott, M. B. and Lyman, S. M. (1968) 'Accounts', *American Sociological Review*, 33(1): 46–62.

Stone, A. (1982) *Autobiographical Occasions and Original Acts*. Philadelphia: University of Pennsylvania Press.

Sullivan, D. and Tifft, L. (2001) *Restorative Justice: Healing the Foundations of Our Everyday Lives*. Monsey, NY: Willow Street Press.

Swora, M. G. (2002) 'Narrating community: The creation of social structure in alcoholics anonymous through the performance of autobiography', *Narrative Inquiry*, 11(2): 363–84.

Tajfel, H. (1981) *Human Groups and Social Categories*. Cambridge, UK: Cambridge University Press.

Tilly, C. (2006) *Why?* Princeton, NJ: Princeton University Press.

Waldram, J. B. (2007) 'Narrative and the construction of "Truth" in a prison-based treatment program for offenders', *Ethnography*, 8(2): 145–69.

Ward, T. and Maruna, S. (2007) *Rehabilitation: Beyond the Risk Paradigm*. London: Routledge.

Chapter 6

Thinking inside the box: prisoner education, learning identities, and the possibilities for change

Emma Hughes

John is studying through distance learning in an English prison. In the first letter that he wrote to the charity that funded his correspondence course he signed his name, followed by his prison identification number. After completing several further courses funded by the charity he wrote to them again. This time he signed his name, followed not by a prison identification number, but by letters earned from the certificates and qualifications he had achieved.

This change in John's self-presentation is typical of that of many of the prisoner-students that I encountered while conducting qualitative research on British prisoners' experiences of distance learning. In this chapter I specifically examine the role that education in prison can play in helping prisoners to develop new identities and new self-perspectives, which are often centred around the notion of being a 'student'. Critically, these new identities are recognized and verbalized by the prisoner-students themselves. It is the students' own perspectives on their identities that will form the basis for what is presented here. The students describe these shifts and changes in their self-perceptions as positive and leading to a greater degree of autonomy in their lives.

Throughout this research the focus has been on the students' own narratives and voices, in keeping with explorations of 'prisoner' education, as opposed to 'prison' education (see, for example, Reuss 1999; Wilson and Reuss 2000). As such, the emphasis remains on the student rather than the system as a whole. This study focuses on the perspectives of distance learners rather than classroom-based students, which offers an opportunity to consider the unique issues and experiences that such students encounter and the implications for their sense of identity. However, because many of the students have previously studied, or are concurrently studying, through prison-based classes as well, their insights are not confined to this more specialized form of education in prison.[1]

Distance learning as a mode of study in prison allows for more advanced-level study, and greater variety of courses, than is typically available through a prison education department. The students who participated in the research were exploring a wide variety of academic and vocational subjects at a full range of levels, from City and Guilds to postgraduate study.[2] In this research 76 prison-based distance learners completed short-answer questionnaires about their current and previous educational experiences, including their time at school; 47 of these respondents then participated in individual semi-structured interviews. At the time of interviews, the learners were studying courses that ranged from accounting to zoology by way of car maintenance theory, counselling skills, computer programming, and nineteenth-century British history.

Drawing from these research findings, I first explore how the students perceive and describe changes in their sense of self. I make reference to how they have noted changes in their estimation of personal abilities and qualities. I discuss how shifting identities can lead to new and different roles being adopted within the prison, which in turn further inform the students' sense of self. I also address how difficulties encountered with their studies may result in challenges to the students' new self-perceptions. In subsequent sections I examine the role of others within and without the prison in affecting these self-perceptions, and consider the consequences of a revised sense of self for future goals and intentions.

Self-perceptions of change

Far from representing an academic prison 'elite', the academic standing of the majority of these students at the outset of their prison experiences reflects the educational underperformance of the prison population as a whole (see, for example, Devlin 1995; Social Exclusion Unit 2002). Some of the distance learners had been unable to read or write when they entered prison. Stories of negative school experiences, of truancy and expulsion, and of leaving school without the equivalent of a high school diploma, were commonplace. As will be seen, education in prison can serve a potentially transformative role for such students, involving the creation of a new, positive, student identity and reassessment of personal attributes (see also Wilson 2000).

By contrast, a few of the distance learners had entered prison with advanced-level qualifications. For those distance learners who came into prison with positive backgrounds in relation to education, work, or community standing, but who have found their pro-social identities disrupted by the consequences of criminal conviction, I will consider the role that education can play in rebuilding 'spoiled identities' (Goffman 1961; Jewkes 2005; Crawley and Sparks 2005).

'I don't feel so stupid'

Among those prisoner-students who had struggled with academics prior to prison, there was evidence that gaining confidence in their mental abilities while in prison could have a significant impact on their sense of self and their estimation of personal abilities. Kevin, studying GCSE psychology, reports that through education his self-perceptions have changed.[3] He no longer 'feel[s] so stupid'. He explains that education has 'give[n] me more self-worth' and he adds: 'I feel better about myself'. He contrasts this with the low self-confidence he had previously felt, particularly when he was unable to help his niece with her maths homework despite being in his twenties.

Indeed, it was not uncommon for students like Kevin to describe how they had previously thought themselves to be 'stupid' or 'thick'. Illustrative of such shifting perceptions, Mike, studying counselling skills through distance learning, explains that: 'a lot of people ... before they went on education [in prison] they were just like me, really thick. But then [they] get a better education and they found they had a meaning to them and so they continued with it.' Mike argues that this experience of discovering a 'meaning to them[selves]', equated with an ability to achieve, is shared by 'an awful lot of prisoners' who study.

The students often express surprise at what they have been able to achieve through their studies. Ed describes how when completing his course assignments he still feels 'amazed that I can understand what I am doing'. This 'amazement' at what he is accomplishing can be read in the context of Ed's previous belief that he was 'never actually good at anything'. Other students talk of education helping them 'realise some potential abilities' and of discovering 'hidden talents' which in turn builds self-confidence.

Sue's statement that 'I'm proving something to myself', and Tony's comment that education 'has given me a lot of belief in myself' are further indicators of education's potential for playing a transformative role in terms of students' self-perceptions and self-assessments. Alex has gained GCSEs and A levels since being in prison.[4] Significantly, while he recognizes the value of these qualifications, he believes that the sense of pride and achievement he has gained is 'more important than [actual] qualifications'.

These comments regarding achievement and discovering new abilities serve as important reminders that for many prisoners educational underachievement has been the norm. The value of achieving academic success cannot be underestimated, particularly within the confines of an environment which by its very nature is associated with failure (see also Reuss 1997). Furthermore, assuming the role of student provides a concrete pro-social identity to assume within the prison, and is often combined with other roles and identities related to the students' educational activities.

'I became a Listener'

Educational experiences can work alongside other prison-based experiences in order to encourage the shifts in self-perception described above. For some students who had previously held low perceptions of their academic capabilities or inclinations, gaining self-confidence elsewhere in the prison was instrumental not only in initiating these shifts in perception, but also for encouraging education enrolment (for a detailed account of motivational histories for education in prison see Hughes 2004, 2007). Therefore, education can be viewed within the context of broader experiences within the prison setting. In particular, I focus within this section on other roles that prisoners may adopt within the prison alongside, and often intertwined with, their activities as students.

Before becoming involved with education during the latest of his many prison sentences, sentences which had included significant time spent in segregation due to disruptive behaviour, Mike participated in a prison scheme run by the Samaritans. This UK charity trains prisoners to act as 'Listeners' for others who need someone to speak to during a mental or emotional crisis. Mike 'became a Listener' after having himself been 'listened to' by another prisoner, an experience he found to be very helpful and personally rewarding.

Working as a Listener proved pivotal for Mike, a self-described 'career criminal'. He talks of awakening a dormant interest in becoming a counsellor and with a newfound confidence went on to take a number of counselling skills courses through distance learning. At the time of interview Mike was voluntarily residing in a prison therapeutic community where he was undergoing further counselling himself, including working to address a drug addiction. Of note, Mike says that he is jokingly called the 'counsellor' by other prisoners because of his contributions to group therapy informed by his academic studies, and because of his availability to act as a Listener.

Ed's decision to undertake education was largely influenced by his being given a job of 'responsibility' in the prison laundry. In beginning to realize that he held mental capabilities, of which he says he was previously unaware, Ed began a course of study that would have significant implications not only for his sense of self, but also for the roles that he would play within the prison. He had entered prison without any academic qualifications, but went on to study sociology at a post-secondary school level. He became editor of the prison's widely read in-house magazine and became the education department orderly, acting as a prisoner assistant for the education department staff. In this latter capacity he oversaw and scheduled my day of interviews.

From a starting point of low self-confidence in his academic ability, Ed's experiences within the prison played a part in building his confidence to the point of trying education. His educational achievements in turn increased his self-confidence and broadened his outlook on his life and future. He observes: 'When I first came here, it was my life is over . . . the criminal record and all that stigma attached, but because of education and my being able to move on, it has actually proved to be the most positive [thing] of my life so far'. Ed sees education as offering a way forward in light of the negativity he associates with a criminal label and identity. Ed has furthermore acquired new, positive identities associated with the roles of 'student', 'editor' and 'education orderly' in the process.

Some of the students came into prison already possessing what they describe as positive, socially oriented identities. For example, the study includes first-time offenders with successful employment and/or educational records. It is here that further insight regarding the potential benefits of education in prison can be drawn from Jewkes (2005) and Crawley and Sparks (2005), who have argued that prison can 'spoil' the positive former identities, including work identities, of long-sentenced prisoners. In effect, the prisoners can suffer the loss of identities and roles that 'locate themselves within the social world' (Jewkes 2005: 369) and they can be left with simply the identity of prisoner.

Education in prison can serve, however, to reinforce such positive identities as were held before prison. This is evident in the case of Doug who writes that he has 'been in marketing and PR most of my life' and refers to having held a position of respect within his local business community. Expecting to serve eight years in prison, Doug is using education to enhance and support his prior relevant skills. Through education, Doug's identity as a person who is involved in business and PR is reinforced. Although he admits to 'very black days' when he cannot see a future, education is helping to restore his 'hope' that there will be options for him upon his release. His education may help to reduce the tarnish of an identity blemished and 'spoiled' through criminal conviction.

Regardless of the initial motivations for educational activity, for those prisoners involved with education, taking courses can provide a means through which to further develop and reinforce emerging and former perspectives, identities and interests. The prisoner-students, through their academic studies and other related activities, are developing and/or renewing self-perceptions that can help to offset the negative identity and image of 'prisoner' and 'criminal' (see also Reuss 1997; Jewkes 2005; Crawley and Sparks 2005). The new way in which John signed his letter as described at the chapter's outset by replacing his prison number with the qualifications he has earned is illustrative of such a shift (Hughes

2000). Additionally, examples above have indicated how the students' educational and related involvements can ultimately feed back into activities and roles that benefit and assist others within the prison environment. This is not uncommon among the distance learners whose educational studies have led to participation in a range of activities within the prison including teaching literacy and numeracy to fellow prisoners.

'This is the real me now'

Previous sections have shown that involvement in education and related activities can increase and sustain prisoners' self-confidence, particularly in relation to mental abilities, and can inform their sense of place and role within the prison. However, the students regularly point to broader consequences for their general sense of self that go beyond the education realm.

Mike, the 'counsellor', reflecting on his educational and therapeutic experiences in prison, remarks that he is no longer that 'horrible' person that he used to be. He explains: 'I've sorted my life out . . . this is what you're gonna get from me now. You're not gonna get that horrible Mike that there was before.' In fact, he refers to himself in terms of: 'this is the real me now'. For Mike, this means no longer feeling the need to be 'false with anybody' and no longer feeling the need to be concerned with an 'image' just to be 'part of a crowd'. He observes that he no longer maintains contact with his former criminal friends outside of prison.

Other prisoner-students also made spontaneous reference to undergoing a sense of personal change when asked to describe what benefits, if any, they experienced through education. For some students this sense of change, and their awareness of this change, is encouraged by their education, as well as through reflection brought about by their criminal conviction. As in the case of Mike, this process of self-reflection is sometimes related to participation in counselling programs. Indeed, the experience of undergoing counselling may serve to further encourage the students to recognize and express awareness of personal change, in this respect, making them ideal candidates for offering reflective responses to research questions.

Bill, aged 35, has 'had a drug problem for 14 years' and has 'been coming in and out of prison for a number of years now'. To merely point out that Bill has, in his current sentence, taken a course on counselling through distance learning, and completed courses within a prison education department, would fail to tell the full story. He offers:

> With this sentence, my perspective on myself and my life has changed tremendously, but that's also through the course that I'm doing on the Drug Therapeutic Community (DTC) [in which he lives]. With regards to the [distance learning] course, I would say that

it's been a part of the process within the DTC as well. This whole sentence for me has been a really good learning experience.

Having completed his DTC program, at the time of interview Bill was working as a resident counsellor for other prisoners still involved in the program, a role he would like to continue in other settings once he leaves prison.

As a result of their varied activities and 'learning experience[s]', it was common for students to report a sense of empowerment, in part through increased knowledge and increased articulacy. Eric explains: 'Knowledge is power, you don't get knowledge by doing a 7 [am] to 5 [pm] factory job or driving huge chunks of cannabis around the country ... with the education that I'm getting and that I'm doing for myself, I can go a lot further than I ever imagined I could.' Mike offers that through his education and therapeutic experiences, as well as his work as a Listener, he has learned to 'to be able to communicate a bit more'. He notes: 'before I would never sit down and talk to you like this [in the interview]'. He adds: 'I think I've matured'. Trevor, who says of education, 'it has relaxed me more', refers to being less aggressive and to 'sort[ing] things out differently' with others, namely through talking. Like Mike, Trevor appears to have developed increased communication skills.

For some students their personal exploration can lead to a new-found desire to take responsibility for themselves and for their post-release plans. Education, Trevor states, 'opens people's eyes to different things'. Explaining his continued interest in education, which he began simply to avoid mopping floors, his statement also signals a degree of empowerment: 'I just wanted to better myself. I want to become self-employed and take my future into my own hands really.'

Ultimately, education, as well as positive experiences of addiction treatment, other forms of counselling, and participation in varied prison activities, can all contribute to a growth in self-confidence, a new sense of perspective, and a new sense of self. Significantly, students report feeling that through their studies and activities they have gained more control over their lives than otherwise might be the case. As Alex suggests: 'Pride is one thing that you can keep yourself in prison. As long as they don't take it you're still an individual.'

'Oh, I'm a failure'

However, while education, as well as other prison-based activities, can serve to boost self-confidence, and can lead to the adoption of new roles and identities for the students, these identities can also be fragile. Fear of failure, as well as actual course failure, may challenge and disrupt the prisoner-students' self-perceptions. While anxiety and fear of failure can be common among mature students returning to education in the community (Young 2000; Brine and Waller 2004), such fears can be magnified within a prison environment that by its nature is already associated with societal failure (Forster 1998). For isolated distance learners, these fears can be even greater.

Jason's experience demonstrates that even those who came into prison with good academic backgrounds, and whose prison studies begin with a degree of success, are not invulnerable to disruptions in their progress and confidence. Jason believes that while undergoing intensive therapy within the prison he overextended his educational commitments as a university student. He failed one of his courses and this led to a considerable crisis of confidence in regard to his academic ability. For Jason, failing his exam: 'made [him] go back to thinking, "oh, I'm a failure"'. His self-doubt increased and this affected his self-perception. When first considering resuming his studies, he reported thinking: '"oh, you failed, you can't do anything, you're worthless", and it keeps coming back again . . .'

While the potential of self-doubt and failure for disrupting academic progress is evident, and the potential personal and psychological conse-quences this may entail must not be minimized, such experiences, in the right circumstances, can nevertheless be reframed in a way that allows students to move forward in a positive and self-empowered way. With support from others within the prison including both staff and inmates, Jason returned to his studies with a new strategy, deciding: 'instead of taking on a big chunk I'll take on something a bit smaller . . . I'm starting to get there . . . just do a little bit each day . . . Now I've got my confidence back again.' Significantly, Jason believes that he is now more willing as a result of his recent experiences to undertake challenges he would previously have avoided and has increased his own self-understanding in the process.

Even the most able and most committed students may be vulnerable to such challenges and self-doubts as are described above. The student identity can be fragile, and maintaining this positive identity and maintaining educational progress within the confines of a prison can be difficult, particularly for distance learners without on-site support from instructors and classmates. It is with this in mind that I turn to consider how others within and without the prison may inform and influence these prisoners' student identities. In particular, I will examine the impact of others on the self-confidence, increased self-determination, and positive sense of self, that numerous students have reported developing and/or reaffirming through their educational and related pursuits.

The role of others

In order to explore how 'others' can serve to reinforce or to undermine the students' changing perceptions and roles, I first consider the influence of those within prison, specifically prison staff and fellow prisoners. Next, I look 'beyond the walls' to assess how family and friends outside prison, as well as external tutors and organisations, can affect the students' self-perceptions. As discussed below, support from others can go beyond the realms of practical advice and encouragement on a particular assignment and can serve to reinforce the students' new and developing identities as well as to validate the roles that they have assumed. However, examples also emerge whereby others question the pro-social roles and identities of the students in ways that may prove disruptive to educational and rehabilitative endeavours.

'You're brilliant, girl'

Prison staff can play an important role in recognizing and encouraging the development of a positive, pro-social identity. Pam explains how she not only received assistance with coursework from prison staff, but describes how officers would tell her, 'you're brilliant, girl', as she worked on her course. Interestingly, she adds: 'sometimes the officers would say things that you don't see'. Students like Ed appreciate the role of responsibility that they were given within prison jobs, roles that allowed them to realize, as Ed put it, 'that maybe I did have some "grey matter"'. In both Pam's and Ed's statements there are suggestions that prison staff are recognizing positive abilities, skills or attributes that the students themselves had been unwilling or unable to see.

Other prisoners are also able to reinforce and encourage such developments and, in particular, can help support and foster the student identity. Some of the prisoners studying through distance learning form informal self-help groups to assist each other with their studies. As distance learners who are removed from their external institutions and unable to participate in internet discussion groups available for many community-based distance learners, this opportunity to associate with other prisoner-students can be of value. The presence of other equally committed students can help to 'normalize' and cement a student identity (Worth 1996: 181; see also Hodkinson 2004).

Mike's nickname of 'counsellor' is also informative in terms of recognition by others around him. His academic interests, his work as a prison Listener, and his contributions to group therapy sessions are being acknowledged and referred to by other prisoners on his wing, if even in a humorous manner. Prison staff also comment upon the emergence of this pro-social identity and his prison therapist has told him that 'from her opinion I would make a good counsellor'. Given the insecurities and concerns that some of the prisoner-students report experiencing, the potential value of these positive affirmations must not be ignored.

'A drug dealer doing Open Uni, now that's funny'

In contrast to these examples of encouragement from prison staff and prisoners, some students report that their educational and related endeavours have been dismissed and derided by prison officers as being (in the case of male students) 'girlie', a 'skive', 'non-macho' and not constituting 'real work'. This is a view that is also shared by some fellow prisoners and can serve as a source of antagonism for prisoner-students. Negative comments and attitudes can contribute to a prison culture perceived to be anti-education in its orientation and policies, and this can adversely affect students' interest in study (see Hughes 2004, 2007, for further exploration of this issue). Crucially, such reactions can also serve to question or undermine a student identity.

Negative attitudes expressed by those in authority within the prison can be particularly damaging, and may have significant consequences for the prisoner-students. Clive, studying with the Open University,[5] said that he had been told by one of the counsellors on the prison's offending-behaviour course: 'a drug dealer doing Open Uni, now that's funny'. Clive was then told he would have to choose between taking his university course or taking the offending-behaviour course. He chose the university course, despite the fact that this might endanger his early release. Apart from pointing to how prison regime requirements might disrupt academic progress, this example is illustrative of how prison officials may serve to reinforce a criminal rather than pro-social identity of a prisoner-student through the labels they use.

Similarly, Steve reports being told by a prison psychologist in relation to his educational endeavours: '[you are] just training yourself to be a better drug-smuggler'. As in the case of Clive above, the legitimacy of the student identity is questioned by an authority figure while a criminal identity of 'drug-smuggler' is reinforced. It is also worth noting that Ed reports that sometimes the officers call you 'stupid' and 'useless' and that 'after a number of times you may begin to believe it'.

Some students describe being harassed by other prisoners because of their educational activities. Jason refers to varying degrees of 'humiliation' that he experienced due to studying. He says: 'I've been called names by other prisoners: they call you names [such as] "snob".' He feels, however, that the more significant animosity, which can amount to bullying, is reserved for those prisoners who turn to education after having previously 'been hanging around with a crowd' in the workshops. In so doing, these new students may appear to be abandoning former roles and identities in a way that might be construed as especially disruptive and threatening to friends and associates who feel that the student is acting 'superior' (see Willis 1977 for insight into the importance of group membership in the lads' counter-school culture; see also Brine and Waller 2004).

That some prisoner-students do feel superior to those prisoners whom they consider to have no future is, however, clearly apparent. For many of the prisoner-students, educational involvement is both a means through which to achieve a non-criminal future, as well as evidence of their distinction from those they consider 'no-hopers'. This distinction may even be seen as a personal bolster within an environment identified with failure and may serve to support the 'student' rather than the 'prisoner' aspect of their identity. As Eric puts it: 'Well, I'm sorry to say but there are a lot of people in prison that there's just no hope for.' Scott likewise differentiates between those who are seeking to change their lives, and those who within the prison are thought of as 'criminals':

> Some people don't care about education. Some people have been into crime all their life and as far as they're concerned, that's how they earn their money. That's up to them if they want to come back to prison. It's not for me. They're seen as criminals – I suppose they are really (*laughs*) – they're seen as criminals and that's how everyone sees them.

As his laugh suggests, the irony of his statement is not lost on Scott, who is himself a life-sentenced prisoner. However, his remark points to a distinction, unrelated to initial offence, between those who are seen to be 'bettering themselves' and those who are thought to be revolving-door prisoners, endlessly cycling through the system. Although such attitudes may potentially contribute to a sense of elitism, these attitudes may partially act as a defence against the hassle the students can receive from their peers.[6]

Nevertheless, Duguid and Pawson (1998) have argued that where anti-education attitudes exist, and their prevalence appears to vary between and within institutions (Hughes 2007), prisoner-students may need to negotiate and manage their dual prisoner-student identity in careful ways. Bruce, who studies maths through the Open University, explains that he makes an effort to keep his textbooks hidden away because they may create a 'barrier' between himself and other prisoners. A practical response such as this may reduce the challenge to a student identity within a prison environment.

'You talk different'

Moving beyond the prison walls, prisoner-students in contact with family and friends outside of prison report that these relationships can provide an additional source of motivation for continuing their educational programs. Crucially, these individuals can also provide further confirmation to a student regarding shifts in their persona and behaviour. Mike, the 'counsellor', explains how his father and sister tell him: 'you're different, you talk different' and '[you are] more approachable now'. He concludes: 'I just want to prove it and let them see the change in me, and I'm glad if they see that change.'

Because distance learning involves educational institutions and tutors external to the prison, this is another area where identity as a student can be either affirmed or tested. In many cases, being a student at a non-prison-based institution is validation for the prisoners, and represents an affiliation through which their identity as 'student' rather than 'prisoner' is paramount. Indeed, distance learning gives the prisoner-students membership in a location that defines all within it primarily as students. However, there can be exceptions. Ali, working on an MA in psychology, has noted frustration with administrative difficulties related to his being in prison and this leaves him feeling that he is not treated as a 'regular' student by the external institution. Unable to register for courses using the same procedure as other students, yet unable to receive timely assistance from an overworked prison education department regulating his studies, Ali has experienced conflict between the identity and demands of being a student and the identity and demands of being a prisoner. Such conflicts where they arise may undermine the important 'normalisation' process of becoming a student considered important for prison-based distance learners (Worth 1996).

However, Ali also has been writing letters on children's education that are regularly published in a community newspaper. Through this he has been contacted by children and their families, some of whom have subsequently come to visit him in prison. He refers to the letters he has received with great pride and pleasure. Ali says that this external contact has served to 'increase my interest' in the subject, and he jokes that he has become a 'celebrity'. This contact represents public affirmation of Ali based on his academic and intellectual activities, in a way not subsumed by his identity and status of prisoner.

The Prisoners' Education Trust, the charity that has funded these distance learners, is another external organization that can validate a student and pro-social identity. Clive is taking courses related to his goal of becoming a physiotherapist. He says: 'For me to realise people such as the Prisoners' Education Trust are willing to give me another chance, makes me want to repay that trust, and one day I'll be able to help others who need help.' Clive's comment, along with similar remarks from other students, suggests considerable gratitude for the generosity that has been shown while also indicating appreciation that the non-prisoner aspect of their identity is recognized. Clive's gratitude that the Trust was 'willing to give me another chance' suggests that the support from the Trust contrasts with the rejection that he may otherwise be expecting because of his prisoner/criminal label. Forming or re-establishing positive associations with individuals and organizations outside of the prison may help to address such concerns, while also offering possible benefits for the future reintegration of the prisoner into the outside world (Woolf 1991; see also Light 1993; Petersilia 2003; and Martinez, this volume, on the value of family ties for successful prisoner reentry).

Future course of action

The most commonly cited reason for undertaking distance learning in prison was to prepare for a brighter future. Students talked frequently of seeking to 'better themselves', and to increase their post-release options especially in relation to employment. It is helpful to assess how the developing of student and other pro-social identities within the prison may assist them in this respect.

As the students make clear, educational achievement provides a means of demonstrating to others that 'change' is and has taken place, that something substantial and positive has been pursued in prison. While the notion of demonstrating change has been discussed in relation to family members, Sue represents this position in relation to job-seeking when she says that through earning a university degree she is hoping to show prospective employers: 'Yes, I've been in prison, I've served a long sentence, but at the end of the day this is what has come out of it, I'm not the person from back then and I've not wasted my time.'

The word 'hope' reappears in the students' narratives, as do other references to more optimistic visions of the future. Although there is recognition of limitations and obstacles that may lie ahead, particularly in relation to employment, through education the students are gaining an increased sense of empowerment and self-determination. As Joe puts it, education 'gives you not only a confidence in yourself, but a confidence that your life is actually going somewhere once you get out of here'. There is a commonly expressed belief that they are doing the best that they can to improve their chances.

Research on desistance can offer further insight into how these personal developments, the sense of change, along with increased self-confidence and agency, might affect the students' future courses of action. Burnett and Maruna (2004) propose that such a sense of personal belief may itself be related to future outcomes. Interviewing persistent offenders before their release from prison they found that 'over 80 per cent [of the interviewees] reported that they *wanted* to go straight, but only 25 per cent thought they would definitely be *able* to go straight' (2004: 395, emphasis in original). Follow-up fieldwork found that 'there seemed to be a strong correlation between self-reported estimates of offending likelihood and self-reports of offending in the second and third waves of interviews', conducted after the participants' release from prison (2004: 395).

Rumgay's (2004) analysis of persistent female offenders leads her to conclude that: 'successful desistance from crime may be rooted in recognition of an opportunity to claim an alternative, desired and socially approved personal identity' (2004: 405). These identities in turn offer pro-social roles and 'scripts' for the offenders to follow. As has been seen, educational programmes in prison and related activities can offer this opportunity to develop or reinforce an identity that does not revolve around being a 'prisoner' or 'criminal'. In as much as the students continue to pursue their studies or related interests, in prison or out, whether through employment, continued education, or hobbies, these chosen identities are strengthened. Rumgay additionally cites the value of 'social support networks' (2004: 413) for encouraging and reaffirming these new identities and roles. It is here that staff and peers within prison, and family, friends, organizations, and agencies outside of prison, can play an integral part.

However, while the Burnett and Maruna (2004) and Rumgay (2004) studies cited above focus on issues relevant to persistent offenders, not all of the participants in this study can be described as persistent offenders. As Patrick points out, the interviewees include first-time offenders like him with successful employment and/or educational records. It is here that the potential benefits of education for 'spoiled identities' are relevant, with education reinforcing such positive identities as were held before prison (Jewkes 2005; Crawley and Sparks 2005).

Whether education in prison is aiding prisoner-students in the formation of new identities or in the reaffirmation of valued identities already held, desistance literature suggests that these positive self-perceptions and identities may assist in the process of reintegration following their release from prison (Maruna 2001; Burnett and Maruna 2004; Rumgay 2004). The students frequently acknowledge the challenges they will confront, particularly in relation to employment. However, through education, positive roles and identities that will help situate the students in the world outside prison are being maintained or created, rather than being destroyed. This may enable the students to respond more effectively to challenges they face in the future.

Conclusion

Many of the distance learners refer to wanting to use their new-found skills and knowledge to give back to their community after release and this is often coupled with taking responsibility for their former actions. The popularity of taking counselling skills classes and aiming to work or volunteer in peer counselling capacities in the future is evidence of such desires. In short, these students talk of wanting to do what Maruna (2001) has described as 'making good'. But as Maruna (2001), Burnett and Maruna (2004), Rumgay (2004) and others have noted, a sense of self-efficacy is an important ingredient for realizing such a plan. I would argue that the persistence and stamina required for distance learning under any circumstances, but particularly within a prison environment, stands these students in good stead. Not only have their studies armed them with qualifications, and new knowledge sets, but their studies have reinforced confidence and perseverance, and encouraged the development of positive roles and identities that may serve to equip them for such difficulties they may face following their release.

However, a culture of needing to negotiate challenges to study in prison might be more costly than beneficial – others who may have become students might have been deterred by anti-education attitudes, conflicting demands within prison regimes, personal doubts and insecurities. These factors may all impact upon decisions to undertake education and, by extension, limit the possibilities for prisoners to experience such positive changes or reaffirmations as have been described herein. With greater institutional support, more prisoners may choose to involve themselves with education while still benefiting from such positive personal developments as described within this chapter.

The challenge I would suggest, therefore, is for prisons to seek to encourage and/or recognize, rather than discourage, the development of such positive identities. The students' experiences suggest that the pathway to finding and developing these new identities can be a meandering one, often the result of accidental circumstances and in many cases not reached until after many years spent in prison, or numerous obstacles overcome. If creating strategies for change in offenders is desired, systems have to be in place to provide a more effective method of signposting, improving the routes, and removing the barriers. Listening to the prisoners' voices regarding their own self-perceptions of change helps to illustrate the ways in which these developments may come about, and how they may best be maintained. For sustained commitment to identity development within prison, this requires thinking inside the box – not just by the prisoners working and reflecting within their cells, but within prison services and corrections departments as a whole. It is not just the prisoners' identities that need to be thought through, but that of the prison service too.

Notes

1 This research was partially funded by the Prisoners' Education Trust, a UK charity that offers grants to prisoners for distance learning courses. All of the students in this study had received grants for distance learning.
2 City & Guilds qualifications are mainly vocational qualifications that are offered in a variety of industry areas. They cover a range of levels from entry level to postgraduate.
3 A GCSE is a General Certificate of Secondary Education. Students typically take a number of these in a range of subjects at the age of sixteen, thereby marking the end of compulsory education.

4 A-level qualifications generally involve two years of study and are designed for students who have completed GCSEs. They are available in a range of subjects and are often used as indicators of suitability for university.

5 The Open University (OU) is the UK's only distance learning based university.

6 The distinction within prisons between those who are seen as 'criminals', and those who are not, is not a new phenomenon and nor is it confined to a distinction between those who are studying and those who are not. For example, Maruna (2001), in interviewing Liverpool desisters, revisits Irwin's (1970) prison term of 'square johns' used to refer to those prisoners who have committed one-off offences, perhaps in a 'moment of passion' (as cited in Maruna 2001: 46). While the crime itself may be extremely serious, the individuals may have not had previous criminal records and are unlikely to commit crime again (Maruna 2001).

References

Brine, J. and Waller, R. (2004) 'Working-class women on an access course: Risk, opportunity and (re)constructing identities', *Gender and Education*, 16(1): 97–113.

Burnett, R. and Maruna, S. (2004) 'So "prison works", does it? The criminal careers of 130 men released from prison under Home Secretary, Michael Howard', *The Howard Journal*, 43(4): 390–404.

Crawley, E. and Sparks, R. (2005) 'Older men in prison: Survival, coping and identity', in A. Liebling and S. Maruna (eds) *The Effects of Imprisonment*. Cullompton: Willan Publishing.

Devlin, A. (1995) *Criminal Classes: Offenders at School.* Winchester: Waterside Press.

Duguid, S. and Pawson, R. (1998) 'Education, transformation and change', *Evaluation Review*, 22(4): 470–95.

Forster, W. (1998) 'The prison service and education in England and Wales', in W. Forster (ed.) *Education Behind Bars: International Comparisons.* Leicester: NIACE.

Goffman, E. (1961) *Asylums: Essays on the Social Situation of Mental Patients and Other Inmates.* Harmondsworth: Penguin.

Hodkinson, P. (2004) *Career Decision-Making, Learning Careers and Career Progression: Nuffield Review of 14–19 Education and Training Working Paper 12* (based on Discussion Paper given at Working Day II, 23 February 2004) [Online]. Available at: *www.nuffield14-19review.org.uk/files/documents38-1.pdf* [Accessed January 2005].

Hughes, E. (2000) 'An inside view: Prisoners' letters', in D. Wilson and A. Reuss (eds) *Prison(er) Education: Stories of Change and Transformation.* Winchester: Waterside Press.

Hughes, E. (2004) *Free to Learn? Prisoner-Students' Views on Distance Learning.* Surrey: Prisoners' Education Trust.

Hughes, E. (2007) *Thinking Inside the Box: British Prisoner-Students' Experiences of Distance Learning*, unpublished PhD dissertation, Birmingham City University, School of Social Sciences.

Irwin (1970) *The Felon.* Englewood Cliffs, NJ: Prentice Hall.

Jewkes, Y. (2005) 'Loss, liminality and the life sentence: Managing identity through a disrupted lifecourse', in A. Liebling and S. Maruna (eds) *The Effects of Imprisonment*. Cullompton: Willan Publishing.

Light, R. (1993) 'Why support prisoners' family-tie groups?', *The Howard Journal of Criminal Justice*, 32(4): 322–9.

Maruna, S. (2001) *Making Good: How Ex-Convicts Reform and Rebuild Their Lives*. Washington, DC: American Psychological Association.

Petersilia, J. (2003) *When Prisoners Come Home: Parole and Prisoner Reentry*. Oxford: Oxford University Press.

Reuss, A. (1997) *Higher Education and Personal Change in Prisoners*, unpublished PhD dissertation, University of Leeds, School of Sociology and Social Policy.

Reuss, A. (1999) 'Prison(er) education', *The Howard Journal of Criminal Justice*, 38(2): 113–27.

Rumgay, J. (2004) 'Scripts for safer survival: Pathways out of female crime', *The Howard Journal of Criminal Justice*, 43(4): 405–19.

Social Exclusion Unit (2002) *Reducing Re-offending by Ex-Prisoners*. London: Office of the Deputy Prime Minister.

Willis, P. E. (1977) *Learning to Labour: How Working Class Kids Get Working Class Jobs*. Farnborough: Saxon House.

Wilson, D. (2000) 'Introduction', in D. Wilson and A. Reuss (eds) *Prison(er) Education: Stories of Change and Transformation*. Winchester: Waterside Press.

Wilson, D. and Reuss, A. (eds) (2000) *Prison(er) Education: Stories of Change and Transformation*. Winchester: Waterside Press.

Woolf, Lord Justice (1991) *Prison Disturbances April 1990: Report of an Inquiry by the Rt Honourable Lord Justice Woolf (Parts I and II) and His Honour Judge Stephen Tumim (Part II)*, Cm. 1456. London: HMSO.

Worth, V. (1996) 'Supporting learners in prison', in R. Mills and A. Tait (eds) *Supporting the Learner in Open and Distance-Learning*. London: Pitman Publishing.

Young, P. (2000) '"I might as well give up": Self-esteem and mature students' feelings about feedback on assignments', *Journal of Further and Higher Education*, 24(3): 409–18.

Chapter 7

Accounts of change and resistance among women prisoners

Barbara Owen

Introduction

Drug treatment has become the latest attempt at rehabilitation in the contemporary prison. In the 1990s, the then California Department of Corrections (CDC) embarked on a massive experiment to introduce prison-based drug treatment in its system.[1] This experiment in personal change is primarily conducted through the therapeutic community (TC) model, which has been implemented throughout corrections with varying success. Often called a 'modified TC', this model relies on the 'community as healer' and is typically a phased programme that combines paraprofessionals with peer leaders. This chapter describes narratives of change and resistance as women prisoners negotiate a new image of 'self' while participating in a prison drug treatment programme, the therapeutic community. Cooley's 'looking-glass self' and Blumer's perspective on symbolic interaction are used to frame this negotiation and redefinition of self. The data reported here are drawn from ethnographic observations of the treatment participants within the therapeutic community and used to illustrate how women experiment and audition changes in definitions of the self and of their situations. While some women resist this process, others experience epiphanies and 'see the light' about the possibilities of changing identity and, ultimately, changing their lives. While much of this narrative is couched in the symbolism and language of the TC, these descriptions also capture the ambivalence of imprisoned women as they try to straddle contradictory worldviews in both trying out the TC and continuing to live in the prison world.

Methods and conceptual framework

The data for this chapter come from descriptions drawn from participant observation and interviews over 16 months in an in-prison therapeutic community. Typical qualitative and ethnographic methods were used here. Berg (2007) offers various definitions of ethnography. Building on Spradley's view, Berg (2007: 171) suggests that ethnography is the work of describing a culture, with the essential core of the activity aiming to understand another way of life from a native point of view. Other definitions include ethnography as a detailed and accurate description of a natural setting and as an examination of social phenomena from the participants' point of view (Berg 2007: 172). In the encounter group, data collection was limited to observation with no questions being posed during the group. For the discussion groups, a focus group methodology was employed. The focus group method as discussed by Bertrand *et al.* (1992) allows the participants to respond freely to questions regarding perceptions and experiences. This qualitative methodology has been advocated in the literature for researchers who 'are interested in examining the context-embedded gendered experiences' (Pollock 2003: 461). Focus groups are 'carefully planned discussion groups designed to obtain perceptions on a defined area of interest' (Javidi *et al.* 1991: 231). This method is particularly valuable for 'understanding collective experiences of marginalization, developing a structural analysis of individual experience and challenging taken-for-granted assumptions about race, gender, sexuality, and class' (Pollock 2003: 461).

In collecting these observations, I 'hung around' the program extensively, observing the range of daily activities and participating where possible. I sat in on every aspect of the program, including attending 'morning meetings' where the plan for the day was announced; sitting in 'caseload' groups, where a range of prepared materials were presented and discussed; and observing the 'encounter group', a structured treatment group where individual women were challenged about an in-programme problem, behavior or attitude. In voluntary focus group discussions held after the treatment day, specific research questions were posed.

In this chapter I suggest that the world of the TC and its effect on its women participants fit closely the model presented by the symbolic interaction perspective. Symbolic interactionists argue that the self is created through an ongoing process of interaction between one individual and others. The concept of the 'looking-glass self' (Cooley 1902) is one of the critical components of a reflective identity and can be applied to the renegotiation of self and identity within the TC. Blumer (1969) sees that symbolic interaction is the process through which the self is created through communication and interaction. The symbolic interaction perspective asserts that reality is a subjective, social construction. Meaning, in Blumer's words, accretes though interaction and over time. As he suggests:

> Symbolic interactionism . . . does not regard meaning as emanating from the intrinsic make up of the thing, nor does it see meaning as arising through psychological elements between people. The meaning of a thing for a person grows out of the ways in which other persons act toward the person with regard to the thing. Their actions operate to define the thing for the person; thus symbolic interactionism sees meanings as social products formed through the activities of people interactions (Blumer 1969: 5).

For symbolic interactionists, the self is primarily a social product of symbolic interaction. The definitions of self, then, are sustained and changed through interaction with others. As such, the self is a dynamic and adaptable entity that is shaped by taking the role of the other. Taking the role of the other is the process of placing yourself in another's position and viewing the world as they do.

The concepts of the looking glass self and the process of symbolic interaction can be used to frame imprisoned women's statements about their *selves* and their negotiated identity and personal change. In the TC, the expectation is that women will see their own problems (and subsequent solutions) by looking through the eyes of another's experience.

Profile of the program participants

At the same time as my fieldwork, the research team from the UCLA Drug Abuse Research Center was conducting a large-scale process and outcome evaluation of the in-prison TC (Prendergast and Burden 2000). These data are derived from their Intake Assessment and describe the demographic profile of treatment participants. The mean age of the program female participants was 35.9, roughly equivalent to the general population at the facility. The average length of stay for the current incarceration was just under three years. African-American women made up about one-third of the population, another third was white and less than one-quarter was Hispanic/Latina. Other racial and ethnic identities made up the remainder of the participant population. Few women reported being married (19 per cent) or 'living as married' (8 per cent), with most women (69 per cent) saying they had never married, were divorced, separated or widowed. Over two-thirds reported that they were unemployed (67.8 per cent) in the 30 days prior to incarceration. The majority of women had been convicted of a drug-related crime (64 per cent), about one-fifth for property crimes and the remainder convicted of crimes against persons (8 per cent) and other crimes (8 per cent). Cocaine/crack was mentioned as the primary drug of choice and problem alcohol use also noted frequently as well. Interestingly, almost one-quarter of the women did not meet the formal diagnostic criteria for alcohol or drug abuse/dependence. Just over half met this DSM-IV criteria for *either* alcohol or drug abuse/dependence, and just over one-quarter met the criteria for *both* alcohol and drug abuse/dependence.

A brief review of the therapeutic community

The therapeutic community (TC) originated in community treatment settings and has been operating in prison settings since the late 1980s. De Leon (2000) has described the community TC as a residential treatment program that provides a highly structured living environment in which staff and participants interact in structured and patterned ways. The National Institute on Drug Abuse (2002: 1) defines therapeutic communities as a residential setting that uses a 'hierarchical model with treatment stages that reflect increased levels of personal and social responsibility. Peer influence, mediated through a variety of group processes, is used to help individuals learn and assimilate social norms and develop more effective social skills.' In this model, the key agent of change is the TC community, made up of both treatment staff and those in recovery. This approach is often referred to as 'community as method' (De Leon 2000: 1). TCs differ from other substance abuse treatment programs in that the community, rather than professionals, is the key agent of change. Peers have a critical role in this change process with peer influence used to help participants learn and assimilate pro-social norms and behaviors.

In addition to the importance of the community as a primary agent of change, a second fundamental TC principle is the notions of 'self-help' and 'mutual self help' which task the individual with some responsibility for the recovery of their peers as part of their own recovery process (NIDA 2002: 2). Other aspects of the 'community as method' therapeutic model focus on changing negative patterns of thinking and behavior through individual and group therapy, community-based learning, confrontation, games, and role-playing (De Leon 2007). NIDA also states that, 'Ultimately, participation in a TC is designed to help people appropriately and constructively identify, express, and manage their feelings' (2002: 3).

Change in behavior is created by the structure of the TC and reinforced through social learning and a social contract with the community. The contract is actualized by: (1) being aware of, confronting, and reporting on one another's negative behavior, (2) acknowledging and reflecting on their own personal negative actions, and (3) striving for honesty, with themselves and others (Phoenix House Foundation 1995: 9).

This view sees that substance abusers must take responsibility for their own recovery through 'fundamental changes in feelings and behavior'

(1995: 9). This responsibility is learned through participation and ultimate immersion in the community itself. In the TC, recovery is facilitated by two main mechanisms: the social structure of the TC and the peer group encounter, both of which deliver the 'theory of right living' (1995: 10).

Welch (2007) examined current research on the prison TC models and has found that, while most studies conclude that prison TC treatment appears to be effective, there are significant gaps in our knowledge about the over-efficacy of this modality. He suggests that our knowledge is mediated by specific methodological limitations, such as selection and attrition bias, dissimilar outcome measures, few statistical controls and potentially low statistical power (Welch 2007: 1484). Another gap involves research on women's experience in prison TCs. In their study of treatment needs of women in prison TCs, Messina *et al.* (2003) found that there are important gender differences relevant to the design of institutional treatment programs and question the extent to which the TC model is appropriate for women offenders. A review of four studies by the National Institute of Justice (2005) found the various treatment programs

> share the premise that the needs of women inmates differ in many respects – physically, emotionally, psychologically, and socially – from those of their male counterparts. The implementation of rehabilitation programs specifically designed with those differences in mind can effectively address the needs of female inmates and identify factors which may impede their ability to succeed post-release (2005: 7).

The Phoenix House Model

In the Phoenix House version of the TC model, substance abuse is defined as a character disorder, involving the whole person, and affects his or her values, beliefs, personality, feelings, behavior and attitude. Observable behaviors are generated by underlying feelings, with a collection of behaviors interpreted as attitude. Rehabilitation, then, requires change in 'virtually every aspect of that person' (Phoenix House Foundation 1995: 7). The whole person is the target of the TC treatment process with substance abuse seen as a symptom of a wide range of incorrect and destructive ways of acting, feeling and thinking. All program participants in this TC were called 'family members'. The concept of mutual self-help was conveyed by the phrase, 'you are you sister's keeper'. One key philosophy of the program was the 'theory of right living'. This 'right living' includes: (1) the centrality of honesty, (2) a focus on the here and now, (3) the value of social responsibility, (4) responsible concern, and (5) 'you *are* what others *see*'. It is this last point ('You are what others see') that is illustrated through observations of the encounter groups and a focus group discussing epiphanies and personal change.

The encounter group

In focusing on immediate, real-time behavior, the encounter is the primary 'engine' that drives the recovery process in the institutional TC. As stated in the Phoenix House clinical manual: 'The peer group encounter is the therapeutic community's most important mechanism for dealing with conduct disorders. Its purpose is to heighten self-awareness of negative behavior by means of confrontation' (Phoenix House Foundation 1995: 51). The manual continues by saying that the peer group encounter is:

> ... designed to raise the awareness about negative behavior and about the feelings that underlie them. By confronting specific negative behaviors, the encounter group helps the individual to identify the underlying feelings behind them, and to make a commitment to change behaviors. The commitment to resolve negative attitudes through positive change in the behavior is crucially important in the development of a mature personality (1995: 9).

The basic encounter has the following goals: (1) to confront specific negative behavior that needs to be modified, (2) to persuade the confronted person to admit (own) responsibility for that behavior, (3) to help the person identify honestly the feelings underlying the negative behavior when it occurred, (4) to have the person make a commitment to change the behavior in the future, and (5) to have the person accept the support of the group in setting realistic goals for altering attitude (1995: 51).

Women were selected to participate in the encounter through several mechanisms. Most commonly, family members 'drop a slip' wherein they 'indict' another program participant for either a very specific behavior ('getting high on the yard') or for more general non-involvement in the program. Less frequently, women can ask to be seen 'in the circle', as encounters are sometimes called. Another type of encounter can be called when an entire room or another group within the program has issues to discuss through this structured interaction. Other encounters, or 'games', can be called when a woman is in danger of being removed from the program for violating rules, or when she is transitioning or graduating from the program.

At the end of an encounter, a breakthrough in acknowledging one's negative behavior is the expected outcome. If the 'game was called' to address some immediate transgression, such as breaking either a prison or a Phoenix House rule, a 'Learning Experience' (LE) or 'Behavioral Contract' (BC) was assigned as a sanction with the goal of promoting some movement toward new behaviors. Another end product of the encounter was to secure 'commitments' from others to help the encountered woman work on her recovery.

Prison culture

In addition to understanding the dimensions of the TC, prison drug treatment programmes should also be examined within the context of prison culture. Prison culture includes the ways in which prisoners define their experience in prison; how they learn to live in prison; how they develop relationships with other prisoners and the staff; and how they change the way they think about themselves and their place within the prison and the free world. As I found in my previous work (Owen 1998), women's prison culture is embedded in a complex social world where women prisoners learn to negotiate its complexity on their own terms, based on their pre-prison orientation and the degree to which they become immersed in the normative world of the prison community. Prison culture is based on a subtle negotiation of time and place, individual identity, and personalized relationships inside and outside the prison community (Owen 1998). Like most experiences for women, their responses to imprisonment and to a new world of treatment norms is a gendered experience. In this gendered context, relationships among the prisoners and with the staff, rules about informing and readiness to participate in treatment have direct relevance to the TC experience. When the culture of the TC is layered onto these pre-existing normative frameworks, it creates yet another cultural stratum that women must negotiate.

One salient aspect of learning how to adjust to the struggle of imprisonment is through the prison code. The prison code is a set of values that prescribe the conduct of a prisoner who is immersed in the prison community. Among male prisoners, common values include 'Don't be a snitch or informer', 'Be loyal to convicts', and 'Do your own time'. Inciardi *et al.* (2000: 1–2) describe the prison code for male prisoners and its relation to therapeutic communities:

> Every correctional facility has its subculture, and every prison subculture has its system of norms that influence prisoners' behavior, typically to a far greater extent than the institution's formally prescribed rules. These subcultural norms are informal and unwritten rules, but their violation can evoke sanctions from fellow inmates ranging from simple ostracism to physical violence and death. Many of the rules revolve around relations among inmates and interactions with prison staff, while others reflect preoccupations with being 'smart', 'tough', and street wise. As such, this prison code often tends

to militate against reform in general, and drug rehabilitation in particular.

Although somewhat weaker than in the male prisons, women's prisons, too, have a stricture against informing on the behavior of other prisoners. For women prisoners participating in the TC, the rules of the convict code often collided with the norms of the TC, particularly those concerning 'snitching', privacy and trusting prison staff. As will be seen below, the encounter was the most obvious area of collision. The encounter is based on confrontation, making behavior public in front of other inmates and prison staff. In confronting the behavior and attitude of the participants, inmates were challenged to choose between the demands of two conflicting normative systems: the prison culture and the demands of the therapeutic community model.

A fuller understanding of the prison-based therapeutic community must be developed within the context of prison culture, especially for women. The prison code may constrain interaction within the TC because full participation in the therapeutic community often conflicts with the proscriptions of the prison code. For example, 'doing your own time' requires, among other things, loyalty to other inmates, protecting inmate interest and avoiding interaction with the prison authorities. However, the TC model is built upon 'responsible concern', a key component of the 'community as healer'. 'Responsible concern' is the self-help process whereby residents learn that responsibility and mutuality in interpersonal relationships are core aspects of the recovery process (Phoenix House Foundation 1995: 11). The manual provides a further elaboration:

> Another value that requires the rejection of the street code is responsible concern. Members learn to demonstrate concern for their peers by directly challenging their negative behavior. In some situations, they must report such behavior to the staff. By subcultural norms, this reporting is a taboo termed 'snitching' or 'dropping a dime'. When one challenges the behavior and attitudes that are the same as one's own, inner conflict typically results (Phoenix House Foundation 1995: 11).

As the manual recognizes, these concepts often conflict with those embedded in the prison code. In the New Choice program, women are often ambivalent as they try to straddle contradictory worldviews of the TC and the prison world. The rules of the informal prison code caution against informing staff about in-prison behavior and, at the same time, the rules of the TC require it. The encounter provides a lens through which to view the inherent conflicts and contradictions in the overlapping constraints of the prison rules, the Phoenix House rules, and the demands of the prison culture. The entire encounter process demands that women examine their own behavior and that of other participants in a very public setting.

Encountering the self

The TC model asks women to discuss their past behaviors and experiences in the encounter as a way to discard old versions of self and create and sustain new definitions and new futures. 'Community' also has a resonant meaning in both the TC language system and the theoretical constructs of symbolic interaction. In the therapeutic community, the 'community is healer', suggesting that recovery is gained by taking on the values and behaviors of those peers who have begun their journey toward the 'pro-social' ideals underpinning the TC model. In symbolic interaction, the community supplies language and other symbols, mediates meaning, and provides the social context for this process (Blumer 1969).

Therefore, the TC process can be seen as a specific version of symbolic interaction: the 'self' as reflected onto others. 'Self-help', from this perspective, gains additional meaning. Within each encounter group, the woman 'being encountered' hears the community's perspective on her behaviors, often through narratives in which the other encounter group members describe their own experience. This narrative ('running my story') is thought to change a woman's view of herself by promoting a redefinition of self. This redefinition, in theory, leads to new, more 'pro-social' behaviors. The concept of the 'looking glass self' and the process of symbolic interaction are sharply illustrated in the encounter group narrative. As women explore their own lives and recount their own experience in this setting, these public events become a looking glass in which women may see their own behaviors in the reflections of others when they are asked 'to see yourself in me'.

While the public world of the program continually reinforces these 'pro-social' definitions of a sober self, there is significant cultural conflict between the TC expectations and the strictures of the inmate culture. Women were often caught in these subcultural crossfires. One salient example is found in the process of 'dropping a slip' or bringing an indictment. Making previously private wrongdoings public through the indictment was the first of many direct challenges to the age-old prison code that advocated 'doing your own time'. It appears that the rules of TC and the demands of prison culture were often in direct conflict, causing some women to consider which side they would choose. Would a woman 'talk the talk' and 'walk the walk' of the therapeutic community? Or would she 'lay in the cut', and continue her ties to the prison subculture, resisting both the redefinition process of her 'sisters' and self-reflection? As an illustration, in one heated but honest encounter, several women expressed the frank opinion that they were unwilling to give up the street life, and as one woman[2] said:

No matter what you tell us here, I know I am going back to the street when I get out of here. When people [sister prisoners] I knew on the street see me in this program, they see it as a betrayal. You have to understand that in the convict world, they see that my being in a program like this is turning on them.

This next example provides one illustration of a woman, Jessica, who was actively resisting, through her actions and statements, any attempt at redefinition. She was indicted by her roommates because she was not participating as a full member of the therapeutic community. Her six roommates, who were more actively participating in the TC, were called 'to the circle' and sat quietly as the staff person began the encounter by challenging the roommates about their own behavior. The staff member asks the entire room why 'they let this go on', allowing Jessica to avoid full participation in the program. In response, Miranda, a roommate who has adopted the symbolic definition of self provided by the TC, opens the encounter by directly confronting Jessica. Miranda tries to reach Jessica by suggesting that all women in the program have the same struggles:

There is something wrong out there on the streets that is bringing you back here. Something that is keeping you angry, making you use drugs. Don't look at this just as a drug program. I know you have other problems – like addiction to money. This is the place to deal with this. I have been in this program nine months and I have been so happy. If you just sit and listen long enough, you will hear your story. We have all been through what you have been through. We are all here to figure it out.

In this quote, Miranda likens her own struggle with addiction to Jessica's problems. In saying, 'We have all been through what you have been through' and stating that she has 'been so happy' in the program, Miranda suggests that such positive emotion is available to Jessica as well. Many times the response to such outpouring of good intention is positive, with the woman under indictment persuaded by peer encouragement and the reflective logic of the encounter. In this example, however, Jessica was unmoved and resisted participating in this process in any way. While the roommates held up their experiences 'on the street' and in the program as a way to see her self, Jessica refused to look. She sat silently throughout the encounter, and when prodded said, 'I don't want to talk.' In another attempt to get Jessica to open up 'to the process', Samantha, a second roommate, 'runs her story' and remarks:

I see a lot of me in you. I did not want to hear what people had to say. You will find mirrors in here. You will see people just like you if you look at their behavior, hear their stories. It is just like how your children learn to act from you. We try to learn how to act by watching each other, by helping each other.

I was an ugly-ass person on the streets. I was my own self-enemy. But now I am too tired and too old for this. Having to put up a fake-ass-shell because the devil has gotten a hold of us. It is time to change.

I am going to go home to my family, to see my grandkids, to a mom with cancer. I have learned from my addiction. I have recognized it and I have worked on it. I am going home with my tools. People aren't going to know me on the streets. I am not going to be the Samantha they knew before.

This first paragraph captures this sense of a duality of self and the looking-glass process as played out in the encounter. In addition to the statement, 'I see a lot of me in you,' Samantha continues by suggesting that other women in the program are mirrors as well. 'People just like you,' she says, 'can be found in here. You will see them if you look at their behavior, hear their stories.' Here is the promise of understanding one's self by observing another – one of the central tenets of symbolic interaction.

Jessica remains unconvinced and says, 'I am tired of this place. The staff, the c.o.'s are only here because it is a job.' Charlotte, a third roommate, then holds up her experience as a mirror in this telling example of self-awareness, as she describes her separate self:

I know when I am loaded I don't think right. You lose touch with reality and don't see things in a clear mind. Your mind is altered and you have cravings. I will have money that I set aside for the rent and you say to yourself, 'just one more'. What is right in my eyes when I am loaded is not right in sobriety.

I am embarrassed when I think about how I acted when I was using. *It is my separate self.* The drugs made me selfish and only think about getting more. You look for a feeling that you really know you'll never get but you always look for it.

Jessica continues to resist these entreaties and says, 'No program can change me. I have the right to have feelings. I am angry – at myself, at the prison – about being away from my family.' The counselor then tells her: 'It is OK to be upset. We are here to learn how to express feelings constructively. We are all here to help you with that and now you need to make a conscious decision to embrace the program. Now, what is your commitment?' Something about this statement moves Jessica. Whether it is accommodation to peer pressure or a genuine reflection, she appears to shift perspectives. With some tears all around, she announces, 'I am going to give this program a chance.' Hugs and congratulations 'close the game' and her roommates promise to redouble their efforts to be their sister's keeper.

In this next example of an encounter, Suzie represents an 'old-timer' who has more or less accepted the TC philosophy. Serving multiple prison terms, she was giving the program experience every chance to change her life and, while mostly in the background ('laying in the cut'), she participated in program activities. In this encounter, she attempts to be her sister's keeper, a behavior directly contrary to the prison norm of 'minding your own business'. Suzie brings an indictment against one of her roommates for 'running the yard' and 'getting high'. Showing 'responsible concern', she has 'dropped a slip' on Ellen in the hope of addressing her 'dope fiend behavior'. This encounter intends to show Ellen that 'everyone sees her' and wants to 'save her life'. Very few women took this step to participate openly in 'outing' the behavior of her sisters in the program. In addition to Suzie, her other five roommates are called to the inner circle to confront Ellen. Suzie begins the encounter by saying:

> I won't sit back and watch you die. I already watched someone die on the streets because of dope. I could not do anything about it on the streets but I can do something about it here. I am an old timer – I have an old number,[3] I have been to prison sixteen times. I have been around heroin my whole life. I brought my brother home dead and I just can't sit here and watch you do this to yourself.

The counselor then followed up by saying: 'Is Suzie the only one who wants to save her life?' Suzie, then, uncharacteristically, began to yell at Ellen, accusing her of lying about her behavior as well. Ellen attempted to defend herself but was silenced by the counselor who said, 'When you get in a mess, you are not only messing with your own recovery, you are messing with everyone's recovery.' With the group extremely still, she continues in asking Ellen, 'Why are you in prison? Can you see that this is the kind of behavior that got you here?' In turning to the group as a whole, the counselor asked them: 'Why is this room letting her sink? Why is this all on Suzie? Is she the only one who cares if she lives or dies? You all need to express yourselves and challenge this kind of behavior.'

Yesinia, another roommate, then said, 'You didn't think you would get caught on your shit. You knew – we knew – you were hanging with people on the yard who are using and selling. We all knew. You broke a cardinal rule [of this treatment program] – you were getting high!' Ellen continued to deny the accusations throughout the encounter, but now the five roommates continued their charges, re-enforcing the statements made by Suzie and Yesinia. At some point, another roommate compliments Suzie for 'speaking on this' with the implicit knowledge that her statements break a critical proscription of the prison code – not 'telling' on another prisoner. She further stated that, 'I know this is the hardest thing you have ever done.' Suzie, in tacitly acknowledging that she purposively broke this rule of the prison code, said, 'You can throw this message out on the yard. I can stand up for myself.' The encounter closed with the counselor saying to Ellen, 'This community will not let you take other people's recovery.' Ellen, sitting silently, offered no response.

The experience of 'being encountered'

I was able to ask questions of women who volunteered to participate in focus groups after the program day. In one of these groups, I asked women to describe the experience of participating in an encounter group. Juanita, a woman who had embraced the community as healer, started by saying:

> At first it is a scary feeling. You are nervous all day long [when you know one is scheduled]. When I first attended one, my stomach flipped like a big dog. I don't know most of these people and I knew there is so much negativity here. I was mad when I was indicted. I got an attitude but you know what you have to do. At first you wonder, what is she talking about? Why is she picking on me? Later, I asked to be seen in group because I thought it would be helpful in my own recovery. I used to feel like everyone here was a hypocrite – groups were 'tit for tat' I thought – how can she tell me what to do?

Andie chimes in to say, 'I didn't like the program at all at first but now see that it can change you.' She continued in saying she understood that 'the community is supposed to heal itself':

> I have seen a change, I have seen good encounters. The house [program] has grown; it has mellowed, there is a better curriculum, I see changes in attitude of everyone here. When I first came in, I was negative but then I actually saw how one person felt and saw myself in that. Some people can't see what is wrong in their lives and they need it pointed out to them. The program works if you want to change. We have to give it a chance.

Within the negotiation of the definitions of self, patterns of resistance and accommodation, many women expressed gratitude for the program experience. Elsie, a woman with multiple prison terms and a lengthy history of 'serious dope fiend behavior', stated:

I now know I am going to go home with a different outlook, a different plan. I have been doing my own inventory, working on my relapse prevention plan. This would not have happened without this program. I may be old but I am not dead. I came in here tired of my old life and they made it available for me to do something different. And I took it. I think this program was successful for me because I fitted my needs with their program. This program has restored my confidence. I saw the change in the program and I saw the change in me.

A lot of what is going on, though, is my own process. They did not give it to me. This program was a chance to get my priorities straight. Reflecting on the lives of other women in the house gave me an added insight into what I was missing by leading the kind of life I did. This program helped me get back in touch. I liked learning from the others that are very different from me. Here, if you can't see it, just listen and maybe you can hear it. We are all mirrors here. Mirrors of each other's lives. And if you can't see it in your life, maybe you can see it in somebody else's life.

'Seeing the light'

In another discussion group, I asked a group of women who were active in all aspects of the TC to discuss how they 'got' it; that is, accepted the new ways of 'thinking, acting and feeling'. I began by asking if anyone knew the term 'epiphany' and one woman replied, 'Is it when you see the light?' We agreed that this was a perfect way of framing our conversation.

Jill, who had discussed with me her growing anxiety about going home, was first to volunteer her answer. Her children and family were far away in another state and they had been estranged for many years. Jill began by saying:

> I was locked up at [another prison] and had been away from my kids for three years. I got some pictures of my youngest kids and was shocked at how much they had changed. They were little the last time I saw them. They had grown so and I realized how much I had missed. It made me throw up and I slid down the door and said to myself, 'This has to stop. I have to change and I can't do it alone.' For the first time, I realized the consequences of my actions and I knew it clicked this time.
>
> Before I had a 'don't give a fuck' attitude. I thought my family would always be there. But now I can see they won't always be there because I have hurt them so much. I am tired of hurting them. And I want them to be proud of me.

Like many of the groups I observed, this heartfelt expression brought tears to the eyes of all of us in this conversation. As Maria offers her sense that:

117

Some of the girls here don't have people or places outside of the life. [This program] is the only time I been around people who are trying to get out of the life. This program made me look at things the way they are. This program gave me the will. I used to make excuses and was always running away from my family. Now I have a clear mind.

Bonita listened carefully to these statements and shyly admitted that:

I have not gotten it yet. I have not seen the light yet. I am too scared to look at the things in my life. I have been in the same patterns since I was thirteen years old and I have to figure out what normal people do. I am terrified. I didn't know what to do, how to change. I never believed that I could change before, but this time I am going to try. I want to feel this. This is my second prison term and I spent the last five years in prison. When I came to the program, I had no intention of stopping using. I thought I would keep selling dope when I went home. I always thought I knew what I was doing. Then a lady came here and told me God has a reason for me to be here. I really want this to happen to me. I know I need to move forward and leave this madness behind.

Everyone nods toward Bonita in encouragement and then Cassie begins to speak:

When I got it, it was like a freaking strobe light. It has come on and off at different times in my life. The light came on in my twenties, my thirties and forties. At [another prison], I realized that I have to accept things as they are. I still have a light, but sometimes it is dim. Yes, I want this craziness to stop. I can't – won't – say never. But I have had eight trips to prison, so who am I kidding? I said I was never coming back many times, but I am too old to fool myself. It's God will and we all have a destiny. I guess prison is mine.

Joanne then says:

I guess the light has always been on for me. I knew what I was doing was wrong, but I had my sunglasses on. We all have our destinies and we have to go through certain things regardless. We never know what our purpose is here. Not to preach or anything. I think my sunglasses are lightening up. My time will come. I have seen people die right in front of me. I have seen terrible shit, but it did not turn me around.

I know I have been selfish my whole life. But when I dropped off my kids to turn myself in to do this time, they were all in tears and I am determined to get myself together for their sakes.

In this statement, Elana saw a version of self reflected in the wishes of her children:

I have been to prison so many times, it seemed like I belonged here. I was partying on the yard and just running all around. A few months ago, I was just kicking it on the yard and I called my kids and they told me what they wanted to be when they grew up. My daughter told me she wanted to be a doctor so she could fix me when men hurt me and my son said he wanted to be an attorney so when the police arrested me, he could go to the jail and pick me up. That was when I asked to be in the program. I knew I had to change all this.

I have had my eyes opened here. Hearing the stories of the women here made me see that I had to get real with myself. I know my children need me. But I always got twisted around on the street and there was this one person that distracted me.

I was pretty bad off before I came here. My boyfriend had grabbed my throat and I had cardiac arrest. When I came to, I called my connection from the hospital and he came and shot heroin through my tube. And I still did not see the light. My husband took the kids away, but I was still using. I had to feed myself through the tube, smoke crack, shoot dope, everything through the tube. I finally got sober but it took a year to get my mind clear. It took me twenty years to figure out a way out of this.

These statements about 'seeing the light' also represent the recognition that their drug-using selves and their sober selves are not only reflected in their own words and actions, but for many, in the words and the lives of their children. In some cases, these reflections on their lives are thrown in sharp relief when confronted with the death of those who were on the same path of addiction and imprisonment. For some, the looking-glass self of the program also reflects the light of sober living.

Conclusion

These accounts illustrate the range of acceptance, accommodation and resistance to new definitions of self in this TC. In the encounter groups and the discussion groups, women reflect on their past troubles, reflecting on the behaviors, feelings and relationships that brought them to prison. Some of the narratives describe a new self, 'a pro-social' person who is prepared to use the tools and experience of the TC to transform their definition of self and develop a recovering identity. Samantha, in the quote above, said that she was now such a different person that she is 'not going to be the Samantha they knew before'. In describing her 'separate self', Charlotte implies that she too is a whole new person. Others, as represented by Jessica and Ellen, are much more tentative in considering any transformation and make only small commitments to change. All in all, seeing change in others is a common thread that supports the assertion that the self is created, maintained and changed through looking at, and listening to, the experience of others.

The encounter, then, can be characterized as a mirror that women hold up to their own experience as a way to examine both their own individual behavior and those of their sisters in the program. The TC provides a context for women to use the encounters not only to show 'responsible concern' for others, but also (and maybe even more importantly) to reflect on their past pain and current needs. These narratives of change show the promise of treatment and the way women see their own pathways to and from prison. While some of these narratives provide strong examples of the resistance to this new definition of self, many women begin to adopt a treatment perspective expressed in their own language over time and begin to accept these new definitions of self and 'more pro-social ways of acting, thinking and feeling'. These observations illustrate that forms of resistance and accommodations shape the reality of the TC. In TC terms, many of the women negotiated this program by 'talking the talk' (that is, participating in the program and giving verbal acquiescence to program demands), but not necessarily 'walking the walk', that is, committing themselves fully to the worldview of the therapeutic community. These narratives also suggest that women were constantly ambivalent about which 'me' was in play. Which self should be displayed while participating in the encounter? The woman who wanted to be 'prison-smart' and not display weakness, or the woman who was prepared to publicly confront her pathways to prison by examining her own behavior? Personal change and planning for the future is reflected in these narratives as women ponder their feelings about themselves, their chances about success in recovery and their hopes and plans for the future.

While it is clear that the narrative redefinition that takes place in the therapeutic community can be an important first step to a clean and sober self, critical aspects of recovery and sobriety remain to be addressed. While social support may be available while participating in the TC, other concrete real-world needs, such as financial support, employment, housing, and re-establishing relationships with children and family remain unaddressed within this individualized definition of a sober reality. One of the most crucial elements required for women's successful reentry is social capital. Yet women offenders as a group experience the highest levels of capital deficits (Reisig *et al.* 2002). Reisig and colleagues found that these social capital deficits can be attributed to women having weaker social networks from which to draw. Flavin (2004) also asserted that along with the material needs of reentry shared by women and men, family support was critical to women's success on parole. Rumgay (2004) concurs in suggesting that parole assistance related to material, social and psychological concerns is correlated with successful reentry. Rumgay adds that successful parole performance is also related to a re-imagining of identity for women offenders. Bloom *et al.* (2003) suggest that reentry initiatives must target women's pathways to offending, including substance abuse and material needs, and address victimization, trauma histories and mental health conditions through comprehensive programs that provide both treatment and socio-economic opportunity. Richie (2001) adds that access to childcare and transportation, safety from abusive partners, and program staff availability beyond business hours, and probation contribute to successful reintegration for women offenders. Other studies have examined the delivery of post-prison services, with comprehensive case management services most closely associated with positive outcomes for women (Pearl 1998; Zhang *et al.* 2006).

Veysey (2008: 1), however, suggests that 'The way into criminality isn't necessarily the way out in reverse.' Discussing the critical importance of changing identity and the need to develop valued social roles, Veysey argues that shedding negative identities requires sustaining a more positive identity through a larger social context. While a new definition of self is essential to any identity transformation, it cannot be sustained on a purely individual level. Without institutional and structural supports, the individualized version of sobriety can only be one step on the pathway to recovery. As Covington (2003: 30) suggests:

A look at the principal themes and issues affecting women in the criminal justice system reveals that women's issues are also society's issues: sexism, racism, poverty, domestic violence, sexual abuse, and substance abuse. While the impact of incarceration and reentry sets the stage and defines the individual experiences of female prisoners, their children and families, and their communities, what is required is a social response. Agencies and actions are not only about the individual; they are also, unavoidably, about family, institutions, and society.

Notes

1 This agency changed its name to California Department of Corrections and Rehabilitation (CDCR) in 2006.
2 All names have been changed to protect individuals' identities and privacy.
3 The prison number indicates when one entered into the system.

References

Berg, B. (2007) *Qualitative Research Methods for the Social Sciences*. Boston, MA: Allyn & Bacon.

Bertrand, J., Brown, J. and Ward, V. (1992) 'Techniques for analyzing focus group data', *Evaluation Review*, 16(2): 198–209.

Bloom, B., Owen, B. and Covington, S. (2003) *Gender-responsive Strategies: Research, Practice, and Guiding Principles for Women Offenders*. Washington, DC: National Institute of Corrections.

Blumer, H. (1969) *Symbolic Interactionism*. Englewood Cliffs, NJ: Prentice-Hall.

Cooley, C. (1902) *Human Nature and the Social Order*. New York: Scribner's.

Covington, S. (2003) 'A woman's journey home: Challenges for female offenders', in J. Travis and M. Waul (eds) *Prisoners Once Removed: The Impact of Incarceration and Reentry on Children, Families and Communities*. Washington, DC: The Urban Institute.

De Leon, G. (2000) *The Therapeutic Community: Theory, Model, and Method*. New York: Springer.

Flavin, J. (2004) 'Employment counseling, housing assistance ... and Aunt Yolanda?: How strengthening families' social capital can reduce recidivism', *Criminology & Public Policy*, 3: 209–16.

Inciardi, J., Martin, S. and Surratt, H. (2000) 'Therapeutic communities in prisons and work release: Effective modalities for drug-involved offenders', Award Number: 97-RT-VX-K004. Washington DC: National Institute of Justice.

Javidi, M., Long, L., Vasu, M. and Ivy, D. (1991) 'Enhancing focus group validity with computer-assisted technology in social science research', *Social Science Computer Review*, 9: 231–45.

Messina, N., Burdon, W. and Prendergast, M. (2003) 'Assessing the needs of women in institutional therapeutic communities', *Journal of Offender Rehabilitation*, 37(2): 89–106.

National Institute on Drug Abuse (2002) *Research Report: Therapeutic Communities*, NIH Publication Number 02-4877. Washington DC: National Institutes of Health.

National Institute of Justice (2005) 'Reentry programs for women inmates', *NIJ Journal*, 252: 2–7.

Owen, B. (1998) *In the Mix: Struggle and Survival in a Women's Prison*. Albany, NY: State University of New York Press.

Pearl, N. (1998) 'Use of community-based social services to reduce recidivism in female parolees', *Women and Criminal Justice*, 10(1): 27–52.

Phoenix House Foundation (1995) *Therapeutic Communities: A Clinical Manual*. New York: Phoenix House Foundation.

Pollock, S. (2003) 'Focus-group methodology in research with incarcerated women: Race, power, and collective experience', *Affilia*, 18(4): 461–72.

Prendergast, M. and Burden, W. (2000) *Quarterly Report on the UCLA-DARC Evaluation of the 1,000 and 2,000 Bed Expansions of the Therapeutic Community Programs for Prisoners*. Los Angeles: University of California, Los Angeles.

Reisig, M., Holtfreter, K. and Morash, M. (2002) 'Social capital among women offenders', *Journal of Contemporary Criminal Justice*, 18(2): 167–87.

Richie, B. (2001) 'Challenges incarcerated women face as they return to their community: Findings from life history interviews', *Crime and Delinquency*, 47(3): 368–89.

Rumgay, J. (2004) 'Scripts for survival: Pathways out of female crime', *Howard Journal of Criminal Justice*, 43(4): 405–19.

Veysey, B, (2008) 'Rethinking reentry', *The Criminologist*, 33(3): 1–5.

Welsh, W. (2007) 'A multisite evaluation of prison-based therapeutic community drug treatment', *Criminal Justice and Behavior*, 34: 1481–502.

Zhang, S., Roberts, R. and Callahan, V. (2006) 'Preventing parolees from returning to prison through community-based reintegration', *Crime and Delinquency*, 52: 551–71.

Chapter 8

Parole supervision, change in the self, and desistance from substance use and crime

Merry Morash

Introduction

In midyear 2000, there were 93,234 women in US state and federal prisons, and this number reached 111,403 by midyear 2006 (Sabol *et al*. 2007b: 5). During the same period, the number of women in jail increased from 70,414 to 661,329 (Sabol *et al*. 2007b: 5). These increases followed two previous decades when the female prison population increased 800 per cent, and the jail population increased 450 per cent (Sourcebook of Criminal Justice Statistics 2006). The nearly three decades of dramatic increases resulted in large part from the war on drugs and get tough sentencing policies (Mauer and Chesney-Lind 2003; Richie 1996, Wellisch *et al*. 1994). Confirming the relevance of drug involvement to women's increasing rates of incarceration, a higher percentage of women than men were in prison because of drug offenses (29 per cent vs 19 per cent) for 2004, the most recent year for which statistics are available (Sabol *et al*. 2007a: 8), and even larger proportions were convicted of offenses committed because of drug-centered lifestyles. Similarly, studies of jails have shown that increasing proportions of incarcerated women have used illegal drugs or abused alcohol (Hartley and Marks 2002; Lo 2004).

The numerous difficulties of women leaving jail and prison have been well documented. High proportions of women offenders with a history of drug use and alcohol abuse have experienced physical and sexual violence as children; prior and current abusive partners; permanently or temporarily lost custody of children; physical illness (often exacerbated by substance use); mental health problems like depression and bipolar disorder; and limited education and work histories (Belknap 1996; Bloom *et al.* 2003; Bureau of Justice Statistics 1991; Covington 1998; O'Brien 2006; Owen and Bloom 1995; Richie 2001). Victimization and drug and alcohol use are connected, because many women have used drugs and alcohol, sometimes for many years beginning before or when they were teenagers, to dampen strong negative feelings rooted in backgrounds of abuse and hardship (Bush-Baskette 2000; Johnson 2004: 12; Kearney 1998: 500; Yahne *et al.* 2002; Young *et al.* 2000). Additionally, either because of a lack of alternatives or a desire to live where drugs are accessible, some women have lived in drug houses or other dangerous places, for example camp trailers or cars (Morash 2007), and such living situations put women at risk for victimization through physical and sexual attacks. Finally, repeated use of some drugs has negative physical effects on the brain, which along with recollections of positive feelings associated with being under the influence of drugs, can trigger the desire to use again (Leshner 1997). These facts demonstrate the many challenges for drug- and alcohol-involved women once they leave prison and jail, their need for positive social support and resources.

Unfortunately, the lifestyle of active drug users can limit social support and resources by disrupting relationships with any pro-social family of origin, partners, grown children, and friends who might provide a listening ear and other emotional and material help. Thus, many women leaving jail and prison must rely on one or more programs and services available to varying degrees depending on their communities (O'Brien 2006). One source of support is through formal parole services, which in some places extend beyond monitoring to providing advice, counseling, and referrals. For women who seek visitation or custody of their children, caseworkers from the state family and children's services agency might provide reunification services that extend to support to mothers. Additional types of community services include community mental health treatment, outpatient and residential substance abuse treatment, methadone maintenance programs, state employment counseling services, and job training programs. Finally, most communities have one or more self-help groups, such as Alcoholics Anonymous (AA) and Narcotics Anonymous (NA). Various parole and community services can provide an alternative to drug use to address negative feelings about self and circumstances, and can help women piece together the elements of a pro-social lifestyle.

Analytical focus

The analysis described in this chapter examined whether and how women with histories of crime tangled with drug and alcohol histories experienced support for stopping use, disengaging from illegal behavior, and changing in ways that supported desistance. One part of this focus was to understand what part, if any, supervising officers played in change and desistance. The women had all left jail or prison prior to entering the study, and they were all in a community supervision program in one of two counties in the same state. One of the counties, called Traditional County,[1] had no special provisions for women offenders, and men and women supervising officers handled mixed-gender caseloads. The other, Gender Responsive County, had an all-female team and their supervisor who worked only with women offenders. (Because the same officers supervised women on probation and on parole, in this chapter, the officers are called *supervising officers* rather than *probation* or *parole officers*.) The focus of this chapter is not on comparing these counties. However, because of county differences, the two-county setting increased the possibility of comparing women with different supervision and related program experiences.

Methodology

Sample

The sample derives from a larger group of all women in the two counties who were under supervision because of at least one felony conviction and who began probation or parole between 1997 and 2000. The subset for the present analysis included only the 41 women who had just served at least 45 days in prison, jail, or the work release center (or some combination of these), and who had regularly used drugs or had problems with alcoholism before incarceration. Many of the women had convictions for offenses that were directly related to drug use (e.g. possession of a controlled substance, manufacture or distribution of a controlled substance, or endangerment of children through exposure to illegal drugs). Others were convicted of offenses – like prostitution, forgery and assault – related to the lifestyle connected to substance use. The most commonly used drugs were methamphetamines, cocaine, crack and heroin, and many women used multiple drugs. The subgroup studied did not include women who were sanctioned to a few days or weeks in jail or work release. Also omitted were three women who moved and were reassigned to supervision in different counties. Thus, all of the women considered in the analysis had the challenges that come after a period of incarceration, including disrupted relations with children and other family members, no recent work except while incarcerated, and disrupted housing arrangements; and all were in one of the two counties during the year after release.

Data sources

Women varied in the number of data sources. For all women, there were supervising officers' detailed chronological reports for the twelve months, official records, and a survey of the supervising officer at the time of release and again twelve months later. The chronological reports were computerized entries in which the supervising officers recorded any information they received about women, such as reports from the police or drug treatment programs, and described their interactions with and responses to women. Other official computerized records were the source of information on convictions and incarcerations going back three years, crimes resulting in the incarcerations, and for the year after release, arrests and convictions, participation in treatment programs and groups, and drug test results. The surveys of supervising officers yielded information on changes in supervision status (i.e. violations of conditions, any sanctions in response to violations, and revocations leading to reincarceration), participation in various groups and programs, and the officers' actions to help and refer women for help in several different areas (e.g. substance abuse, parenting, mental health). In addition, an attempt was made to interview all women in the sample just after release and twelve months later.

Interviews/data collection

Repeated efforts were made to contact women for interviews, and if they could not be contacted for the first interview, efforts still were made to interview them later in the year. Reasons for no interview included being on the run ('absconded status'), being impossible to locate or contact (e.g. no phone, supervision complete, and no known address), and refusal. The proportion of women interviewed just after release was 70.4 per cent (19/27) in Gender Responsive County and 57.1 per cent (8/14) in Traditional County, and the corresponding proportions interviewed at year's end were 74.1 per cent (20/27) and 57.1 per cent (8/14). Contact with women for interviews depended in part on information from the supervising officer, and that information depended on the level of supervision. The proportion of women who had very limited supervision and were reincarcerated, rearrested, or absconded by the end of the year (referred to as *failures*) was much lower in Gender Responsive compared to the Traditional County (3.7 per cent, or 1 of 27 women versus 42.9 per cent, or 6 of 14). This difference explained the higher Gender Responsive County interview rate. Thus, the nature of supervision (limited or not), the year-end outcomes (failure or not), and whether interviews were accomplished were interdependent. Dropping women who were not interviewed from the analysis would remove the high proportion of *failures* in Traditional County, and would create a misleading picture. Thus, all of the women were included in the analysis, though some lacked interview material. Methods of establishing credibility were to use multiple sources of information whenever possible to support a finding and to examine and try to explain negative cases for patterns that were identified.

Like the surveys of officers, the interviews with women included questions about help and referrals provided by the officer for specific reasons (e.g. job preparation, mental health). Women described changes in themselves and their circumstances at the year-end interview in response to open-ended questions about what programs or experiences they found most helpful, and how they had been helped during the year. Some women identified supervision as most helpful. Those who identified other programs were asked whether supervision had referred them, and if not, how they had come to enter the program. Supervising officers also described referrals and changes in their chronological case notes. When interview material is being cited below, information is attributed to the woman. When the chronological case notes are being cited, the supervising officer or the case notes are the attributed source.

Supervision levels and outcomes

Women varied considerably in the level of supervision they received and in their outcomes by the end of the year. Since these variations are central to the discussion of women's experiences, they are described next. Table 8.1 summarizes the intensity of supervision and year-end outcomes by county.

Limited supervision (officially called limited or low) indicates that women mailed in monthly reports or just mailed in any required fees and

Table 8.1 Intensity of supervision and one-year post release outcomes for women in gender responsive and traditional county

Intensity of supervision	Outcome	Gender responsive	Traditional
Limited	*Failure*, no evidence of positive changes	3.7% (1)	42.9% (6)
Medium or high	*Failure*, no evidence of positive changes	18.5% (5)	7.1% (1)
Medium or high	*Failure*, some positive changes	18.5% (5)	21.4% (3)
Medium or high	*Failure*, doing better towards end of year	14.8% (4)	
Medium or high	*Making it*, but still using, some positive changes	22.2% (6)	7.1% (1)
Medium or high	No longer using (*beyond use*)	11.1% (3)	7.1% (1)
Other forces account for positive outcome	*Making it* or *beyond use*	11.1% (3)	14.3% (2)
Total		65.9% (27)	34.1% (14)

restitution. *Higher levels of supervision* (officially called medium or high) involved frequent office visits, home visits, drug tests, and monitoring through phone calls and checks with relatives, professionals and employers. Like the level of supervision, the various outcomes were determined by examining the data. Women *failed* when they had their supervision revoked and were reincarcerated, were reincarcerated for some other reason by the time of the last interview, or committed a new offense other than using drugs in the year after release. When women agreed to a 'sanction' of a short period (hours to a few weeks) in jail or work release, this was not counted as a failure. All of the women who failed continued using drugs for at least part of the year. Positive changes also were identified through repeated readings of the data, and they included not just internal changes, but also lifestyle and skill changes, such as leaving a criminal partner, finding a safe place to live, and acquiring parenting skills. Some women had positive changes, but still failed. Women who were *making it* continued using drugs but did not have the other indicators of failure, and some had positive changes. Two additional outcomes were: (1) being *beyond drug use* for the entire year, which involved no drug use and occurred with positive changes and no indicators of failure, and (2) making it or abstaining, but due to some influence other than supervision, such as assistance from a source unrelated to supervision or a last chance for child custody.

Wraparound services

One theme that reoccurred through the data was the receipt of multiple services that addressed a large variety of a woman's needs. This pattern dovetailed with what are called *wraparound services*, defined by Covington (2002: 140) as a holistic and culturally sensitive plan for each individual that draws on a coordinated continuum of services located within a community. Wraparound services respond to offenders who have multiple goals and needs that should be met in a coordinated way by one or more providers (Covington and Bloom 2003: 1; Reed and Leavitt 2000). Women who were *beyond drug use* (i.e. had desisted from using drugs since the beginning of parole) most fully epitomized recipients of wraparound services. To a lesser extent, women using drugs but otherwise *making it*, and women who seemed to do a turn around for the better during the year, also had multiple sorts of continuous intervention. Interview responses of women *beyond drug use* to questions about the 'most helpful' programs and groups suggested that they viewed assistance from multiple sources, which varied by woman, as one coordinated intervention.

Tina is an example of a woman who received wraparound services within a comprehensive program that was part of supervision, and who attributed getting useful assistance to supervision. Before the start of supervision, she had used heroin for 26 years. She was in a methadone maintenance program. Tina told the supervising officer that she had anxiety disorder and ADHD (Attention Deficit Hyperactivity Disorder), and many years ago she began taking heroin to 'solve' these problems. After supervision began, because of her ADHD, she found it very difficult to work more than part time as a waitress, and when she lost that job because the boss felt she was too nervous, she worked sporadically at jobs like selling food at a lunch cart. Previous work as a prostitute had left Tina with an STD that had gone untreated and caused her pain, and for a while this contributed to her inability to work. Tina's husband of eight years had used methamphetamines in the past, but he had stopped using drugs four years ago and was working as a counselor in a drug treatment center. He had custody of their two children, and they had an agreement that if she had used recently, she would stay elsewhere. Tina struggled with the multiple problems of addiction, illness, lack of steady full-time work, mental illness, and a learning disability. In response to questions about what had helped her the most during the year, Tina said, 'supervision, including the intensive substance abuse program and electronic surveillance'. The supervising officer had required that Tina attend the intensive substance abuse treatment program, and electronic surveillance was one part of that program. Tina described the multiple needs that were met within the intensive substance abuse treatment program, which she said helped her with her self-esteem, her children, her relationship with her husband, and her addiction.

Omara also received wraparound services. She had first been arrested for running away at age thirteen, and as a juvenile had spent time in a detention center, a group home and a foster home. Beginning in adolescence, she had used marijuana, cocaine, crack, ecstasy and alcohol. She told the supervising officer that her parents had forced her to give up a child to adoption. Convicted of a drug charge, she had just been released after spending fifteen months in prison. Upon release, she was able to live with her father, she held a very low-paying job ($150 a week), and she was involved with a boyfriend whom she described as 'psychologically abusive and controlling'. She did not use any drugs during the year.

Omara identified the Gender Responsive County self-esteem group as most helpful, and she said that the supervising officer had referred her to two psychologists, one who helped her with 'loss issues' resulting from giving up her child, and the other who helped her with prescription medication. Like Tina, Omara viewed supervision as central to connecting her to a variety of services.

Women who used drugs during the year, but who were in other ways *making it*, also had involvement with groups, programs and helping professionals. However, involvement did not seem to be as multifaceted and continuous as for women *beyond drug use*, as illustrated by Judy's situation. Her background was similar to Omera's and Tina's, and included the use of multiple drugs beginning at age ten, self-harm in what she described as a 'cry for help', and loss of two of her three children. For three weeks shortly after release, Judy was on a waiting list for the type of substance abuse treatment program recommended by the substance abuse evaluator. The officer wrote: 'will be on the [urinalysis for drugs] calendar and in groups until she can enter treatment'. After Judy completed the program she faced homelessness. The supervising officer noted efforts to locate housing, and serendipitously the treatment program just then opened transitional housing available for a year. When there were gaps in services, the Gender Responsive County supervising officers typically filled in to monitor and provide controls, a support group, and concrete assistance, and thereby ensured continuity in services and involvement for the women.

Supervising officers' actions could directly precipitate women's connecting to programs, groups and services. Although she had used drugs like powder cocaine and heroin beginning around the age of eighteen, Fran had been arrested and convicted for the first time at age 30, after she forged and cashed checks that her abusive intimate partner had stolen. At the very beginning of the year, the supervising officer noted telling Fran that substance abuse treatment was a priority, so she might have to change jobs because the work schedule interfered with her attending two required weekly outpatient sessions. After Fran had a positive drug test, she spent a brief period in jail and was released to take part in residential treatment. She finished the program, attended required AA and NA meetings, and attended the program's aftercare groups. Persistent monitoring and the emphasis on substance abuse treatment resulted in a common outcome: women's continued substance use was quickly detected, and abstinence and participation in more intense treatment and then aftercare services were required to avoid revocation.

Katie is another example of a Gender Responsive County woman who had a new arrest, and whose supervising officer coordinated multiple resources specifically tailored to her circumstances. Katie had a long history of addiction and prostitution. Early in the year, she was arrested for assault during a fight over drugs. The police report indicated she was very 'high' at the time. The supervising officer involved her in the self-esteem group and a special program that provided multiple services for women in the sex trades. After Katie spent a brief period in jail waiting for a residential treatment opening that never materialized, the supervising officer patched together a place in a transitional housing program for women offenders and intensive outpatient treatment. Katie also took part in grief counseling because of the loss of a child. For the last nine months of the year, she did not use drugs, and there were several positive changes in her life, including getting away from an abusive pimp.

Women's interview responses reflected that they saw individualized wraparound services as very helpful to them, particularly when compared to past supervision. Making such a comparison, Sandy said that supervision was 'more personalized' and 'they are interested in my individual progress'. Julie said that compared to previous supervision, the current experience was better because 'it is more flexible and personal'. Katie said that being on parole had helped her the most because the supervising officer 'knows my needs'. Women who experienced some level of success during the year expressed appreciation of an individually tailored, needs-focused approach that linked them to specific, multiple services.

Avoiding failure: elements of helpful interventions

Responding to a series of open-ended questions about the nature and effects of the programs that had been most helpful during the year, women identified the common elements: monitoring and controls, opportunities to share and deal with feelings, specific skills gained, group support, and improved self-perceptions. The sources of helpful elements varied considerably between women, and they included interactions with the supervising officer, participation in groups and programs required by the officer, and participation in groups and programs unrelated to supervision.

Monitoring and controls

Women who viewed monitoring and controls as helpful were concentrated in Gender Responsive County in three subgroups: (1) women *beyond drug use*, (2) those who seemed to be *making it* despite drug use, and (3) those with a new arrest but then seemed to be *making it* for the months before the year ended. Much of the monitoring they described was accomplished by frequent drug tests and home visits, checking with relatives and professionals for 'relapse behavior', frequent required office visits, and participation in intensive programs, including those that were residential. As an example, Jo described the intensive substance abuse treatment program as imposing controls when she explained how 'harsh' it was compared to other programs: 'I had to clean up my act. Otherwise, I would have ended up locked up again.' In another example, Jen described the controls in a substance abuse treatment program: 'They don't mess around. If you break the rules you're out of there.' Controls were manifested when supervising officers met continued drug use with not only increased monitoring and treatment, but also increasingly harsh sanctions, starting with community service work hours or participation in a weekend work crew, and progressing to days in work release or jail. Monitoring and controls were delivered by supervising officers, the programs and groups they required women to attend, or both.

Sometimes monitoring and controls extended to place of residence, use of money, and job search efforts. The range of targets is evident from

Sandy's experiences. Her supervising officer informed her that the trailer where she was living was not adequate housing and she should find a studio apartment; she could not accept a loan of money from a convicted felon; she should stop spending time repairing a car for another person in lieu of finding a job. The officer also reviewed Sandi's budget on a regular basis, and determined that she needed to include phone costs and not let her boyfriend pay for the phone after he was required by his supervising officer to live apart from her. At one point in the year, the officer told Sandy to call daily with an update on her job search efforts. Later, the officer denied her request to move to the state where her children lived, and told the child and family services worker that she did not recommend that the children be allowed to visit. Sandy was not the only woman who was directed and scrutinized by an officer who tried to change her decisions and lifestyle in areas beyond stopping drug use, desisting from crime, and meeting formal requirements of supervision (like holding a job or paying court fees).

At least some heavily supervised women felt the oversight helped them. Julie explained how drug testing helped. She never knew when she had to come in, so she had to be ready every day. This got her into the 'good habit' of routinely calling in and being prepared. She explained, 'supervision gave me boundaries for not crossing that line and getting in trouble again'. Although the supervising officer watched her closely and denied many of her requests, Sandy was generally positive about the experience. She told the interviewer that the alcohol and drug treatment group she attended as 'part of supervision' had been most helpful to her. Other women expressed similar sentiments, for instance reporting that residential treatment was most helpful because it was 'strict enough to work' (Fran) or that frequent drug testing 'helped me keep clean' (Jo). For the women who at the end of the year seemed to be doing fairly well, the intrusiveness of supervision did not preclude its helpfulness. Research on correctional programs in other settings, for men as well as women (Andrews and Kiessling 1980; Paparozzi and Gendreau 2005), has shown that carefully orchestrated and consistently applied monitoring and graduated sanctions, combined with needs assessment and a large array of treatment interventions, are most effective in preventing recidivism. The women in the present study seemed to confirm this, since they did find controls helpful, but found that other resources and support, which are described next, were also essential in the change process.

Dealing with feelings

A second commonly identified helpful element was programming that helped women deal with their feelings constructively without using drugs or alcohol. This was the case for three Gender Responsive County women *beyond drug use,* and two who did use drugs during the year, but still had positive changes and were *making it*. Women explained the several ways they benefited from understanding, expressing and coping with their feelings. Tina, as described above, struggled with the multiple problems of addiction, physical illness, difficulties working, and a learning disability and anxiety disorder that left her nervous and unable to concentrate. She said that in the intensive substance abuse treatment program she 'could express myself freely and get any input I needed. I learned about my emotions, how to understand my emotions.' Susan had been living with a psychologically abusive and controlling boyfriend, and she was dependent on boyfriends or her father for a place to live. She said about the self-esteem group: 'I liked best being able to loosen up and talk about my feelings. Especially after leaving prison . . . I was there 16 months . . . I was very angry at the system. It was very helpful to relax and think about things.' Dana had lost two of her children aged two and four to foster care, and her six-year-old child was in a treatment program. She had been charged with burning him, but told the supervising officer that he was burned because he set fires. She said that she had quit drugs on her own, and then drank alcohol heavily. She told the interviewer that a court-ordered drug and alcohol group helped her 'talk about things more openly and not having to rely on people to get my own feelings out'. It gave her skills in coping with her feelings, including anger. Given the abuse in the backgrounds of women who used drugs, the way they lived and the places they lived when actively using, incarcerations, mental and physical health problems, dispersed children, past and ongoing abuse, and limited means of self-support, they would be expected to have powerful and complex negative feelings. Their comments suggest that an increase in women's capacity for dealing with such feelings enabled them to move further from substance use and crime. The groups and counseling sessions that they found helpful made it possible for them to identify and express their feelings in a setting that they perceived as accepting and safe. The women linked their increased capacity to understand their own feelings with being able to control them.

Other specific gains and skills

Some women who were *making it* by the end of the year mentioned each of the following areas of change as elements of helpful interventions: knowledge about substance abuse, problem-solving and coping skills, and concrete employment-related skills. About knowledge gained, Joan said that in NA, she learned to 'actively tell myself that alcohol is a drug and is part of my family history'. Problem-solving and coping skills included learning to 'break down problems into rational steps' (Jen), 'completing what I start, setting and reaching goals' (Fran), recognition of 'stress points and how to cope with problems that made you do wrong before' (Dana), and developing 'new avenues of thought and actions to deal with my problems . . . break the cycle of "I do this because I have always done it"' (Sandy). Employment-related gains included computer skills learned in a federally supported training program (Julie) and learning 'how to retain a job' (Kristin). Although women had agency to make changes in themselves, it seemed that wraparound services, including easy access to state employment services, and the program and relationship elements of monitoring, controls and addressing powerful negative feelings enhanced women's opportunity to avoid drugs and alcohol. These findings about supports for specific gains held for women *beyond drug use*, and those who still used for at least a part of the year, but were otherwise *making it*.

Group support

Group support from other women who were offenders and drug users, or who had other shared troubles, was linked to abstinence from drugs. Joan told the interviewer that NA had been especially helpful to her because: 'This is an actual house whose sole purpose is for NA activities, support, and socializing. There were social activities. Good friendships are created there. It helps me stay clean and sober through networks of support.' Florence described the support she received from the 'adults molested as children' group, and she compared it to the less helpful group she had attended in prison: 'What makes it a good group is being believed and encouraged but not forced to talk about your feelings.' She described the counselor as 'very understanding and loving'. Other women who commented on helpful group support talked about group leaders who they could relate to and who were accepting, about friendship and unity and trust in the group, which was sometimes due to exclusively women participants, and easy access to group members for help. Many of the groups where women found helpful support met frequently and over a long period.

Improved self-perceptions

Women *beyond drug use* connected their experiences in groups to improved self-perceptions. A sense of being 'normal' that resulted from interaction with women with similar experiences was one reason for the connection. Talking about the group for adults molested as children, Florence said that while listening to others, she realized she was not 'the only person who had done something wrong'. She went on to say, 'I get embarrassed when I do things wrong', and that she had learned to accept herself and that she did not have to impress other people. Susan described how the self-esteem group helped her: 'I've never experienced anything like that since I was always in and around negative people and situations, and was always putting myself down.' Three other women (Fran, Dana, Kristen) who made it through the year even though at some point they used drugs talked about how supervision itself and/or programs connected to it improved their self-esteem, and made them feel they did not have to depend on others for happiness.

Women who failed

Of the 27 Gender Responsive County women, eleven (40.7 per cent) ended the year absconded or were reincarcerated by the end of the year, and did not have a period of desistance and positive changes before the year's end. This proportion was even higher in Traditional County, where ten out of fourteen women (71.4 per cent) had a negative outcome. Analysis of the data on women who failed provided additional insight into the process of positive change by revealing why it sometimes did not occur.

Consistent with common practice in Gender Responsive County, several women who failed were monitored closely and referred to multiple services, but the year still ended badly for them. Margaret was most recently arrested for starting a car with pliers and stealing it, and she told the interviewer that during the year she also carried out burglary, forgery, and delivery and possession of drugs. The supervising officer noted that Margaret seemed proud of her record, which included convictions for stalking a police officer and self-admissions of repeatedly manufacturing and dealing methamphetamines. Margaret told the interviewer that the workshop offered by state employment services was 'boring', and although she told the officer she was 'emotionally messed up', she did not follow up on a referral for mental health help.

An exception in Traditional County, Barrie was supervised at a high level. She had fifteen prior arrests for offenses that included contempt of court, failure to appear, forgery, possession of a controlled substance (methamphetamines), and possession of a forgery instrument. The supervising officer wrote that when confronted with a positive test for methamphetamines, Barrie said the officer must be lying, because she did not use drugs. Barrie told the interviewer how she resisted interventions, saying she had not wanted a job or a home since being on supervision and had done the 'exact opposite of what they ask me to do'. She said, 'I have a problem with people telling me what to do. I like the fact that I can finish my jail time and be done with my supervision, and I don't have to report after I'm released from jail.' Both Margaret and Barrie exercised their agency to counteract and reject interventions that others found to be most helpful. They actively resisted change, and they valued identities that included defiance and lawbreaking. Others did not seem to cling to identities that reflected valuation of a lawbreaking lifestyle, but they became reinvolved with drugs or with people who supported illegal activity, and drifted back into illegal behavior.

Besides women's rejection of interventions or drift away from them, inadequacies in interventions could explain continued substance use and criminality. Leslie had a drug use history that started at age ten, and she had used numerous different drugs, most recently cocaine and heroin. She had been with the same man for most of that time, and they were arrested together several times. Jail staff referred Leslie to substance abuse treatment, but at the end of the year she told the interviewer she had been supporting herself through dealing drugs and prostitution. Although she saw benefits to treatment ('it was confidential, and the people are warm and sincere'), she pointed to these deficits:

> There is a time limit to how long you can be in the program – people are graduating that don't seem ready – and the support is completely over once you leave. They [staff] say that certain things will be worked on but the staff don't follow through. [The program needed] more structure, no tolerance for being late, [and there were problems with] cross talk and people showing up late and nobody seems to care.

The positive aspects of the program may have been counteracted by the lack of structure and controls. Leslie's brief involvement with a program was very different from the long-lasting support groups described by women who did better during the year.

Other women who failed also described programs that seemed like weak interventions. Marilyn had been expelled from school because of drug use, and had been using marijuana and methamphetamines daily for fifteen years. She was convicted most recently after she and her boyfriend, both high on methamphetamines, drove a stolen car in an attempt to escape from a pursuing police officer. At the end of the year, she had absconded. During the year, she resisted the supervising officer's efforts to counsel and refer her, and told the interviewer that NA was most helpful to her, because it was 'non-committal' and there was 'nothing mandatory about it'. Similarly, Ellen, a long-time drug user, described a low intensity substance abuse treatment program she located through an advertisement: 'It kept me clean for a little while and was a place to detox.' Different from other programs, it did not pressure her to 'tell them my business'. Meg, who had a very long history of using multiple drugs and who remained involved with her intimate partner, who dealt drugs, also chose to participate in a program because it would not push too hard to address what the supervising officer described as 'anger and childhood issues'. Before the year ended, Meg left the program and was arrested for possession of a controlled substance. Women who failed avoided programs and interactions that promoted their talking about their feelings, and if they took part in any programs, they opted into those that left them relatively unaffected and untouched by other people. This result was in part a choice of the women, and in part a result of a supervision style that did not require women to attend high intensity programs and the nature of some programs.

Conclusion

Consideration and comparison of the data on women who made it through the year and those who did not suggested a sequence of events that led to women's positive changes, and it also showed how supervision and program and group experiences shaped change. For many women, supervision, sometimes reinforced by substance abuse treatment programs, was crucial in setting limits on drug use and making it unpleasant or difficult for women to continue using drugs. Just as important, supervision used requirements and referrals to put women in touch with safe environments where they could express and learn to handle strong negative feelings, places where they could learn about addiction and basic life skills, and group support that made them feel accepted and that provided the opportunity for friendship. Both supervising officers and programs could provide women with access to multiple places to learn skills and obtain social support. An essential ingredient in making the progression from abstinence to positive changes in networks and self, however, was women's willingness to reveal their feelings, shift away from partners who continued to break the law, and alter self-perceptions that included lawbreaking and non-conformity as positive. In the absence of some self and lifestyle changes, women could avoid monitoring and controls and stay out of groups and programs that gave them opportunities and knowledge to change.

Published research on recovery from drug and alcohol addictions is helpful in determining the consistency of the present research findings with the results of other studies of women's recovery from addictions. Kearney (1998) identified parts of the recovery process: awareness that alcohol and drugs were causing more stress than they were relieving, abstinence, dealing with negative emotions leading to substance use, recognizing and avoiding self-deceptive thinking patterns, accessing support sources, and developing the self. In the present study, the women's statements supported Kearney's conclusion about the importance of abstinence, dealing with negative emotions, changes in self-perception (developing the self), and reliance on support sources.

Prior research on women who use drugs and/or break the law has confirmed the helpfulness of specific program elements identified through the present study. The relevance of changed self-perceptions to women's addiction recovery has been shown in research (Cocozza *et al.* 2005; Giordano *et al.* 2002). Additionally, Covington (1994) found in research on women in twelve-step programs that the first step in recovery was expansion and growth of the self, and research by Veysey *et al.* (2007) showed how identity transformation, or what Maruna (2001) described as relinquishing an old self, promoted movement away from crime and drug use. Relevant to social support, Covington (1998: 148) drew on theory of women's development to reach the conclusion:

If we are trying to create treatment for women to help them to change, grow and heal from addictions, it is critical that we place them in programs and environments where relationship and mutuality are core elements. The system needs to provide a setting where women can experience healthy relationships with their counselors and each other.

The conclusion is based in theory that has emphasized that women's identities and actions are heavily influenced by their relationships with other people (Covington and Surrey 1997). The women in the present research described helpful relationships with other program participants and with program staff as accepting, warm and healthy. Collectively, the present and other studies show that changed self-perception and new social support are part of the process through which women give up drug-oriented lifestyles and drug-use supporting identities.

Kearney's (1998) analysis of multiple studies also showed that the match of helping resources with women's needs – which is the essence of wraparound services – was an influence on how smoothly and successfully women accomplished recovery work. Other studies have shown that case management approaches that match women's needs to multiple services are effective with women offenders who use drugs (Martin and Inciardi 1993; Rhodes and Gross 1997). Also consistent, Bloom *et al.* (2003) drew on multiple theoretical frameworks and related research and concluded that women offenders needed programming to address gender-related problems like prior trauma and grief, employment-related services to improve financial standing, and a style of community supervision that resulted in comprehensive and collaborative services. In other studies, O'Brien (2002) described helpful programming for women coming out of prison that provided 'longer than average' stays and at exit had employment, housing and mentoring; and Johnson (2003) wrote about how the same halfway house that O'Brien studied addressed multiple areas of need, including employment skills, understanding and coping with past histories of physical or sexual abuse, and substance abuse. The present research and other studies consistently show the effectiveness of long-lasting, multifaceted, and intensive programming to address women's multiple needs as they become salient over time.

Especially in Gender Responsive County, where there was the clearest connection between supervision and positive changes, and where higher proportions of women described being supported in various stages of abandoning drug use, supervising officers were very directive, exerted controls through sanctions that included brief jail stays and lengthy residential substance abuse treatment, and monitored many aspects of women's day-to-day lives. Several women found heavy monitoring helpful, though some disliked or resisted it or were ambivalent. It may be that such monitoring and response moves some women to feel that drugs

139

create more stress than they relieve, creates periods of forced abstinence, or creates reasons not to use drugs, and thereby promotes abstinence.

What is striking about how women experienced interventions as helpful is the complexity and the individualized nature of the supervising officers' controls, referrals, and requirements for women to participate in different interventions. Women who put drug use behind them or had other positive changes during the year were more often in groups and programs where they felt their self-perceptions improved, they gained concrete life or job skills, they had positive support, and they were treated as 'individuals' and their particular needs were addressed. For some women, these positive benefits occurred unrelated to supervision, but for most supervising officers matched women to tailored interventions, and sometimes the officers were the glue and the force that held multiple or sporadically available interventions together.

Note

1 To protect confidentiality pseudonyms are used for counties and women.

References

Andrews, D. A. and Kiessling, J. J. (1980). 'Program structure and effective correctional practice: A summary of CaVic research', in R. Ross and P. Gendreau (eds) *Effective Correctional Treatment*. Toronto: Butterworths.

Belknap, J. (1996) 'Access to programs and health care for incarcerated women', *Federal Probation*, 60: 34–9.

Bloom, B., Owen, B. and Covington, S. (2003) *Gender-responsive Strategies: Research, Practice, and Guiding Principles for Women Offenders*. Washington, DC: US Department of Justice, National Institute of Corrections.

Bureau of Justice Statistics (1991) *Women in Prison*. Washington, DC: Government Printing Office.

Bush-Baskette, S. (2000) 'The war on drugs and the incarceration of mothers', *Journal of Drug Issues*, 30: 919–28.

Cocozza, J., Jackson, E., Hennigan, K., Morrissey, J., Reed, B., Fallot, R. and Banks, S. (2005) 'Outcomes for women with co-occurring disorders and trauma: Program-level effects', *Journal of Substance Abuse Treatment*, 28: 109–19.

Covington, S. (1994) *A Woman's Way Through the Twelve Steps*. Center City, MN: Hazelden Educational Materials.

Covington, S. (2002) 'A woman's journey home: Challenges for female offenders and their children', a paper produced for a conference funded by the US Department of Health and Human Services, 30–31 January 2002. Available online at: *www.urban.org/UploadedPDF/410630_FemaleOffenders.pdf* [accessed 21 March 2008].

Covington, S. (1998) 'Women in prison: Approaches in the treatment of our most invisible population', *Women and Therapy Journal*, 21: 141–55.

Covington, S. and Bloom, B. (2003) 'Gendered justice: Addressing female offenders', in B. E. Bloom (ed.) *Gendered Justice: Women in the Criminal Justice System*. Durham, NC: Center for Gender and Justice. Available online at: *www.centerforgenderandjustice.org/pdf/4.pdf* [accessed 21 March 2008].

Covington, S. and Surrey, J. (1997) 'The relational model of women's psychological development: Implications for substance abuse', in S. Wilsnak and R. Wilsnak (eds) *Gender and Alcohol: Individual and Social Perspectives*. Piscataway, NJ: Rutgers University.

Giordano, P. C., Cernkovich, S. A. and Rudolph, J. L. (2002) 'Gender, crime, and desistance: Toward a theory of cognitive transformation', *American Journal of Sociology*, 107: 990–1064.

Greenfeld, L. A. and Snell, T. L. (1999) *Women Offenders. Bureau of Justice Statistics Special Report, December*. Washington, DC: US Department of Justice.

Hartley and Marks Publishers Inc. (2002) *Trends in Substance Abuse and Treatment Needs Among Inmates, Final Reports*. New York: The National Center on Addiction and Substance Abuse at Columbia University (CASA). Available online at: *www.ncjrs.gov/pdffiles1/nij/grants/197073.pdf* [accessed 21 March 2008].

Johnson, H. (2004) *Drugs and Crime: A Study of Incarcerated Female Offenders*, Research and Policy Series No. 63. Canberra: Australian Institute of Criminology. Available online at: *www.aic.gov.au/publications/rpp/63/RPP63.pdf* [accessed 21 March 2008].

Johnson, P. C. (2003) *Inner Lives: Voices of African American Women in Prison*. New York: New York University Press.

Kearney, M. H. (1998) 'Truthful self-nurturing: A grounded formal theory of women's addiction recovery', *Qualitative Health Research*, 8: 495–512.

Leshner, A. I. (1997) 'Addiction is a brain disease, and it matters', *Science*, 278: 45–7.

Lo, C. C. (2004) 'Sociodemographic factors, drug abuse, and other crimes: How they vary among male and female arrestees', *Journal of Criminal Justice*, 32: 399–409.

Martin, S. S. and Inciardi, J. A. (1993) 'Case management approaches for criminal justice clients', in J. A. Inciardi (ed.) *Drug Treatment and Criminal Justice*. Thousand Oaks, CA: Sage.

Maruna, S. (2001) 'Making good: How ex-convicts reform and rebuild their lives', Washington, DC: American Psychological Association.

Mauer, M. and Chesney-Lind, M. (2003) *Invisible Punishment: The Collateral Consequences of Mass Incarceration*. New York: Free Press.

Morash, M. (2007) 'Probation/parole tactics and outcomes for women in Gender Responsive and Traditional County', a paper presented at the annual meeting of the American Society of Criminology, November, Atlanta, Georgia.

O'Brien, P. (2002) *Evaluation of Grace House: Using Past Experience to Inform Future Results*. Chicago: Jane Addams College of Social Work.

O'Brien, P. (2006) 'Maximizing success for drug-affected women after release from prison: Examining access to and use of social services during reentry', *Women and Criminal Justice*, 17: 95–113.

Owen, B. and Bloom, B. (1995) 'Profiling women prisoners: Findings from national surveys and a California sample', *Prison Journal*, 75(2): 165–85.

Paparozzi, M. A. and Gendreau, P. (2005) 'An intensive supervision program that worked: Service delivery, professional orientation, and organizational supportiveness', *The Prison Journal*, 85: 445–66.

Reed, B. G. and Leavitt, M. (2000) 'Modified wraparound and women offenders in community corrections: Strategies, opportunities and tensions', in M. McMahon (ed.), *Assessment to Assistance: Programs for Women in Community Corrections*. Lanham, MD: American Correctional Association.

Rhodes, W. and Gross, M. (1997) *Case Management Reduces Drug Use and Criminality Among Drug-involved Arrestees: An Experimental Study of HIV Prevention Intervention*. Washington, DC: National Institute of Justice and National Institute of Drug Abuse.

Richie, B. E. (1996) *Compelled to Crime: The Gender Entrapment of Battered Black Women*. New York: Routledge.

Richie, B. E. (2001) 'Challenges incarcerated women face as they return to their communities: Findings from life history interviews', *Crime and Delinquency*, 47(3): 368–89.

Sabol, W. J., Couture, H. and Harrison, P. M. (2007a) *Prisoners in 2006*. Washington, DC: US Department of Justice.

Sabol, W. J., Minton, T. D. and Harrison, P. M. (2007b) *Prison and Jail Inmates at Midyear 2006*. Bureau of Justice Statistics Special Report No. NCJ 217675. Washington, DC: US Department of Justice.

Sourcebook of Criminal Justice Statistics (2006) Available online at: *www.albany.edu/sourcebook/pdf/t6142006.pdf* [accessed 21 March 2008].

Veysey, B. M., Heckman, J., Mazelis, R., Markoff, L. and Russell, L. (2007) *It's My Time to Live: Journeys to Healing and Recovery*. Washington, DC: Substance Abuse and Mental Health Services Administration, US Department of Health and Human Services.

Wellisch, J., Prendergast, M. L. and Anglin, M. D. (1994) *Drug-Abusing Women Offenders: Results of a National Survey*, Research in Brief, October. Washington, DC: National Institute of Justice.

Yahne C. E., Miller, W. R., Irvin-Vitela, L. and Tonigan, J. S. (2002) 'Magdalena Pilot Project: Motivational outreach to substance abusing women street sex workers', *Journal of Substance Abuse Treatment*, 23: 49–53.

Young, A. M., Boyd, C. and Hubbell, H. (2000) 'Prostitution, drug use, and coping with psychological distress', *Journal of Drug Issues*, 30: 789–800.

Chapter 9

Identity change through the transformation model of the public safety initiative of LIFERS, Inc.

M. Kay Harris

At a maximum-security state prison in Graterford, Pennsylvania, a group of long-term prisoners initiated a movement to end the culture of crime and violence that they viewed as wreaking havoc on urban communities. Acting out of belief that they had been instrumental in creating and sustaining the same types of public safety problems they saw their loved ones, neighbors, and an endless stream of youth being subjected to, members of the Public Safety Initiative (PSI) of LIFERS, Inc. concluded that they needed to become a meaningful part of the solution. They crafted a model for achieving that goal by working for transformation at the individual, institutional and community levels.

The PSI model relies heavily on positive peer intervention to spur changes in thinking and behavior. PSI members challenge one another 'to reflect on past behavior, the cost and effect on our families, our communities, and ourselves, in an effort to cause a cognitive transformation – thinking in a new way through self-discovery – that becomes self generating' (Lifers Public Safety Initiative, n.d.). The process begins with individual soul-searching, facilitated by peers who have already turned away from crime and deviance, in order to confront ways in which the beliefs, values, and mores of street-crime culture interfere with leading a productive, honorable life. The quest then turns to the exploration of new ways of thinking that accept responsibility for the well-being of self and others. The expectation is that people who come around to this new way of thinking not only will live as upstanding citizens, but also will work tirelessly to help pull others out of the street-crime culture and to eliminate the culture itself.

With roots in a number of earlier projects, including an anti-crime summit the group led in the prison in April of 2003, the Public Safety Initiative was launched formally in 2004. A series of intensive discussions within the lifers' organization on the causes of crime and violence in urban communities led to the conceptualization of a culture of street crime theory. That work was reflected in an article written by members of the steering committee that appeared in the December 2004 issue of *The Prison Journal* (Lifers Public Safety Steering Committee 2004). In August 2005, a day-long conference was held at the prison in connection with the World Congress of Criminology that focused the attention of more than 100 criminologists from around the world on those ideas. More recently the group's attention has been focused heavily on advancing their comprehensive strategy for ending the street-crime culture. Toward that end, PSI has developed proposals, organized task groups and an external advisory board, and carried out a series of projects to build community partnerships and enhance the quality of community life.

Sterling, a PSI leader, summarizes the group's overall, multiple-level vision of transformation in the following way:

> Transformation is coming from one state of existence that's unfavorable to another level of existence that's favorable for life and for people. More specifically, it means what we have done here. We have, under these difficult circumstances, made a decision to transform ourselves, our thinking, inside this environment and thus transform our environment. So to me, the transformative movement means moving from individuals to populations inside the prison to the external community, specifically to transform neighborhoods that are crime-ridden, without safety and without economic opportunities. And as people who have violated those norms before, this transformation, having gone through it ourselves here collectively, we would now say, 'Let's unify.' Now that we've seen our mistakes, we made a decision to build where we once tore down, to become protectors of the community instead of those who harmed it.

Approach, scope and purposes of this chapter

This chapter focuses on selected aspects of the work of the Public Safety Initiative directed at change on the individual level among incarcerated men who formerly were involved in street crime. It centers on accounts of personal transformation and the approach used to achieve it that were derived from interviews of 29 PSI participants completed in the spring and summer of 2007 at Graterford prison.[1] The discussion also draws on my more general knowledge of PSI obtained through serving as an active volunteer and external member of the organization's steering committee for the last several years. Far from being a disinterested observer, I readily acknowledge that I undertook the work of helping to document and report on PSI's efforts to promote cognitive transformation and to reduce crime and violence because of my enthusiasm about the group's mission and activities.

The interviews of PSI members were conducted with a structured, open-ended interview guide that had two main parts. One section focused on the nature of the PSI transformation model and the other addressed the meaning of transformation in the lives of individual participants. Lasting from one to six hours – typically around two – the one-on-one sessions were held in a private office in one of the treatment areas in the prison. I was allowed to take notes by hand, but not to tape record the interviews. All of the names used are pseudonyms and all respondents were advised of their rights as human subjects.

Because I was investigating the PSI model, I sought a targeted rather than a random sample of members to interview, drawing heavily on steering committee members and others who helped lead and shape the overall initiative or specific projects. Those interviewed volunteered to participate after being provided with a description of the purpose and nature of the planned sessions and assurances of the confidentiality of their responses.[2] Most of the men have been incarcerated for much of their adult lives, including some for more than 30 years. By far the most common sentence being served by those I interviewed was life without the possibility of parole.[3] These facts reflect the seriousness of the conviction offenses and criminal records of the research participants. All but two of the people interviewed were people of color, primarily African American.

The men I interviewed represent an important and understudied population. As Presser (2008: 7) has noted, little qualitative research has focused on violent offenders and most of the work that has been done on this population has been for the purposes of understanding causes of their involvement in crime rather than their experiences in turning away from it. Giordano et al. (2002: 1052, 1054) also have noted the importance of including as research subjects long-term offenders convicted of more serious crimes, especially males and people of color. Yet more than a few people have questioned me about the value of focusing on transformation among long-term prisoners who may never get out of prison, asking how we can know whether the changes reported are real and will prove to be enduring.

The problem of gauging whether avowed personal transformations of any sort are genuine and will prove to be lasting is, of course, a universal one. It simply is not possible to know with certainty what goes on in people's hearts and minds or how people will behave in the future, either in prison or if at liberty in the community. We can track people over time, but affirming the value of long-term follow-up studies should not detract from recognition that we can learn things from the way in which people describe and make sense of their own paths that is not accessible through any other means. As Maruna (2001) argues, a phenomenological approach to criminology provides a valuable supplement to positivist methods, allowing us to explore 'criminal decision making through an examination of the offender's self-project – the self-image they are hoping to uphold, the ends they aim to achieve, and their strategies for creating meaning in their lives' (Maruna 2001: 33, citations omitted).

At the time I conducted the interviews, my primary purpose was to develop a better understanding of PSI's transformation model. My focus on the model meant that the matter of the identities of the individuals I was interviewing was not in the forefront of my thinking. Yet in seeking to obtain a better understanding of the central concept of transformation, I asked those I interviewed whether or not they considered themselves transformed and what transformation has meant in their own lives. Only later did I come to appreciate how much my inquiries had probed into the identities of the men.

Within criminology, particular attention has been devoted of late to trying to better understand the process by which once active offenders desist from crime (for example Presser 2008; Farrall and Calverley 2006; Laub and Sampson 2003; Terry 2003; Maruna 2001; Shover 1996). Although there is not universal agreement that identity change is a necessary element of successful desistance from crime, Maruna (2001) is among the respected scholars who make the case that a marked change in the propensity or inclination toward criminal activities tends to go hand in hand with a new way of looking at the world or constructing reality. Listening to the accounts of people like the PSI members interviewed for this study can help shed more light on the self-definitions and world-views of people who report that they were once actively involved in criminal activity but no longer are. In particular, this type of information can help illuminate the perceived role of agency and cognitive shifts toward desistance, two factors whose contributions may have been underestimated using other methods (see Giordano *et al.* 2002). In addition, a focus on PSI as an organizational resource in facilitating the desistance of other incarcerated offenders and in promoting alternative values to those reflected in traditional prisoner cultures and codes brings a dimension to research on identity change among offenders that has been largely neglected.

The subsequent sections of this chapter address two main themes. The next major section is devoted to fleshing out the meaning of transformation and identity change for PSI members, investigating both how these terms are conceptualized and what they have meant in the lives of those interviewed. The subsequent major section explores the role of PSI in inspiring, facilitating and sustaining transformation, elaborating on ways in which PSI functions as a self-help or mutual aid organization and how the very existence of PSI may contribute to desistance from crime and other pro-social ends.

The meaning of transformation and identity change

Members of the Public Safety Initiative describe their individual-level model of change as one involving cognitive transformation. Cognitive theory holds that thinking determines feelings and behavior and that by changing a person's interpretations and understanding, new responses can emerge (Kurtz 1997: 15). Frequently using the shorthand expression 'thinking in a new way' to describe the intended outcome of their positive peer intervention efforts, PSI members are of the view that as former participants in the culture of street crime they are uniquely qualified to penetrate, confront and help alter the perceptual reality of other incarcerated men who still are enmeshed in that culture. Using a perspective similar to the position that 'almost all deviants share an "antisocial logic" or a "small set of cognitive habits that define their orientation toward life"' (Bush, cited in Maruna 2001: 74), participants in PSI seek to challenge the ways of thinking that their criminal peers use to rationalize and justify criminal activity and to support and assist them in finding more pro-social ways of thinking. The result sought is a shift in identity from active member of the street-crime culture to transformed, former offender serving as a crime prevention activist.

McAdams reports that 'psychologists have found it difficult to state exactly what identity is and, perhaps more importantly, what it is not' (1985: 17). Noting that the concept cannot be measured in any precise way because it cannot be delimited (1985: 17), he has developed an understanding of identity as a life story. It is 'an individual's story which has the power to tie together past, present, and future in his or her life. It is a story which is able to provide unity and purpose' (1985: 17–18; see also McAdams 2006: 280–92). Of course, the individual's story develops within a larger socio-historical context, which colors, shapes and constrains it in important ways (McAdams 1985).

Transformation denotes changes that are marked, far-reaching and multifaceted. Yet that is hardly a clear-cut definition. Similar to the issues frequently raised around how to operationalize 'desistance' (see for example Maruna 2001: 45–8; Farrall and Calverly 2006: 17–18), that general description leaves unresolved how sweeping or enduring change has to be in order to qualify as transformation. What is clear is that the very notion of identity transformation represents shifts that are so broad and deep they can be thought of as a kind of conversion (Terry 2003: 96), though not necessarily a religious or spiritual one. In the context of people who are turning away from criminal behavior, Toch has argued that '[t]he individual is only truly reformed when he or she has acquired new purposes, a fresh set of meanings, and a satisfying new role' (in Maruna 2001: xvi). In saying this, he underscored Maruna's point that 'those who are reformed have had to relinquish an old self and invent a new one' (2001: xvi). PSI members would say that such individuals have been transformed, rather than reformed. Identity transformation thus involves a process of biographical reconstruction or mentally rewriting the script of one's life story, for which the individual draws on available subcultural and societal concepts, ideologies and other resources.

How PSI members describe identity transformation

In responding to open-ended questions about the meaning of transformation, Cleveland starts by mentioning the importance of a phenomenon featured in the literature on change – readiness or openness to change (see for example Proschaska *et al.* 1992; Giordano *et al.* 2002: 1000–3). Yet as Terry's (2003) research on men succeeding in overcoming the effects of criminal convictions and addiction reminds us, motivation to change is not enough. His research subjects first 'had to know that living differently was possible' (2003: 97). This is one way in which the existence of PSI has proved useful in facilitating the change process among participants; PSI members attest to and model the possibility of thinking and acting in new ways.

Once Cleveland began to contemplate the possibility of change and consider the types of adjustments he could make, he credits his involvement with PSI as helping him undertake the process of altering his thought patterns and choices, and then his behavior. At the same time, Cleveland's narrative also gives credit to his own agency and achievement; first, in investigating the meaning and utility of cognitive transformation, and second, in learning how to keep old response patterns in check. PSI opened up his awareness of the possibilities for change, but he had to work hard to accomplish the transformation.

Upon entering this institution, I didn't really believe I could be totally transformed. In fact, I didn't have the desire to be transformed. PSI has afforded me an opportunity to dig deep inside and challenge myself: 'What can I do differently?' And I believe that's what I'm doing. Do I still have the old behaviors inside? I believe I do. Do I exhibit those behaviors by acting them out? I believe I've arrested that through this transformational process. The single most important key to transformation is thinking in a new way. I'm sold on that. Cognitive change. I looked it up, dissected it. If a person thinks differently, I think you act differently.

Bishop's discussion of the meaning of transformation presents a similar fundamental contrast between previously held and current world-views. His comments also reflect his understanding of transformation as requiring complete consistency between the values espoused and the behaviors practiced.

It's basically your approach on life, so you're constantly confronted with how you've been seeing things, and now taking on these values and beliefs of transformation, how you see things now. For instance, if you come out of a criminal background, you want to get out of jail. Your first instinct on how to get money to get out of jail would be some criminal activity to raise the money. Now, for me, the test of was I really into transformation was not just not being willing to participate in criminal acts to raise some money, but also not soliciting money from anyone involved in criminal activity. That was the test for me. Had I really come over the line? It's these type of choices that's based on this new value system.

The comments of a third PSI member, Antwan, also juxtapose the way in which he thinks as a transformed person with how he thought about things in earlier parts of his life. Spelling out what it means to him to think more responsibly, Antwan is one of a number of those interviewed who talk about the importance of using a conscious process of analysis and anticipating likely future outcomes as key components of cognitive transformation.

Transformation for me is thinking in a responsible way. I told somebody the other day, reflecting back on when I was younger, I didn't really consider the feelings of other people or the outcome of my actions. It's like a guy says in a commercial I see on television. He says, 'I don't think. I just react. Bam, bam.' In my youth, I didn't really think out the outcome.

Transformation is when you begin to think more futuristic. You begin to think in long-term perspective. I'm thinking about the future in a way that's always productive, your next move. You're cognizant of the direction in which your decisions are leading you. If you want a positive outcome, you're gonna make positive decisions to achieve that.

Levon underscores the crucial linkage in a transformed person between changes in thinking and changes in behavior. For him, the resultant shifts will be dramatic enough that one's associates will mark them. He also conveys the importance of the fact that transformation is movement in a positive or progressive direction and begins to identify some of the other core values of the PSI transformation model, including care and compassion. Furthermore, Levon's comments call attention to the fact that because PSI is based in a prison, participants may have to travel an even greater distance in the process of becoming transformed than would be true for people outside. As they embark on the path to transformation, incarcerated men must overcome not only their own personal conditioning, but also the associates and institutional forces within the prison setting that would tend to push them in the opposite direction.

> What transformation means to me is that when guys on the street see you, you become unrecognizable to the guys around you. A fundamental shift in thinking comes out in your actions. With transformation you change the way a person responds to stress and sees the value in other human beings. Transformation is a shifting from one way of thinking to another and the actions produced are wholesome, geared to helping others. Part of the transformation process is to do something to build up compassion for others. In prison, it builds hate and they carry it back into the streets.

Transformation and desistance from crime

PSI members see desistance from crime as a necessary but not a sufficient element of transformation. The men I interviewed uniformly stress that transformation leads to turning away from crime and other deviance, but they also emphasize, as Toch has put it, that it involves substantially 'more than discontinuance of undesirable conduct' (in Maruna 2001: xvi). Thus, although the Public Safety Initiative, as its name suggests, is concerned with reducing crime and violence, discussion of the transformation model at the heart of the movement does not necessarily begin with, or even center on, a change in criminal behavior.

In the following passage, for example, Levon identifies the importance of becoming less selfish and more concerned about other people as a precursor to desistance from crime.

> I can tell if a guy is at least on the road to transformation. It puts you in a different place – that you care for other people – and then you just stop committing crimes. They change who they used to be. They are always reaching out to other people. Not just saying, 'I'm gonna go get education.'

Asked if not committing crime is a good indicator of transformation, Russell says,

> I wouldn't think that inaction is a definite sign of transformation. Someone might stop committing crime because they've come into an understanding that it's harmful to them as an individual.

Russell's comments are consistent with a distinction Presser (2008) makes in assessing differences in moral reform among the violent (and formerly violent) men in her study. By contrasting weak and strong evaluation, Presser seeks to evaluate the depth of change reflected in her research subjects' narratives. As she summarizes this distinction, 'the weak evaluator is a "simple weigher" of alternatives who determines whether he or she desires one alternative more than the other' (Presser 2008: 101), while 'the strong evaluator judges *desires themselves* as more or less desirable . . . The strong evaluator takes into account what kind of person he or she wants to be' (2008: 101, emphasis in original).

This gauge is a helpful antidote to the notion that a simplistic hedonistic calculus is all that needs to be taken into account when decisions are being made, especially when a person is evaluating major life choices (see for example Giordano *et al.* 2002). The idea of strong evaluation is illustrated well by Terry in discussing his own path and the role of twelve-step programs in moving from being a heroin addict with a history of repeated imprisonment to living 'a relatively "normal" life' (2003: 101) as a criminology professor. He says:

> Perhaps the most significant thing I've learned is that it's not so much what I'm doing (such as job or marriage) but how I'm doing it that best defines the quality of my life. How do I treat people? What are my motives and how much are they related to my selfish interests? Do I make the world a better place? How am I living today compared with last year, or 10 years ago? How do I hope to be living tomorrow? In 12-step programs, we learn that our chances of staying clean are enhanced when we work on improving ourselves by becoming better human beings. (Terry 2003: 101)

Members of PSI consistently discuss transformation as involving a fundamental change in who they aspire to be as persons, stressing new-found growth in selfless concern for others, desire to be a part of the solution to problems of crime and violence and a willingness to take personal action on multiple levels to achieve needed change. As Myles expresses it, 'You can see someone on the path of transformation through their positive actions, through their selfless commitment to remaking the world around them for the better.'

The evolutionary aspect of transformation as PSI conceptualizes it is captured in the caterpillar to butterfly analogy adopted as a salient image for what the group is seeking to achieve. Saying, 'We are all, and particularly me, a work in progress,' Jerome goes on to declare,

> It's the closest thing I can recall or relate to of metamorphosizing, metamorphosis. The process a butterfly goes through from caterpillar to cocoon to butterfly. We affirm that when a person is transformed

cognitively, that there's no turning back because there's nothing to turn back to. Once you've been exposed to yourself and the fallacy of a lot of our behavior, why would anyone want to turn back to that? Can the butterfly go back to being a caterpillar?

At the same time, while virtually everyone involved in PSI argues that once a person has been transformed it is not possible to return to what he was like before, Jerome and others continue to stress that being trans-formed is not a passive state. They believe that working to empower others to become transformed serves to reinforce the changed identity of a transformed person. This is reflected in the following observation that Jerome makes after his comment above:

But you have to pay dues. We've made mistakes. Transforming ourselves, we believe we can be reasonably sure that we are transformed or remain transformed by reaching back to others who are still leading some of the same destructive lifestyles which we ourselves had once led. Mind you, before the behavior comes the thought process, the thinking. So in reaching back to others we have to engage them in conversation with regards to there possibly being a problem with their thinking.

The organizational contributions of PSI to identity change

Thus far, the contributions of PSI to the identity change process may sound similar to those expected from other, state or privately run cognitive intervention programs (see for example MacKenzie 2006: 112–34, 337–8). The following section highlights a number of notable features of the PSI model that may be difficult or impossible to provide in programs run by correctional staff or contractors, but which may prove to be significant in promoting transformation in a population like the one described here. Some of these attributes of the PSI model deserve attention as important elements common to self-help and mutual aid approaches. Other features may be distinctive to the particular model adopted by PSI.

Leaders of the Public Safety Initiative describe it as a movement; a movement to end the culture of crime and violence. They stress that it is more than a program. Yet focusing specifically on the aspects of PSI that are concerned with cognitive transformation reveals that PSI shares a number of significant features with well-known peer support or mutual aid groups. Importantly, rather than fitting what is perhaps the traditional view of self-help groups as alternative sources of treatment, PSI is consistent with a perspective on mutual support organizations that emphasizes their role as normative communities (Kurtz 1997: 10). In this sense, PSI provides the valuable ingredient of a 'rehabilitative [or transformative] subculture' (Braithwaite 1989) or replacement culture.

In reflecting on the organization's major goals, Russell describes PSI as a normative community that provides a social model for those involved:

I would think that they [the goals] are to bring about a condition which ends the way of thinking that creates a sense of responsibility to a culture that is detrimental to the well-being of the individual, the community and people as a whole. Besides ending the violence and the culture of crime that produces the violence and allows the criminal activity to be accepted, I think it's a social model that would unite people in the development of themselves and the people they come in contact with, their collective responsibility to themselves and the communities. I think the strongest principles or goals of it is to bring about dignity in all human beings.

The notion of PSI serving as a social model is also relevant to the way in which members conceptualize and frame the nature of the assignments they have in reaching out to engage their peers in transformative work. Kareem articulates a view of transformation as opening up awareness of the individual's connection to a larger community, which in turn engenders a sense of responsibility for addressing the problems within that larger whole.

Transformation is a verb, not just a noun. So, if you stop committing crimes, that only makes you a desister. Transformation is a connection movement. It's a movement geared towards seeing yourself as being a part of a larger community. It means that you are obligated, responsible for being involved. So if I see a young guy on the road to prison, it's my job to intervene in his life in whatever way I can. That's your job as a transformed man. It becomes a responsibility. That's not just your kids, they're my kids. That's not just your community, that's my community. You not gonna be able to help everybody, but you have to contribute to the betterment of everyone around.

Myles' comments also reflect a view of PSI as a social model. He describes one of the main tasks of PSI leaders as working to 'flip the switch' of a person who starts out with self-serving motivations in order to turn that individual on to the value and joy of working to make positive changes in the community.

I think the base motivation [for getting involved with PSI] is to make a difference, but individuals have different focuses as to where they want to make a difference. We're learning in PSI that we have to pave the avenues toward those different focuses. That's a large part of what the movement is. That's our initial work, the enrollment – to flip the switch from being satisfied with their lifestyle to questioning their lifestyle. We have to continue to find ways to get and hold their attention long enough for that switch to be flipped. Unfortunately, quite often it's the lure of doing something positive to impress the parole board, and in the moment that we have their attention, we attempt to get them to focus on deeper issues.

In functioning as normative communities, self-help groups serve to help re-educate members by providing alternative world-views through which they can reframe how they think of and define their difficulties (Kurtz 1997: 15). PSI members stress that because many, if not most, men who come to prison were thoroughly enmeshed in the values associated with the culture of street crime, transformation requires re-examining and changing almost everything they were used to thinking and doing.

In discussing how his life before he experienced transformation through PSI differs from what it is like now, Marshall describes how all-encompassing and multifaceted transformation has been for him. He also identifies a strong linkage between his sense of self and his behavior. He observes that when he had a poor assessment of his self-worth, he acted in shallow and selfish ways.

It affects every part of my life. It affects the way I carry myself every day. It affects what I do with my time, the company I keep, the way I raise my family when I go home. It affects everything. The way I think, most of all. Before, when I first came to jail, I'd be makin' wine, smokin' weed, in frivolous conversations about who had more of this or that on the street, how tough I was, trying to impress my peers through negative stuff. I wasn't readin'. If I was, it wasn't no value. I just cared about myself. I definitely didn't worry about how what I did affected other people, as long as it satisfied me. I had really low self-esteem. I didn't think I deserved better.

Marshall's description is consistent with Terry's findings based on the life histories of 20 men struggling to overcome the effects of heroin addiction and incarceration that 'perhaps the greatest barrier people like the fellas [his research subjects] have to face . . . is their deeply held belief that they are inferior human beings' (Terry 2003: 9). In his interviews, Terry found that negative self-assessments can be mitigated by strong social support (Terry 2003: 9). His research subjects identified development of new reference groups as pivotal in coming to see themselves differently and changing the direction of their lives. This was all the more critical the more 'prisonized' a person was in the sense of having used the prison culture as his reference group (Terry 2003: 76). Terry therefore reached the conclusion that 'addicts and ex-convicts who are trying to do good will benefit by developing new relationships and self-concepts that either exclude or depreciate their old values. At the same time, they need to be accepted within new social worlds and not condemned for past actions' (Terry 2003: 14).

Although Terry refers primarily to social support provided by family relationships or involvement in twelve-step programs (Terry 2003: 9), interviews with PSI members make it clear that PSI functions as an important pro-social and affirming reference group for its participants. This is consistent with the view that '[e]mpowerment flows from the community aspect of a self-help group' (Kurtz 1997: 26). 'Empowerment occurs when one becomes able to take action for oneself and in behalf of others. The first sign of it is a dawning belief in oneself; one experiences growth of self confidence, which is usually accomplished within a group of others facing the same ordeal' (1997: 26).

Emphasizing the importance of the cognitive elements of transformation and their linkage to personal choice, Jeff asserts that the correctional programs he participated in were not delivered in ways that treated him as being truly capable of choosing. He also argues that his involvement with PSI has had effects on him beyond those that may have come simply from maturation, education, or spiritual growth. More specifically, he believes that his work with PSI gave him a new sense of his own identity and power.

> I was a dog trainer on the outside. It's repetitive. 'Stay.' 'Sit.' 'Good.' 'Stay.' 'Sit.' It's exactly the same in the [prison-run] programs here. They don't deal with why am I capable of making good choices for myself. They don't get deep down inside ... I know when the time comes, I'm not gonna go through that revolving door. It's not because I'm [more than 50] years old, or because I got an education, or because I got spiritually enlightened. It's because I got to know myself. It's because I know the system and I want to be involved in changing it. That's what PSI does.

In addressing the value of social support from his peers in PSI to his investment in the transformation process, Marshall speaks to the importance of the belief and message that he got from PSI members that he is capable of change, even if that does not happen overnight.

> Another thing ... was that I had people that took an interest in me and really went out of their way to help me. And I think that was one of the most important things. All my life I had people tellin' me what I couldn't do. And they [PSI members] was tellin' me, 'You can be anything you want. You can change. It's not too late.' Without that

support, I don't know if I'd been able to do it by myself, to see the good in me. That's why I like PSI. Sometimes you gotta go out of your way to reach people even if they reject you at first. People in the community expect change overnight. They're real impatient. They want to give you like this revelation and expect you to change. I think it's gonna be a gradual process but it's gonna happen as long as people are committed, cause if I could change, there's hope for anybody.

Similarly, in speaking to what he sees as the main strengths of the PSI transformation model, Manhattan stresses the importance of the support and connections he obtains from the group. 'Strengths, for me, it was the love they gave. It made you feel like you was a part of something.' Jesse also identifies the value of the intellectual, emotional and social supports available through PSI, as well as the role models, in responding to a question as to why people would be motivated to participate.

The strength of the people that created the program – the study, the literature, the time and effort they have put in – I really commend the guys and you, yourself, who are behind us. These are the people that people think the worst of, but they are presenting such helpful and such spiritual information wherein these men just didn't give up on life. They give me, they help motivate me to give me a message that I should change, not only to help myself but to help somebody. These guys, the men in PSI, the simple things I don't even think about, it makes their day, like when guys talk about positive things with their family, for example.

Utilizing the analogy of a plant needing a good environment in which to grow and flourish, August elaborates on the value of PSI group sessions in providing social support in the transformation process, saying:

Once I decide that I'm gonna try to be a good human being and once I understand and look at the ashes of myself, to rebuild from the ashes I need an environment and people that would encourage me to continue this growth process. You need the company of good human beings around you to encourage you and help you grow – to become a good human being. It's almost like a plant. You have to have an environment where life can grow and I think that's what the positive transformation sessions are about. You tell 'em, 'It's okay to be a good person.' It's growth in that process. I believe that everybody in that environment all receive nutrients – all of us. When you're talking to other people about being right and good, it kind of adds cement to your moral fiber.

The role of PSI in reworking one's story

Maruna argues that ex-offenders desisting from crime 'need to account for and understand their criminal pasts (why they did what they did), and they also need to understand why they are now "not like that any more"' (Maruna 2001: 7). The central idea is that the reworking of one's story, as within Alcoholics Anonymous or Narcotics Anonymous, 'is itself the recovery process' (Maruna 2001: 113). As Terry (2003) describes it, 'Through the process of storytelling, members are able to gain a sense of shared identification with one another and also rethink or recreate their life history in such a way that they begin to see themselves as worthwhile human beings living meaningful lives' (2003: 100).

PSI can supply a critical ingredient in the re-authoring of lives by helping participants find a causal interpretation of the condition or behavior that is undergoing change that will not make those involved feel disempowered from being able to do something about it (Kurtz 1997). The PSI model serves this important function by elaborating the role that the culture of street crime is believed to play in accounting for how young people get drawn into and stay involved in criminality and related deviance. Likewise, the fact of participation in the PSI cognitive transformation process can help explain how and why the individual has been or will be able to achieve dramatic change.

Levon articulates these key points in noting that PSI's transformation model is conceptualized in such a way that it puts the onus for change on the individual, while at the same time, by emphasizing the pull and power of the street-crime culture, it places the individual's past behavior in context. This avoids an implication that men who have been involved in criminal activity are categorically different from non-offenders or 'regular people'. This is important because acceptance of the idea that offenders are simply 'bad people', besides being dehumanizing, suggests that they are unable to change. Thus, by providing this 'replacement discourse' (Maruna 2001: 167) to one of criminal essentialism, PSI is supplying a critical ingredient in helping ex-offenders re-author their lives. PSI's conceptualization also helps clarify why addressing the tangible needs of people coming out of prison for housing, jobs and the like, without addressing the attraction of the street-crime culture, often is not sufficient for insuring that those individuals do not return to crime.

> Sure, making it in the community has to do with jobs, education and all that. But that's not enough. They [Department of Corrections] have programs like 'Citizenship', 'Thinking for a Change' and 'Character Development' that are based on cognitive intervention, and they're all fine programs. They even had prisoners facilitating them. We kind of took them over and did it through the PSI model. We thought, 'At least we can really challenge these guys by putting the PSI twist on

it.' We were teaching from a perspective that is aware of the culture of street crime, not just focusing on the individual. 'It's not who you are, this culture, it's what you do. You just get caught up in this thing.' From the DOC perspective, it's about making the person wrong. The culture gives a guy cover. He says, 'I just got caught up in this thing.' We say, 'You ain't got to appeal to those guys [members of the street-crime culture]; give that up.' DOC comes from the past – what a guy did. We try to look at the future.

The PSI stance reflects a delicate balance in its conceptualization of agency and accountability. On the one hand, it acknowledges the powerful pull of the enticements of the street-crime culture and the forceful push of the hardships associated with racism, poverty, urban decay, and other forms of oppression in drawing people into criminal behavior (see Lifers Public Safety Steering Committee 2004). On the other hand, the PSI position is that neither one of these forces, nor the two of them combined, provides an excuse for past antisocial behavior. The argument is that participants chose to seek the psychological and economic rewards associated with street crime despite knowing deep down that the violence and other forms of harm they inflicted were wrong. Thus they fully deserve to be held accountable for the choices they made. The emphasis on the culture of street crime provides a context for past criminality, but, as Levon stresses, 'Giving a guy cover [from the conclusion that he is simply a bad person] is not the same thing as evading responsibility.'

Maruna argues that desisting offenders need to perceive 'structural opportunities to achieve the sort of agency [power, self-respect] and communion [love, connection] they could obtain through criminal behavior' (cited in McAdams 2006: 236). However, identifying meaningful opportunities to take purposeful action and to 'expand, defend, or express the self' or to 'join with others in bonds of love, friendship, and community' (2006: 244) and accomplish other-oriented goals can be exceedingly difficult in prisons and jails. This reality means that PSI (and organizations like it) can serve as a critically important resource in meeting the needs among incarcerated populations for agency and community.

Supporting their peers in achieving agency through non-criminal means is a centerpiece of PSI work. All forms of self-help, whether individual, group, community or national, tend to focus on the promotion of latent inner strengths (Kurtz 1997). As is true with other models of peer support, PSI emphasizes self-determination, self-reliance and self-empowerment. Members aim to 'assist those who are a part of the culture of street crime to take responsibility for their own lives, and to assume control of their own futures' (Lifers Public Safety Initiative, n.d.). The common sense and experiential wisdom of participants are validated and respected as relevant (Kurtz 1997) within both group and one-on-one working sessions.

Comments made by PSI members suggest that for many participants, the road to transformation has included making a transition from being weak evaluators to becoming stronger ones (Presser 2008). They describe moving from making choices for selfish and narrow reasons to making decisions guided by considerations beyond self-interest. This suggests that it is possible for people to learn to engage in stronger types of evaluation and identifies another valuable role that PSI plays in the transformation process. PSI members can help their peers appreciate the differences between weak and strong forms of assessment and their differing implications, as well as modeling how to live in accord with the latter type of evaluation.

Self-help groups typically provide their members a defined path or 'steps' for developing new ways of living built on experiential knowledge. Although PSI has not yet issued what Myles describes as 'an instruction manual for life', the PSI approach includes at least two additional ways of influencing their peers' thinking that are critical to successful transformation. First, they assist with pathways thinking by helping their peers examine the thoughts they have about their ability to produce one or more workable routes to their goals. Second, they help their peers with agency thinking by encouraging them to focus on the thoughts they have about their ability to start and continue movement on their selected pathways toward their goals (Snyder *et al.* 2006). Because both pathways and agency thinking are needed for a person to experience hope (Snyder *et al.* 2006), PSI is fueling hope while also helping to empower their peers and encourage agency when it offers these types of assistance.

Taking responsibility, redemption and generativity

In reaching out to their peers and engaging in projects designed to arrest the development of street-crime culture, PSI members are acting as change agents. As Toch describes this phenomenon, 'Having undergone a transformation, [they] feel competent and motivated to assist others with problems' (in Maruna 2001: xvi). Over and above the ways in which such activities may benefit the recipients directly, they afford PSI members bountiful opportunities to take on responsibility and to exercise generativity; opportunities that may be associated with desistance from crime, especially among populations whose access to and ability to expend various forms of capital is limited (Barry 2007; Giordano *et al.* 2002).

'Taking on responsibility' involves 'the desire, opportunity, incentive and capacity to be trusted with a task of benefit to others' (Barry 2007: 24). In that PSI members frequently view themselves as being obligated to seek to repair the damage that their own criminal and other antisocial behaviors helped to create, as well as the more general collateral damage that their very participation in the culture of street crime may have engendered, participation in PSI provides multiple avenues for taking on responsibility. 'Generativity' refers to 'an adult's concern for and commitment to promoting the well-being of future generations' (McAdams 2006: 49). In calling for members to lead the charge in collective efforts to transform the street-crime culture in order to prevent future generations from continuing the cycle of violence that participants formerly helped perpetuate, PSI engages participants in many forms of generative endeavors.

Not surprisingly, given the centrality of taking responsibility and generativity to PSI's goals, many members address these themes by identifying specific desires to reduce victimization and build safer communities. Such descriptions often follow a 'redemption script' (McAdams 2006; Maruna 2001) in which something that was negative is turned into something positive. Myles offers a classic example of such a script in discussing his own reasons for being involved in the work of PSI.

> My community has helped to create me even through my criminal lifestyle. In that culture I earned the credentials to enable me to be effective now in the work of PSI. It was my street cred's that put me in a position to be a PSI leader, and on the other side of those experiences – the drug-motivated, criminal ones – I came to realize that I was indebted to that community not only for the destruction that I left in my wake, but because that was the furnace where my mantle was formed – where I was molded. I need to save the children who are growing up in the unchecked violence that I started from the death that awaits them. PSI is my vehicle to do that.

It is important to recognize that PSI provides a venue for members to act on some of their central strivings consistent with what they come to see as their life's purpose. This is all the more significant because it takes place in a prison setting where it can be extremely difficult to find meaningful opportunities to pursue generative goals. Indeed, some of the greatest misery associated with imprisonment, especially long-term confinement that extends into middle and old age, arguably stems from the sense of stagnation associated with it (see for example Johnson 2002).

Thaddeus describes the desire of transformed prisoners to help change things for the better in a colorful way, and in so doing suggests that he sees something like generativity – making a difference – as a fundamental duty associated with involvement in PSI.

> When you're a convict, it's raining every day. It may be sunny outside, but it's raining in here. If you can help save somebody from that, especially somebody who you can see is headed in the wrong direction, you can make a real difference . . . And I believe we're all put on this earth to make a difference in one way or the other.

Somewhat paradoxically, at the same time that many PSI members identify freedom as something they obtain through transformation, they also speak to developing a new sense of obligation that comes along with the other profound changes they experience. This is related to the commonly expressed view of transformation as empowering, an effect that almost requires continuing action on the part of the person who has been transformed. As Jerome puts it,

When you talk about PSI, transformation is something real, real radical. It's like putting gas in the gas tank. It has an empowering element that makes you want to get up and go. You got to do something. You just have to.

The commitment to engaging in positive peer intervention is discussed by PSI members as a virtually inescapable concomitant of personal transformation, as well as being a core part of the PSI model. This leadership and service role becomes a consuming part of the identity of participants. Jerome expresses this moral-imperative perspective power-fully:

For me to change and not be engaged in peer intervention, it's like selfish. What's the difference of me winning the lottery and my family's in poverty and me moving to Beverly Hills? What I believe makes or gives substance to what we do is when we can reach back and have influence on the lives of others. And in that way we're not just preaching to the choir. We're confronting people just like ourselves. The same struggles, the same quirks, basically good people. But they haven't discovered it yet. So in part, I guess you could say that our work is about waking up the genius within.

In underscoring the importance of the active nature of involvement in PSI's transformation work – especially that it operates through positive peer intervention – Jerome also highlights the catalytic effects of the ambitious nature of PSI's goals.

What turns me on about the PSI model is the declaration about ending the culture of crime. You've got to be gutsy to do that. Even people on the outside don't want to tackle that, to make such a gutsy commitment. The peer intervention – going back out on the block to talk about PSI. I can only pray we can plant some seeds in the head of a brother going home soon . . . It engages you in the work. This is not a passive movement. Once we've accepted ownership of these problems, we have to get up and do something. It's this for me: to change or transform, so what? That's good, but come on. Where we get our momentum is when other people buy into this declaration.

Conclusions

Based on the belief that changed thinking leads to changed behavior, members of the Lifers Public Safety Initiative at SCI-Graterford utilize positive peer intervention to encourage and assist adherents to street-crime culture in a process of soul-searching designed to accomplish cognitive transformation. Adopting a view of identity change as a revision of one's life story, this chapter has explored how men who report having accomplished such a transformation describe and interpret both the process of re-authoring their life stories and the significance of this shift in identity to their lives today.

In exploring the connections between the PSI version of transformation and desistance from crime, this chapter has made clear that PSI members who see themselves as transformed also see themselves as desisters, but they do not see all who describe themselves as desisters as being transformed. In the view of PSI members, offenders may stop engaging in crime on the basis of 'weak evaluation' (Presser 2008), fearing an extended sentence or a return to prison or simply being burned out, for example. Transformation, on the other hand, is understood as a much more all-encompassing shift in identity than simply turning away from criminal activity. Like the butterfly that has sprouted wings, the transformed offender experiences a new-found sense of freedom and personal power. It is this power and a desire for redemption that helps impel those who experience transformation to embrace new responsibilities as peer helpers, role models and crime prevention activists.

The stories highlighted here of personal transformation and the ongoing efforts of the men who have been transformed illuminate how even long-term prisoners can craft lives full of meaning and make valuable contributions to their incarcerated brethren, the institutional environment and future generations. The interviews paint a picture of highly generative adults whose aspirations and activities are far removed from the popular stereotypes of hardened, uncaring prisoners. By finding important ways to take responsibility and exercise their redemptive and generative aspirations, the men involved in PSI are applying themselves creatively and on a sustained basis to building strong, harmonious communities.

This chapter also has highlighted ways in which PSI may be conceptualized as a mutual aid or peer-support organization, at least with respect to its cognitive transformation efforts. The findings suggest that PSI represents a significant resource in efforts to encourage offenders to change their lives and desist from crime and to reduce misbehavior both within and outside of correctional institutions. The experience-based theoretical work done by PSI members has proven to be of great value in assisting participants in the re-authoring of their life stories, both in spotlighting the role of the culture of street crime in drawing people into criminality and in offering a replacement discourse to explain how and why dramatic shifts in identity can be accomplished. PSI also contributes to these goals in serving as an alternative normative community and pro-social reference group. PSI offers a social model within which participants can find meaning and purpose in taking on responsibility to enhance the quality of community life and help make the world a better place for future generations.

Notes

1 I would like to express my appreciation to David Diguglielmo, Superintendent of SCI-Graterford, and his staff, especially Robert Dromboski of the Psychology Department, and to Bret Bucklen of the Office of Planning, Research, Statistics and Grants of the Pennsylvania Department of Corrections, for their support in allowing me to conduct these interviews, and to Temple University for providing me a study leave during which this research was conducted.
2 I owe a tremendous debt of gratitude to the members of the Public Safety Initiative of LIFERS, Inc. who participated in these interviews. Their generosity, openness and insights, along with their dedication to arresting crime and violence, are a continuing source of admiration and inspiration for me.
3 Life sentences represent murder convictions. Under Pennsylvania law, first-degree murder is punishable by life or death and the penalty for second-degree murder is mandatory life in prison. Life sentences carry no parole eligibility.

References

Barry, M. (2007) 'The transitional pathways of young female offenders: Towards a non-offending lifestyle', in R. Sheehan, G. McIvor G. and C. Trotter (eds) *What Works with Women Offenders*. Portland, OR: Willan Publishing.

Braithwaite, J. (1989) *Crime, Shame and Reintegration*. Cambridge: Cambridge University Press.

Farrall S. and Calverley A. (2006) *Understanding Desistance from Crime: Emerging Theoretical Directions in Resettlement and Rehabilitation*. New York: Open University Press.

Giordano, P. C., Cernkovich, S. A. and Rudolph, J. L. (2002) 'Gender, crime, and desistance: Toward a theory of cognitive transformation', *American Journal of Sociology*, 107(4): 990–1064.

Johnson, R. (2002) *Hard Time: Understanding the Reforming the Prison*. Belmont, CA: Wadsworth.

Kurtz, L. F. (1997) *Self-Help and Support Groups: A Handbook for Practitioners*. Thousand Oaks, CA: Sage.

Laub, J. H. and Sampson, R. J. (2003) *Shared Beginnings, Divergent Lives: Delinquent Boys to Age 70*. Cambridge, MA: Harvard University Press.

Lifers Public Safety Initiative (n.d.) 'Fact sheet: Ending the culture of street crime: A paradoxical solution to ending the crime culture'. Philadelphia: LIFERS, Inc.

Lifers Public Safety Steering Committee of the State Correctional Institution at Graterford, Pennsylvania (2004) 'Ending the culture of street crime', *The Prison Journal*, 84(4): 48S–68S.

MacKenzie, D. L. (2006) *What Works in Corrections: Reducing the Criminal Activities of Offenders and Delinquents*. Cambridge: Cambridge University Press.

Maruna, S. (2001) *Making Good: How Ex-Convicts Reform and Rebuild Their Lives*. Washington DC: American Psychological Association.

McAdams, D. P. (1985) *Power, Intimacy, and the Life Story: Personological Inquiries into Identity*. Homewood, IL: Dorsey Press.

McAdams, D. P. (2006) *The Redemptive Self: Stories Americans Live By*. New York: Oxford University Press.

Presser, L. (2008) *Been a Heavy Life: Stories of Violent Men*. Urbana and Chicago: University of Illinois Press.

Prochaska, J. O., DiClemente, C. C. and Norcross, J. C. (1992) 'In search of the structure of change', in Y. Klar, J. D. Fisher, J. M. Chinsky and A. Nadler (eds) *Self Change: Social Psychological and Clinical Perspectives*. New York: Springer-Verlag.

Shover, N. (1996) *Great Pretenders: Pursuits and Careers of Persistent Thieves*. Boulder, CO: Westview Press.

Snyder, C. R., Scott, T. M. and Cheavens, J. S. (2006) 'Hope as a psychotherapeutic foundation of common factors, placebos, and expectancies', in M. A. Hubble, B. L. Duncan, and S. D. Miller (eds) *The Heart and Soul of Change: What Works in Therapy*. Washington DC: American Psychological Association.

Terry, C. M. (2003) *The Fellas: Overcoming Prison and Addiction*. Belmont, CA: Wadsworth.

Chapter 10

Formerly incarcerated persons' use of advocacy/activism as a coping orientation in the reintegration process

Thomas P. LeBel

Introduction

Erving Goffman's (1963) *Stigma: Notes on the Management of Spoiled Identity* is universally considered the seminal treatise on the subject of stigma. Goffman defined stigma as 'an attribute that is deeply discrediting' (1963: 3), and suggested that 'criminals deal with blemishes of individual character' (1963: 4). It is now generally believed that formerly incarcerated persons are stigmatized and discriminated against in society (see e.g. LeBel 2006; Petersilia 2003; Travis 2005). Garland (2001: 180) argues that 'the assumption today is that there is no such thing as an "ex-offender" – only offenders who have been caught before and will strike again'. Moreover, Petersilia (2003: 19) states that the plight of felons is best summed up as: 'a criminal conviction – no matter how trivial or how long ago it occurred – scars one for life'. This chapter examines how formerly incarcerated persons attempt to overcome this 'spoiled identity' by supporting and/or becoming involved in advocacy-related activities to change the public's perception and treatment of prisoners and former prisoners.

Stigmatized persons cope with stigma and discrimination in a wide variety of ways including avoidance and withdrawal (Jones *et al.* 1984; Link *et al.* 1991), concealment and secrecy (Goffman 1963; Herman 1993; Link *et al.* 1991), and by educating the public and engaging in political activism (Anspach 1979; Link *et al.* 2002). A qualitative study by Siegel

(1998) of how gay and bisexual men deal with their HIV/AIDS status describes stigma-coping strategies along a reactive–proactive continuum. Reactive strategies such as concealment and selective disclosure of one's stigmatized status, whereas proactive strategies include pre-emptive disclosure, public education, and social activism. So, for formerly incarcerated persons, some conceal their 'ex-convict' status at all costs while others are engaged as activists attempting to change the public's negative treatment of former prisoners. Corrigan and Watson (2002) call the wide pattern of responses from concealment and withdrawal to activism the 'fundamental paradox of self-stigma'.

Concealment of one's stigmatized status is both a highly individual strategy and a reactive or defensive one that attempts to avoid or mitigate the stigma but does not directly challenge it (Goffman 1963; Siegel *et al.* 1998). Research has consistently shown that stigmatized individuals attempt to 'pass' as normal (Goffman 1963), or more generally strive to keep their stigmatized status a secret from others (e.g. Anspach 1979; Herman 1993; Jones *et al.* 1984; Link *et al.* 1991). Several scholars have criticized Goffman's (1963) groundbreaking work on stigma and much of the stigma-related research that followed as being heavily biased toward the examination of 'protective' and 'defensive' management strategies (e.g. for critiques see Anspach 1979; Herman 1993; Kitsuse 1980; Rogers and Buffalo 1974; Siegel *et al.* 1998). For example, Anspach (1979) asserts that most studies using the labeling perspective portray the deviant as 'powerless, passive, and relatively uninvolved in the labeling process', and do not 'provide *sufficiently* for the possibility of politicized deviants, collectively engaged in attempts to reweave the fabric of identity' (1979: 767). Anspach (1979: 766) uses the concept of 'identity politics' to refer to social movements that 'consciously endeavor to alter both the self-concepts and societal conceptions of their participants'. In a similar vein, Kitsuse (1980: 9) proposed the concept of 'tertiary deviance' to refer to the stigmatized person's 'confrontation, assessment, and rejection of the negative identity imbedded in secondary deviation, and the transformation of that identity into a positive and viable self-conception'.

Sociologists (e.g. Anspach 1979; Kitsuse 1980) began to observe in the 1970s that political activism was beginning to represent a viable collective alternative to the previous individualistic responses to stigma discussed by Goffman (1963). Examples of collective responses from stigmatized groups include the activism by persons with mental illness, physical disabilities, HIV/AIDS, and those who are gay/lesbian. According to Kitsuse (1980: 2), these new activists 'declared their presence openly and without apology to claim the rights of citizenship' and began to demand 'institutional equality' (Anspach 1979: 770). Van Tosh *et al.* (2000), for example, provide a history of the mental health consumer movement, which emphasizes the importance of activism in the lives of some persons with mental illness. Advocacy or activism of this sort involved more proactive and collective attempts on the part of stigmatized persons to change public perceptions and create a more positive identity (Anspach 1979; Kitsuse 1980; Sayce 2000). Therefore, unlike the coping strategies of concealment and avoidance/withdrawal, advocacy/activism involves some form of 'coming out' of stigmatized individuals to 'confront stigma in the hope of 'breaking through' social prejudice' (Siegel *et al.* 1998: 6; Gill 1997; Jones *et al.* 1984; White 2001). Rogers and Buffalo (1974: 105) refer to this type of coping orientation as the 'fighting back' phenomenon.

Formerly incarcerated persons and advocacy/activism

There is a paucity of literature on formerly incarcerated persons' support for and/or involvement in advocacy-related activities. One exception is a study from the early 1970s of former prisoner groups in Chicago. McAnany *et al.* (1974: 8) reported that these groups formed 'to bring about changes in criminal justice, and especially the correctional system . . . to inform the public about the inequities and irrationalities of the criminal justice system, and to politicize prisoners and ex-prisoners to seek political redress and system change through collective action'. In a re-emergence of activism that was more common in the 1960s and 1970s, it appears that former prisoner advocacy groups are again 'coming out' to confront the stigma faced by prisoners and former prisoners in society. There are a number of groups advocating for policy reforms in the criminal justice system with a large contingent of prisoners and former prisoners in leadership positions and as members (see Appendix). These groups include national organizations such as Convict Criminology, Critical Resistance and the Prison Moratorium Project; All of Us or None located in California; and several organizations located in New York City (the Center for NuLeadership on Urban Solutions, the Fortune Society, and the Women's Prison Association (WPA)). These grassroots organizations provide a voice to formerly incarcerated persons and give them the opportunity to be engaged in attempts to change public policy. For example, All of Us or None is a national organizing initiative of formerly incarcerated persons and persons in prison. On its website and in its brochure, this organization states that, 'Advocates have spoken for us, but now is the time for us to speak for ourselves. We clearly have the ability to be more than the helpless victims of the system.' Moreover, All of Us or None argues that 'It's OUR responsibility to stop the discrimination, and to change the public policies that discriminate against us, our families, and our communities' (*www.allofusornone.org/about.html*). One policy development from the Center for NuLeadership on Urban Solutions addresses identity issues and involves advocacy to encourage the use of people-first language such as 'people currently or formerly incarcerated' instead of dehumanizing language such as 'offenders' and 'ex-convicts' (see *www.citizensinc.org/centerfornuleadershiponurban.html*). Meanwhile, several of the other organizations are interested in 'developing a group of leaders equipped to craft solutions to the problems facing incarcerated and formerly incarcerated persons' (see, for example, the Women's Advocacy Project (WAP) at *www.wpaonline.org/institute/ wap.htm*).

Characteristics of formerly incarcerated persons potentially related to an advocacy/activism orientation

Social identity theorists (e.g. Ellemers 1993; Lalonde and Cameron 1994; Tajfel and Turner 1986; Wright and Tropp 2002) argue that a limited number of factors determine a person's preferences for behavioral responses to membership in a disadvantaged or stigmatized group. The factors most relevant for formerly incarcerated persons include identification with other similarly stigmatized persons and the perceived fairness and justness with which the group is treated in society.

Group identification

Goffman (1963: 21) extensively discusses the formation and purpose of organized groups of stigmatized individuals and posits that 'among his own, the stigmatized individual can use his disadvantage as a basis for organizing life'. Along these lines, in Chicago, McAnany *et al.* (1974: 27) found that 'the ex-offender groups were formed to confront the stigma, which these prisonized persons were running away from. Thus, the self-change could be, and often was, expressed in terms of identification with prisonized persons as a group, with the understanding that with this group identity came a group obligation.' The groups insisted that there is a 'common bond' between all persons who are formerly incarcerated and that 'helping 'the brothers' was essential for continued group identity' (McAnany *et al.* 1974: 28). By providing a supportive community and a network of individuals with shared experiences, these groups can be interpreted as transforming an ostensibly individual process into a social movement of sorts (Hamm 1997).

Considerable research evidence indicates that stigmatized persons who do not identify with the group (low group identifiers) prefer individualistic strategies such as concealment or attempting to leave the group, whereas persons who strongly identify with the disadvantaged group (high group identifiers) are more likely to endorse and engage in group-level strategies such as advocacy and collective action (Branscombe and Ellemers 1998; Deaux and Ethier 1998; Ellemers 1993; Ellemers *et al.* 1997; Major 1994; Simon *et al.* 1998; Wright and Tropp 2002). In addition, identification may need to include an element of 'group pride' for it to lead to collective action (see Britt and Heise 2000; Ellemers *et al.* 1999). Therefore, it is thought that the more formerly incarcerated persons identify with similarly stigmatized others, the more they will endorse advocacy/activism as a coping orientation.

Perceived unjustness and unfairness of the criminal justice system

The criminal justice literature is replete with examples of how unjust America's criminal justice system is, especially in regard to people of color (e.g. Mauer 1999; Tonry 1995). Former prisoners themselves often articulate that the system is unfair and unjust (e.g. Ross and Richards 2003). McAnany and colleagues (1974: 26) in their study of former prisoner groups found that most of the interviewees perceived the prison experience 'as a basically unjust situation' and postulated that this view 'creates a positive identification – that of victim – for those who undergo it'. Moreover, Maruna (2001) reported that 'in the desisting self-story, the "System" may need more reform than the recovering individual himself or herself . . . In fact, rather than overcoming a "criminal value system", the interviewees saw themselves as recovering from *society's* value system in some sense' (2001: 107).

The more that disadvantaged group members perceive the treatment and status of their group to be unfair, unjust and illegitimate, the more likely it is that they will engage in advocacy-related activities such as collective action to change the status quo (Corrigan and Watson 2002; Major 1994; Wright and Tropp 2002). In fact, the questioning of legitimizing myths that sustain inequalities among groups is believed to be a necessary condition for all protest and liberation movements (Crocker *et al.* 1998: 510; see also Wright and Tropp 2002: 220). Consequently, it is likely that formerly incarcerated persons who perceive the criminal justice system as unjust will be more likely to support and become involved in advocacy-related activities.

Mass incarceration of persons of color

It is also possible that race and ethnicity, rather than a common bond or common fate that all returning prisoners face, may partially drive advocacy-related activities to change the criminal justice system. For the prisoner reintegration discussion, Petersilia (2003: 30) argues that race is the 'elephant sitting in the living room'. Black males are more than six times as likely as white males to be incarcerated (Sabol *et al.* 2007), and about one in every nine black males between 20 and 34 years of age is incarcerated (Pew Center on the States 2008). Moreover, Pager (2007) has found that a person's race (i.e. African-American) has a negative impact on employment prospects, equal to or greater than the impact of having a criminal record. Based on facts such as these, it is not surprising that Anderson (1999: 66), in *Code of the Streets*, reported that 'the criminal justice system is widely perceived as beset with a double standard: one for blacks and one for whites, resulting in a profound distrust in this institution'. Wynn (2001: 170) similarly reported that inmates on Riker's Island in New York City 'often speak of the "conspiracy theory", an intentional plan by the power brokers of society, meaning white men, to accomplish through imprisonment what was undone by slavery's abolishment: to keep them in check'. In response to the mass incarceration of persons of color many advocacy groups appear to place at the forefront of their activities the elimination of race and class bias in the criminal justice system (see for example Critical Resistance and the Center for NuLeadership on Urban Solutions). Therefore, the race/ethnicity of formerly incarcerated persons may be strongly related to their advocacy/activism orientation.

Advocacy/activism orientation and psychological and behavioral outcomes

The coping strategy that a stigmatized person uses has been linked to psychological and behavioral outcomes. Link and colleagues (1991, 2002) found that the use of reactive and defensive coping strategies (e.g. concealment and avoidance-withdrawal) were harmful in terms of the psychological well-being and employment status of persons with mental disorders. In contrast, Shih (2004: 175) posits that 'successful individuals view overcoming the adversities associated with stigma as an empowering process'. Moreover, Jones and colleagues (1984: 132) argue that the self-esteem of stigmatized individuals will increase 'to the extent that the individuals come to view themselves as other than helpless, dependent, and worthless'.

There is growing evidence that proactive strategies are indeed related to more positive outcomes (see LeBel 2008 for a review). Link and colleagues (2002) found that a coping strategy that challenges stigmatizing behavior has a significant positive impact on self-esteem. Similarly, Wahl (1999) found that 'involvement in advocacy and speaking out are self-enhancing, and the courage and effectiveness shown by such participation help to restore self-esteem damaged by stigma' (1999: 476; see also Rosario et al. 2001; Shih 2004). In addition, becoming involved in advocacy-related activities can give meaning, purpose and significance to a formerly incarcerated person's life (Connett 1973: 114). For example, Elaine Bartlett, a formerly incarcerated person, asserts that her advocacy work to overturn New York State's Rockefeller Era Drug Laws gives her a sense of purpose and makes her feel proud for reinventing herself and accomplishing something (Gonnerman 2004).

It is well documented that former prisoners suffer from many 'civil disabilities' such as statutory restrictions placed on public and private employment, voting, eligibility for public assistance and public housing, financial aid to attend college, parenting and divorce, firearm ownership, criminal registration, and the like (e.g. Legal Action Center 2004; Mauer and Chesney-Lind 2002; Uggen *et al*. 2006). Travis (2002) refers to these restrictions as 'invisible punishments'. Much of the advocacy-related activity of formerly incarcerated persons focuses on changing these social policies that create barriers to successful reentry (see, for example, the Fortune Society's new David Rothenberg Center for Public Policy [DRCPP], *www.fortunesociety.org/04_advocacy/rothenberg.html*). Therefore, support for and/or involvement in advocacy/activism among formerly incarcerated persons may be negatively related to criminal attitudes and thinking that one will recidivate because it indicates a desire to lead a law-abiding life.

Study objectives

This study is largely exploratory in nature and appears to be the first to examine the advocacy/activism orientation of formerly incarcerated persons. The main objective of this study is to address three research questions: (1) To what degree do formerly incarcerated persons support and/or engage in advocacy to change public perceptions of prisoners and former prisoners? (2) What factors account for any differences in the advocacy/activism orientation? and (3) Is the endorsement and reported use of advocacy related to psychological well-being, criminal attitude, and the forecast of rearrest?

Methodology

Sample and data collection

A formerly incarcerated person is defined as: 'someone who has served a prison sentence for a felony conviction'. A purposive and targeted sampling technique was employed to recruit 229 male and female formerly incarcerated persons from New York City and Upstate New York. Sampling was aimed at recruiting adults, aged 18 and older, who were currently receiving prisoner reintegration services of some kind. Participants were recruited from six organizations (Father Peter Young's Housing, Industry, and Treatment Network [PYHIT]; the Fortune Society; Exodus Transitional Community [ETC]; the Women's Prison Association [WPA]; the Osborne Association; and the Center for Community Alternatives [CCA] – The Syracuse Recovery Community Service Program [SRCSP]) that provide a variety of services (e.g. counseling, drug/alcohol treatment, education, job training, and other employment services) to former prisoners who come to them voluntarily or due to parole and court mandates. Female former prisoners were oversampled for this project. Whereas women make up only 6.4 per cent of the adults released from prison in New York State in 2003, they make up 15 per cent of this sample.

This is a cross-sectional study and the method of data collection is a self-completed questionnaire using a paper and pencil format that was delivered to groups of former prisoners at each of the organizations. Data collection was completed between April and September, 2004. The questionnaire asked about a variety of topics concerning life as a formerly incarcerated person, including perceptions of stigma, social identity as a former prisoner, coping strategies, psychological well-being, demographics, and criminal history. The questionnaire primarily utilized a fixed-choice 'closed' format with response sets ranging from five to eight items. The majority of participants completed the questionnaire in 30 minutes or less.

Analytical method

Ordinary Least Squares (OLS) regression analysis is used to determine how well a set of variables explains the score on the advocacy/activism orientation scale. This OLS regression analysis provides information on the characteristics of formerly incarcerated persons that are most strongly related to the advocacy orientation. The mean substitution method is used to account for missing data, and following the suggestion of Cohen and colleagues (2003), a missing-data dummy variable is included in the OLS regression equation. The relationship between the advocacy/activism orientation and psychological well-being (self-esteem and satisfaction with life), criminal attitude, and the forecast of rearrest is examined using correlation analysis.

The fifteen independent variables and four variables measuring psychological outcomes and criminality are discussed in the section below and descriptive statistics are displayed in the results section. As the key construct in these analyses, special attention is given to describing the advocacy/activism orientation scale.

Measures

Advocacy/activism orientation
Louis and Taylor (1999) make a distinction between two types of collective action (or activism) behavior: leadership behaviors associated with organizing group members and instigating collective action, and supportive behaviors that involve joining an existing group and/or participating in collective action already organized by someone else. They argue that most studies of collective action have examined individuals engaged in leadership behaviors, whereas a larger percentage of disadvantaged

persons more strongly endorse group support actions (Louis and Taylor 1999). This study concentrates on group support actions instead of leadership behaviors in order to capture the greater proportion of formerly incarcerated persons interested or participating in advocacy/ activism related activities.

The advocacy/activism orientation indicates support for and/or involvement in activities to change the public's (negative) perception and treatment of prisoners and former prisoners. The three indicators have been worded in a general way so that recently released prisoners could have the possibility to either strongly agree or strongly disagree with each statement. The specific indicators include:

- I'm willing to be part of an organized effort to teach the public more about prisoners and former prisoners.

- I'm currently trying to change the way that prisoners and former prisoners are treated in society.

- I'm involved in activities designed to fight public misunderstanding about prisoners and former prisoners.

Higher scores on this scale indicate stronger endorsement of an advocacy orientation. This scale, as well as all to follow, was constructed by adding the scores together and dividing by the number of items in the scale (see Spector 1992, about the summative method).

Demographic characteristics
Demographic characteristics include age, gender, and race/ethnicity.

Social bonds
Education level is scored using three categories ranging from 0 (did not complete high school or earn a GED) to 2 (some college or more). Employment status has been dichotomized with 1 indicating employed full-time and 0 representing all others. Respondents were also asked about their relationship status, if they are single or have a significant other.

Remorse
Remorse is increasingly being linked to the desistance and recidivism process (see e.g. Braithwaite 1989; LeBel *et al.* 2008). To measure remorse, participants were asked to respond to the statement, 'I am sorry for the harm caused to others by my past criminal activities.'

Program-related item
A question determines if respondents attend the program voluntarily or as a requirement of community supervision.

Criminal history
The criminal history of participants was measured in several ways: number of felony convictions in lifetime, prison time served in lifetime (log transformed to account for positive skew), and current community supervision status. Each of these measures involves self-report.

Normalization
The geographic concentration of returning prisoners in the most socially and economically disadvantaged inner-city communities has recently become a topic of interest for prisoner reentry researchers (see e.g. Travis 2005). Three items (e.g. 'A kid growing up today in the neighborhood where I grew up will probably end up in prison some day') were combined to form a normalization scale where higher scores indicate that serving time in prison is seen as a likely occurrence and is not considered shameful in the neighborhood where the respondent grew up.

Group identification

Group identification represents the extent to which respondents identify or feel close ties with other formerly incarcerated persons. The three indicators in this scale are similar to items used by many researchers to measure group identification (see e.g. Ellemers *et al.* 1997). The specific items include: 'I have a number of things in common with other former prisoners'; 'I identify with other former prisoners'; and 'Former prisoners need to stick together'.

Stigma
Respondents were asked for their perceptions of what they believe 'people' think about all former prisoners in general. Items were modified from Link's (1987) devaluation-discrimination scale for persons with mental illness and Harvey's (2001) scale concerning stigma and race. In addition, several new items were developed (see LeBel 2006). The nine-item scale includes many of the stereotypes of formerly incarcerated persons (e.g. dangerous, dishonest, untrustworthy).

Unjust laws
Formerly incarcerated persons' attitudes and beliefs about how fair, just and legitimate they perceive the criminal justice system and laws to be were measured by their response to the statement, 'Unjust laws have put many people in prison'.

Psychological well-being
The psychological well-being of respondents is measured with the Rosenberg Self-Esteem Scale (Rosenberg 1965). In addition, a single question from Andrews and Withey (1976) was used to measure former

prisoners' 'global' well-being: 'How do you feel about your life as a whole?'

Criminal attitude and forecast of rearrest

Pro-criminal attitudes are measured with a scale of three items (e.g. 'To get ahead in the world you may have to do some things that are illegal'). Participants were also asked to predict or forecast the probability that they will recidivate (see e.g. Dhami *et al.* 2006): 'Realistically, how likely or unlikely is it that you will be arrested for a new crime in the next three years?'

Results

Descriptive statistics

Descriptive statistics are presented in Table 10.1. The sample of formerly incarcerated persons has a mean age of 36.14 years, is 85 per cent male, and is 58 per cent black, non-Latino. The modal response category for education is having a GED or high school diploma (44 per cent), while 19 per cent of the sample is employed full-time. Fifty-two per cent of the sample reported having a significant other of some sort. On average, participants have served 87 months in prison in their lifetime (median = 60 months) and have 2.18 felony convictions. Nearly half (46 per cent) of the participants reported voluntarily attending the reintegration program, while about one-third were not under any form of correctional supervision. Most participants agreed or strongly agreed (74 per cent) that they feel sorry for the harm caused to others by their past criminal activities, and many identified strongly with other former prisoners (M = 5.12). The means of the group stigma scale (4.68) and the normalization scale (4.29) are above the mid-point (neither agree nor disagree). More than two-thirds (69 per cent, M = 5.69) of participants agreed or strongly agreed that 'unjust laws have put many people in prison'.

The crime-related measures have relatively low means indicating that respondents reported that they were unlikely to get rearrested and disagreed that it is permissible to do something illegal to get ahead in the world. For the psychological well-being measures, self-esteem is quite high (M = 5.44), but satisfaction with life (M = 4.38) is closer to the mid-point of the scale (mixed feelings).

Advocacy/activism orientation scale

Table 10.2 displays means, standard deviations, factor loadings, and Cronbach's alpha for the advocacy/activism orientation scale. Higher scores indicate attitudes and behaviors that support this proactive orientation. The three indicators have means ranging from 4.08 for

Table 10.1 Descriptive statistics

Characteristic	Description	Mean	(SD)
Age	Years	36.14	(9.68)
Gender	0=female; 1=male	0.85	(0.36)
Black, non-Latino	0=all others; 1=Black, non-Latino	0.58	(0.49)
Partner	0=single; 1=have a significant other	0.52	(0.50)
Education level	0=did not earn GED or receive high school diploma; 1=GED or high school graduate; 2=some college or more	1.02	(0.75)
Employed full-time	0=not employed full-time; 1=employed full-time	0.19	(0.39)
Remorse	Sorry for harm caused to others by past criminal activities. 1=strongly disagree; 7=strongly agree	5.74	(1.70)
Voluntarily attend program	0=attend program as a requirement of supervision; 1=voluntarily attend program	0.46	(0.50)
Time served	Prison time served in months (log transformed)	4.13	(0.85)
Felony convictions	Number of felony convictions (lifetime)	2.18	(1.02)
Supervision status	0=on parole, work release, or probation; 1=not under correctional supervision	0.32	(0.47)
Normalization	Normalization of prison experience in the neighborhood where the respondent grew up. 1=strongly disagree; 7=strongly agree. 3-item scale. $\alpha=0.69$.	4.29	(1.50)
Group identification	The extent to which respondents identify with other former prisoners. 1=strongly disagree; 7=strongly agree. 3-item scale. $\alpha=0.55$.	5.12	(1.06)
Stigma (group)	Perceptions that formerly incarcerated persons are stigmatized. 1=strongly disagree; 7=strongly agree. 9-item scale. $\alpha=0.87$.	4.68	(1.11)
Unjust laws	Unjust laws have put many people in prison. 1=strongly disagree; 7=strongly agree.	5.69	(1.45)
Self-esteem	Rosenberg's Self-esteem Scale. 1=strongly disagree; 7=strongly agree. 10-item scale. $\alpha=0.78$.	5.44	(0.95)
Satisfaction with life	'How do you feel about your life as a whole?' 1=terrible; 7=delighted	4.38	(1.19)

Criminal attitude	Measure of pro-criminal attitudes. 1=strongly disagree; 7=strongly agree. 3-item scale. α=0.65.	2.66	(1.39)
Forecast of rearrest	Likelihood of rearrest for new crime in next 3 years. 1=very unlikely to be rearrested; 5=very likely to be rearrested.	2.08	(1.09)

Note: SD=standard deviation.

reported involvement in activities to fight public misunderstanding to 5.39 for willingness to be part of an organized effort to teach the public about prisoners and former prisoners. The scale mean is 4.76 (SD=1.31) with an alpha of 0.597. A principal component analysis shows that all three indicators load on a single factor that explains 55.50 per cent of the variance.

Explaining the advocacy/activism orientation

Table 10.3 displays the results for the OLS regression model predicting the advocacy/activism orientation. The table reports the unstandardized coefficients (metric slopes), standard errors, standardized coefficients (Betas) and statistical significance (at $p \leq 0.05$) for each of the independent variables. This analysis yielded a significant equation, $F_{(16, 228)}=4.950$, $p<0.001$, $R^2=0.272$, indicating that the set of predictors accounted for a substantial amount of the variance in the advocacy orientation scale. Table 10.3 shows that four of the independent variables predict this orientation.

Table 10.2 The advocacy orientation scale

Indicator	Mean (SD)	Factor loading
Willing to be part of organized effort to teach public	5.39 (1.67)	0.690
Currently trying to change the way treated in society	4.81 (1.67)	0.796
Involved in activities to fight public misunderstanding	4.08 (1.83)	0.745
Scale	4.76 (1.31)	
Eigenvalue		1.67
Total variance explained		55.50%
Alpha		.597

Note: N=229. Principal component factor analysis was used. SD=standard deviation. 1=strongly disagree, 7=strongly agree.

In this sample, formerly incarcerated persons most supportive and/or engaged in advocacy-related activities are older, black, non-Latino, identify more strongly with other prisoners and former prisoners, and reported voluntarily attending the reintegration program. A comparison of the standardized coefficients indicates that group identification (Beta = 0.233) has the largest impact on the advocacy orientation, while black, non-Latino (Beta = 0.195) has the next largest impact.

Table 10.3 Regression analysis results for the advocacy/activism orientation scale

Variable	B	SE B	Beta
Age	0.020*	(0.009)	0.149
Gender (male)	−0.300	(0.241)	−0.083
Black, non-Latino	0.513***	(0.158)	0.195
Partner	−0.242	(0.158)	−0.093
Education level	−0.095	(0.111)	−0.054
Employed full-time	−0.131	(0.206)	−0.040
Remorse	0.051	(0.047)	0.067
Voluntarily attend program	0.474**	(0.173)	0.178
Time served	0.005	(0.111)	0.003
Felony convictions	0.061	(0.088)	0.047
Supervision status (none)	0.089	(0.188)	0.031
Normalization	−0.049	(0.057)	−0.057
Group identification	0.285***	(0.082)	0.233
Stigma (group)	−0.051	(0.079)	−0.043
Unjust laws	0.097	(0.055)	0.108
Missing data dummy	0.440*	(0.221)	0.126
Constant	1.907**	(0.689)	
R^2	0.272		

Note: N = 229. Mean substitution is used for missing data. ***$p \leq 0.001$, **$p \leq 0.01$, *$p \leq 0.05$.

Table 10.4 Relationship between the advocacy/activism orientation and outcomes

Characteristic	Advocacy orientation scale
Criminal attitude	−0.159*
Forecast of rearrest	−0.155*
Satisfaction with life	0.155*
Self-esteem	0.105

Note: Correlations are shown (two-tailed). Pairwise deletion is used for missing data. N ranges from 221 to 226.
*$p \leq 0.05$.

Relationship between advocacy/activism orientation and psychological well-being, criminal attitude, and forecast of rearrest

In the next step, the relationship between the advocacy orientation and respondents' self-esteem, satisfaction with life, criminal attitude, and forecast of rearrest was examined. Table 10.4 displays the correlations (Pearson's r, two-tailed) and statistical significance (at $p \leq 0.05$) of each of the relationships. The results show that the advocacy orientation is negatively related to having a criminal attitude and thinking that one is more likely to be arrested in the next three years. Meanwhile, only one of the psychological well-being measures, satisfaction with life, is significantly positively related to having an advocacy orientation. In summary, the advocacy/activism orientation has a positive relationship with one of the psychological well-being measures and a negative relationship with both criminality measures.

Discussion

Formerly incarcerated persons advocacy/activism orientation has not been previously measured or analyzed in any systematic way. This study had three main objectives: to measure the advocacy/activism orientation in a sample of formerly incarcerated persons; to determine the factors that are most strongly related to the advocacy orientation; and to ascertain if the advocacy orientation is related to psychological well-being, criminal attitude, and the forecast of rearrest. A scale with three indicators was used to measure the advocacy/activism orientation. The mean for the scale was quite high (M=4.76), the internal consistency of the scale was adequate ($\alpha = 0.597$), and a principal component analysis indicated that all three indicators loaded on a single factor. Overall, the formerly incarcerated persons in this study appear quite willing to support and engage in advocacy/activism to change the public's negative views and treatment of former prisoners, and a smaller portion report already making efforts in this regard.

Nearly two-thirds of the sample (65 per cent) agreed or strongly agreed that they are willing to be part of an organized effort to educate the public about prisoners and former prisoners. A substantial number of respondents agreed or strongly agreed that they are currently trying to change the way prisoners and former prisoners are treated in society (42 per cent) or are involved in activities to fight public misunderstanding (30 per cent). Although only about one-third of the respondents indicated active involvement in advocacy-related activities, these findings suggest a desire to become involved in organized efforts to educate the public about issues confronting persons currently or formerly incarcerated. It is notable that many recently released prisoners currently engaged in prisoner reentry programming see themselves as advocates/activists. The endorsement of this sort of proactive strategy by formerly incarcerated persons indicates that they are active participants and not merely passive victims of the stigmatization process (see e.g. Anspach 1979; Kitsuse 1980; Sayce 2000 for a similar argument for other stigmatized groups). These findings also suggest that organizations engaged in advocacy-related activities to change the criminal justice system could successfully recruit many new members from the thousands of prisoners released each year.

The OLS regression analysis provides the first empirical evidence regarding explanations for formerly incarcerated persons' advocacy/activism orientation. Formerly incarcerated persons most supportive and/or involved in advocacy-related activities identify more strongly with other former prisoners, are black, non-Latino, voluntarily attend the reintegration program, and are older. Identification with other formerly incarcerated persons was found to have the strongest relationship with the proactive strategy of advocacy/activism. This finding supports the literature indicating that high group identifiers will be more supportive of advocacy and collective action (Ellemers *et al.* 1997; Simon *et al.* 1998; Wright and Tropp 2002). However, group identification, especially in the form of prisoner cohesion and unity, is often aggressively resisted by prison officials (Irwin 1980). The practice of separating and isolating prisoners continues after release as well. Petersilia (2003: 83) reports that 61 per cent of the States require 'no association with persons with criminal records' as a condition of parole supervision. Based on the findings that group identification is positively related to advocacy and the advocacy orientation is negatively related to criminality, corrections administrators should change these non-contact policies and consider the potential benefits of pro-social peer groups for released prisoners (see especially LeBel 2007).

Major *et al.* (2002: 308) posit that 'individuals who are highly identified with their stigmatized group may have a wider range of coping strategies available to them than those who are less identified'. The findings reported here support this assertion and indicate that our understanding of how formerly incarcerated persons cope with stigma in a proactive manner can benefit from examining their social identity as former prisoners and particularly how much they identify with their peers.

In this sample, black, non-Latino formerly incarcerated persons reported engaging more in advocacy than their white, non-Latino and Latino peers. This finding of support for and involvement in proactive coping strategies by African-Americans appears to be a direct response to racial disparities in prison populations throughout the United States (PEW Center on the States 2008; Sabol *et al.* 2007). Many advocacy organizations attempting to reform the criminal justice system specifically target race and ethnicity issues for change (e.g. Critical Resistance, the Center for NuLeadership on Urban Solutions, the Prison Moratorium Project). The finding of substantially higher levels of African-American involvement in advocacy-related activities highlights the need to examine formerly incarcerated persons' perceptions of simultaneous stigmas (e.g. due to their race/ethnicity, HIV/AIDS status, mental illness, etc.), and the impact that these perceptions may have on their social identities and use of coping strategies (see e.g. Corrigan *et al.* 2003; LeBel 2008). Perhaps it is the recognition of these additional types of perceived devaluation and discrimination that motivate formerly incarcerated persons to become engaged in advocacy.

Formerly incarcerated persons who are older supported advocacy/ activism more than their younger counterparts. It is possible that older respondents, through their more extensive experiences with the criminal justice system, more clearly see the need for active attempts to change the system. It is also possible that an advocacy orientation is developmental in some way and reflects the maturity of older individuals. Respondents who reported attending the program voluntarily also have higher scores on the advocacy/activism orientation scale. This finding suggests that formerly incarcerated persons might attend the program and possibly remain engaged with the organization because participation provides opportunities to become involved in some form of advocacy-related activity (see e.g. McAnany *et al.* 1974). Also, it is possible that an organization may promote or reinforce advocacy ideologies among participants in some of its programs.

The argument that coping by endorsing advocacy efforts will be related to respondents' belief that the criminal justice system and laws are unfair and unjust was not fully supported in this study. The perception that 'unjust laws have put many people in prison' was only a marginally significant predictor ($p = 0.078$) in the regression model explaining the advocacy orientation. This was unexpected as most (if not all) advocacy groups focusing on criminal justice issues target unfairness and injustice of some kind (see e.g. All of Us or None, the Fortune Society, McAnany *et al.* 1974).

The relationship between the advocacy orientation and psychological well-being and criminality was examined. The literature on activism and collective action among members of disadvantaged groups suggested that advocates would have higher levels of psychological well-being (Jones *et al.* 1984; Link *et al.* 2002; Wahl 1999). It was also postulated that advocacy among formerly incarcerated persons would be negatively related to criminality because much of this activity focuses on reducing barriers that make it difficult to succeed after release from prison. Each of these relationships was at least partially supported in this study as the advocacy/activism orientation was found to have statistically significant correlations with satisfaction with life, criminal attitude and the forecast of rearrest. Involvement in advocacy-related activities might improve recently released prisoners' satisfaction with life by giving their life purpose, meaning and significance (see e.g. Connett 1973; Gonnerman

2004). An advocacy orientation might act as a buffer against criminality as formerly incarcerated persons strive to remove barriers that make their own reintegration and that of other released prisoners more difficult. Consequently, the advocacy orientation is more strongly endorsed by persons who do not think it is permissible to break the law to get ahead and who think that the likelihood of their own rearrest is lower. Thus, these activists appear to be striving to reintegrate into society and lead a law-abiding life.

Conclusion

This study provides preliminary evidence of the benefits of formerly incarcerated persons support for and/or involvement in advocacy as a coping orientation. The advocacy orientation is related to formerly incarcerated persons' psychological well-being, and in particular their satisfaction with life as a whole. Moreover, the results indicate a basic incompatibility between an advocacy/activism orientation and criminal attitudes and behavior. These findings suggest that involvement in advocacy-related activities might have potential in facilitating the successful reintegration of some formerly incarcerated persons.

Collective action by groups of stigmatized persons to change laws and other social policies have been documented for persons with physical disabilities, gays/lesbians, persons with mental illness, persons with HIV/AIDS, and other disadvantaged groups (Anspach 1979; Kitsuse 1980; Van Tosh et al. 2000). These sorts of empowerment-oriented, proactive, and collective attempts to change public perceptions and create a more positive identity are increasingly being thought to be stigmatized persons' 'most effective and enduring route to reducing prejudice' (Major et al. 2000: 217; see also Herman 1993; Parker and Aggleton 2003; Sayce 2000; Shih 2004). A benefit of social activism over individualistic strategies such as concealment is that any improved treatment will spill over across a variety of situations and improve the lives of other similarly stigmatized persons (Goffman 1963; Major et al. 2000).

Today, formerly incarcerated persons are increasingly speaking out, giving back to help others (LeBel 2007), and becoming politically active. For example, in May 2008 nearly 100 formerly incarcerated persons traveled from New York City to the state capital (Albany) to lobby lawmakers to reform sentencing laws and to adopt legislation to protect their employment and voting rights (Virtanen 2008). The findings from this study suggest the potential for political organizing among recently released prisoners as many are supportive of advocacy/activism.

Nicole Cook, a graduate of *ReConnect* – the Women in Prison Project's advocacy and leadership training program for formerly incarcerated women, states that:

One thing I recognize as an advocate: people respect you more when they see you are not afraid to stand up for what you believe in . . . Now you have a chance to prove to yourself and to everyone else, that 'I made it – I was incarcerated, I felt worthless, hopeless, and all the other negative emotions you go through when in prison'. To transform into a person who speaks out and advocates for other women, that's awesome. (Correctional Association of New York 2008: 5)

Becoming involved in advocacy-related activities that contribute to pro-social changes may aid formerly incarcerated persons in shedding the negative connotations of the 'ex-convict' identity, while also giving their lives purpose and meaning. Therefore, becoming involved in advocacy appears to help transform formerly incarcerated persons from being part of 'the problem' into part of 'the solution' as they fight back to produce broad and fundamental policy changes in the criminal justice system to increase the likelihood that other soon-to-be released prisoners can 'make it' in a law-abiding way in society.

Moving forward, research is needed to develop better measures for the advocacy/activism orientation, to learn how and why formerly incarcerated persons become involved in advocacy-related activities, to study leaders of these advocacy organizations, and to document the development of this growing social movement.

Appendix: Advocacy groups involving formerly incarcerated persons

All of Us or None (*www.allofusornone.org*)
Center for NuLeadership on Urban Solutions (*www.mec.cuny.edu/spcd/caddi/nuleadership.asp*)
Convict Criminology (Ross and Richards 2003; see also *www.convictcriminology.org/*)
Correctional Association of New York – Women in Prison Project (*www.correctionalassociation.org/WIPP/*)
Critical Resistance (*www.criticalresistance.org*)
Fortune Society (*www.fortunesociety.org/*)
Prison Moratorium Project (*www.nomoreprisons.org*)
Women's Prison Association (WPA) (*www.wpaonline.org/*)

Acknowledgements

The author wishes to thank the executive directors and staff of the prisoner reintegration programs where this study was conducted: Father Peter Young's Housing, Industry, and Treatment Network (PYHIT); The Fortune Society; Exodus Transitional Community (ETC); The Women's Prison Association (WPA); The Osborne Association; and The Center for Community Alternatives (CCA) – The

Syracuse Recovery Community Service Program (SRCSP). Moreover, the author is particularly grateful to the formerly incarcerated men and women who participated in this study.

References

Anderson, E. (1999) *Code of the Street: Decency, Violence, and the Moral Life of the Inner City*. New York: W. W. Norton and Company.

Andrews, F. M. and Withey, S. B. (1976) *Social Indicators of Well-Being*. New York: Plenum.

Anspach, R. R. (1979) 'From stigma to identity politics: Political activism among the physically disabled and former mental patients', *Social Science and Medicine*, 13 (A): 765–73.

Braithwaite, J. (1989) *Crime, Shame, and Reintegration*. Cambridge, UK: Cambridge University Press.

Branscombe, N. R. and Ellemers, N. (1998) 'Coping with group-based discrimination: Individualistic versus group-level strategies', in J. K. Swim and C. Stangor (eds) *Prejudice: The Target's Perspective*. San Diego, CA: Academic.

Britt, L. and Heise, D. (2000) 'From shame to pride in identity politics', in S. Stryker, T. J. Owens and R. W. White (eds) *Self, Identity, and Social Movements*. Minneapolis, MN: University of Minnesota Press.

Cohen, J., Cohen, P., West, S. G. and Aiken, L. S. (2003) *Applied Multiple Regression/Correlation Analysis for the Behavioral Sciences*, 3rd edn. Mahwah, NJ: Lawrence Erlbaum Associates.

Connett, A. V. (1973) 'Epilogue', in R. J. Erickson, W. J. Crow, L. A. Zurcher and A. V. Connett (eds) *Paroled But Not Free*. New York: Behavioral Publications.

Correctional Association of New York (2008) 'An advocate's perspective: The Coalition for Women Prisoners 2008 Advocacy Day', *CA Bulletin*, Spring/Summer: 4–5.

Corrigan, P. and Watson, A. C. (2002) 'The paradox of self-stigma and mental illness', *Clinical Psychology: Science and Practice*, 9(1): 35–52.

Corrigan, P., Thompson, V., Lambert, D., Sangster, Y., Noel, J. G. and Campbell, J. (2003) 'Perceptions of discrimination among persons with serious mental illness', *Psychiatric Services*, 54(8): 1105–10.

Crocker, J., Major, B. and Steele, C. (1998) 'Social stigma', in D. T. Gilbert, S. T. Fiske and G. Lindzey (eds) *The Handbook of Social Psychology*, Vol. 2, 4th edn. New York: McGraw-Hill.

Deaux, K. and Ethier, K. A. (1998) 'Negotiating social identity', in J. K. Swim and C. Stangor (eds) *Prejudice: The Target's Perspective*. San Diego, CA: Academic Press.

Dhami, M. K., Mandel, D. R., Loewenstein, G. and Ayton, P. (2006) 'Prisoners' positive illusions of their post-release success', *Law and Human Behavior*, 30: 631–47.

Ellemers, N. (1993) 'The influence of socio-structural variables on identity enhancement strategies', in W. Stroebe and M. Hewstone (eds) *European Review of Social Psychology*. Vol. 4. Chichester, UK: Wiley.

Ellemers, N., Kortekass, P. and Ouwerkerk, J. W. (1999) 'Self-categorisation, commitment to the group and group self-esteem as related but distinct aspects of social identity', *European Journal of Social Psychology*, 29: 371–89.

Ellemers, N., Spears, R. and Doosje, B. (1997) 'Sticking together or falling apart: In-group identification as a psychological determinant of group commitment versus individual mobility', *Journal of Personality and Social Psychology*, 72(3): 617–26.

Garland, D. (2001) *The Culture of Control: Crime and Social Order in Contemporary Society*. Chicago: University of Chicago Press.

Gill, C. J. (1997) 'Four types of integration in disability identity development', *Journal of Vocational Rehabilitation*, 9: 39–46.

Goffman, E. (1963) *Stigma: Notes on the Management of Spoiled Identity*. Englewood Cliffs, NJ: Prentice-Hall.

Gonnerman, J. (2004) *Life on the Outside: The Prison Odyssey of Elaine Bartlett*. New York: Farrar, Straus and Giroux.

Hamm, M. S. (1997) 'The offender self-help movement as correctional treatment', in P. Van Voorhis, M. Braswell and D. Lester (eds) *Correctional Counseling and Rehabilitation*, 4th edn. Cincinnati, OH: Anderson Publishing.

Harvey, R. D. (2001) 'Individual differences in the phenomenological impact of social stigma', *Journal of Social Psychology*, 141(2): 174–89.

Herman, N. J. (1993) 'Return to sender: Reintegrative stigma-management strategies of ex-psychiatric patients', *Journal of Contemporary Ethnography*, 22(3): 295–330.

Irwin, J. (1980) *Prisons in Turmoil*. Boston: Little, Brown and Company.

Jones, E. E., Farina, A., Hastorf, A. H., Markus, H., Miller, D. T. and Scott, R. A. (1984) *Social Stigma: The Psychology of Marked Relationships*. Hillsdale, NJ: Erlbaum.

Kitsuse, J. I. (1980) 'Coming out all over: Deviants and the politics of social problems', *Social Problems*, 28(1): 1–13.

Lalonde, R. N. and Cameron, J. E. (1994) 'Behavioral responses to discrimination: A focus on action', in M. P. Zanna and J. M. Olson (eds) *The Psychology of Prejudice: The Ontario Symposium*, Vol. 7. Hillsdale, NJ: Erlbaum.

LeBel, T. P. (2006) *Invisible Stripes? Formerly Incarcerated Persons' Perceptions of and Responses to Stigma*. Unpublished dissertation, University at Albany, State University of New York. Dissertation Abstracts International, 67 (2-A), 731A. (UMI No. 0419–4209).

LeBel, T. P. (2007) 'An examination of the impact of formerly incarcerated persons helping others', *Journal of Offender Rehabilitation*, 46(1/2): 1–24.

LeBel, T. P. (2008) 'Perceptions of and responses to stigma', *Sociology Compass*, 2(2): 409–32. DOI: 10.1111/j.1751–9020.2007.00081.x

LeBel, T. P., Burnett, R., Maruna, S. and Bushway, S. (2008) 'The "chicken and egg" of subjective and social factors in desistance from crime', *European Journal of Criminology*, 5(2): 131–59.

Legal Action Center (2004) *After Prison: Roadblocks to Reentry: A Report on State Legal Barriers Facing People with Criminal Records*. New York: Legal Action Center. Available online at *www.lac.org/lac/index.php* [accessed 31 March 2008].

Link, B. G. (1987) 'Understanding labeling effects in the area of mental disorders: An assessment of the effects of expectations of rejection', *American Sociological Review*, 52: 96–112.

Link, B. G., Mirotznik, J. and Cullen, F. T. (1991) 'The effectiveness of stigma coping orientations: Can negative consequences of mental illness labeling be avoided?' *Journal of Health and Social Behavior*, 32: 302–20.

Link, B. G., Struening, E. L., Neese-Todd, S., Asmussen, S. and Phelan, J. C. (2002) 'On describing and seeking to change the experience of stigma', *Psychiatric Rehabilitation Skills*, 6(2): 201–31.

Louis, W. R. and Taylor, D. M. (1999) 'From passive acceptance to social disruption: Towards an understanding of behavioural responses to discrimination', *Canadian Journal of Behavioural Science*, 31(1): 19–28.

Major, B. (1994) 'From social inequality to personal entitlement: The role of social comparisons, legitimacy appraisals, and group membership', in M. P. Zanna (ed.) *Advances in Experimental Social Psychology*, Vol. 26. San Diego, CA: Academic Press.

Major, B., Quinton, W. J. and McCoy, S. K. (2002) 'Antecedents and consequences of attributions to discrimination: Theoretical and empirical advances', in M. P. Zanna (ed) *Advances in Experimental Social Psychology*. Boston, MA: Academic Press.

Major, B., Quinton, W. J., McCoy, S. K. and Schmader, T. (2000) 'Reducing prejudice: The target's perspective', in S. Oskamp (ed.) *Reducing Prejudice and Discrimination*. Mahwah, NJ: Lawrence Erlbaum.

Maruna, S. (2001) *Making Good: How Ex-convicts Reform and Rebuild their Lives.* Washington, DC: American Psychological Association.

Mauer, M. (1999) *Race to Incarcerate.* New York: New Press.

Mauer, M. and Chesney-Lind, M. (eds) (2002) *Invisible Punishment: The Collateral Consequences of Mass Imprisonment.* New York: The New Press.

McAnany, P. D., Tromanhauser, E. and Sullivan, D. (1974) *The Identification and Description of Ex-offender Groups in the Chicago Area.* Chicago, IL: University of Illinois Press.

Pager, D. (2007) *Marked: Race, Crime, and Finding Work in an Era of Mass Incarceration.* Chicago, IL: University of Chicago Press.

Parker, R. and Aggleton, P. (2003) 'HIV and AIDS-related stigma and discrimination: A conceptual framework and implications for action', *Social Science and Medicine*, 57: 13–24.

Petersilia, J. (2003) *When Prisoners Come Home: Parole and Prisoner Reentry.* New York: Oxford University Press.

Pew Center on the States (2008) *One in 100: Behind Bars in America 2008.* Washington, DC: The Pew Charitable Trusts.

Rogers, J. W. and Buffalo, M. D. (1974) 'Fighting back: Nine modes of adaptation to a deviant label', *Social Problems*, 22(1): 101–18.

Rosario, M., Hunter, J., Maguen, S., Gwadz, M. and Smith, R. (2001) 'The coming-out process and its adaptational and health-related associations among gay, lesbian, and bisexual youths: Stipulation and exploration of a model', *American Journal of Community Psychology*, 29: 113–60.

Rosenberg, M. (1965) *Society and the Adolescent Self-image.* Princeton, NJ: Princeton University Press.

Ross, J. I. and Richards, S. C. (2003) *Convict Criminology.* Belmont, CA: Wadsworth/Thomson Learning.

Sabol, W. J., Couture, H. and Harrison, P. M. (2007) *Prisoners in 2006* (NCJ 219416). Washington, DC: US Department of Justice, Bureau of Justice Statistics.

Sayce, L. (2000) *From Psychiatric Patient to Citizen: Overcoming Discrimination and Social Exclusion.* New York: St Martin's Press.

Shih, M. (2004) 'Positive stigma: Examining resilience and empowerment in overcoming stigma', *Annals of the American Academy of Political and Social Sciences*, 591: 175–85.

Siegel, K., Lune, H. and Meyer, I. H. (1998) 'Stigma management among gay/bisexual men with HIV/AIDS', *Qualitative Sociology*, 21(1): 3–23.

Simon, B., Loewy, M., Sturmer, S., Weber, U., Freytag, P., Habig, C., Kampmeier, C. and Spahlinger, P. (1998) 'Collective identification and social movement participation', *Journal of Personality and Social Psychology*, 74(3): 646–58.

Spector, P. E. (1992) *Summated Rating Scale Construction: An Introduction.* Newbury Park, CA: Sage.

Tajfel, H. and Turner, J. C. (1986) 'The social identity theory of intergroup behavior', in S. Worchel and W. G. Austin (eds) *Psychology of Intergroup Relations.* Chicago: Nelson-Hall, 7–24.

Tonry, M. (1995) *Malign Neglect: Race, Crime, and Punishment in America.* New York: Oxford University Press.

Travis, J. (2002) 'Invisible punishment: An instrument of social exclusion', in M. Mauer and M. Chesney-Lind (eds) *Invisible Punishment: The Collateral Consequences of Mass Imprisonment.* New York: New Press.

Travis, J. (2005) *But They All Come Back: Facing the Challenges of Prisoner Reentry.* Washington, DC: Urban Institute Press.

Uggen, C., Manza, J. and Thompson, M. (2006) 'Citizenship, democracy and the civic reintegration of criminal offenders', *Annals of the American Academy of Political and Social Sciences*, 605: 281–310.

Van Tosh, L., Ralph, R. O. and Campbell, J. (2000) 'The rise of consumerism', *Psychiatric Rehabilitation Skills*, 4(3): 383–409.

Virtanen, M. (2008). 'Ex-convicts join ranks of lobbyists in Albany', *The Albany Timesunion*, 20 May. Available online at: *www.timesunion.com* [accessed 22 May 2008].

Wahl, O. F. (1999) 'Mental health consumers' experience of stigma', *Schizophrenia Bulletin*, 25: 467–78.

Ward, G. K. and Marable, M. (2003) 'Toward a new civic leadership: the Africana Criminal Justice Project', *Social Justice*, 30(2): 89–97.

White, W. L. (2001) *The Rhetoric of Recovery Advocacy: An Essay on the Power of Language.* Available online at: *www.bhrm.org/advocacy/rhetoric.pdf* [accessed 25 March 2008].

Wright, S. C. and Tropp, L. R. (2002) 'Collective action in response to disadvantage: intergroup perceptions, social identification, and social change', in I. Walker and H. J. Smith (eds) *Relative Deprivation: Specification, Development, and Integration.* Cambridge, UK: Cambridge University Press.

Wynn, J. (2001) *Inside Rikers: Stories from the World's Largest Penal Colony.* New York: St Martin's Press.

Chapter 11

Lessons learned about offender change: implications for criminal justice policy

Russ Immarigeon

Abstract

Current approaches to policy and practice in the area of offender rehabilitation programs and prisoner reentry emphasize the need to deliver services that offenders will use upon release from prison. While these are crucial aspects of successful reentry, this volume emphasizes the connection between offender-centered mechanisms and their individual experiences with innovative change efforts. This combination of factors – the provision of the basic resources necessary to live in communities upon release from prison and the acquisition of the social supports and tools necessary for the identity shifts – presents a fuller picture of the identity transformation process. But, it is argued here, program interventions, however meritorious, are missing an important remedial beat when they avoid, or simply neglect, the location of social programs within the framework of criminal justice operations. In particular, the failure to contrast the relative merits of prison-based versus community-based programming augurs poorly for the maximum capacity of rehabilitation-oriented interventions.

Over the past 40 years, American criminology and criminal justice studies have produced a wealth of empirical findings and theoretical perspectives that aim to improve our understanding of criminal activities and official responses to them. Changing criminal behavior has always been at the forefront of most criminal justice sanctions. Throughout American history, prosecutors, judges, probation and parole officers, prison administrators, and even defense attorneys have attempted to affect 'criminal thinking', at least to the extent that imposed penalties were presumed to address the characteristics, causes, or consequences of criminality.

But criminal justice has long been in a sickly state, and efforts to transform criminal behavior have fared poorly over the years. Nowadays much hope and optimism is given to prospects for the implementation and outcomes of empirically tested programming. But while the 'What Works?' movement holds promise, the realities of everyday practice often gnaw at the possibilities of such hope and optimism.

In this context, it seems foolish, or at least short-sighted, to avoid the glaring light of historical experience. The archaeologist James C. Garman, writing about the contemporary importance of studying nineteenth-century institutions of social control, recently observed that, 'we have become a punitive society seeking retribution against criminals; the discourse of reform is now secondary to the discourse of retribution'. Furthermore, he suggested that we have seemingly abandoned critical reflection on the power of the institutions that enable or enact punishment. 'Unlike our Jacksonian forebears,' Garman noted, 'we rarely interrogate the idea of imprisonment as society's mechanism for punishing the deviant; we look instead for ways to make it cheaper, more efficient, and more effective in meetings its primary goal of separating criminals from society' (Garman 2005: 6–7).

There has been much reflection about criminal justice in recent decades, and a good share of this attention has been critical of existing practices. Witness, for example, the increasingly common use of such terms as 'mass imprisonment' and even the 'prison-industrial complex'. Widespread reference to 'restorative justice', I suggest, is also partially attributable not just to academic acumen, but also to practitioner and popular anxiety and dissatisfaction with the banality of 'law and order' rhetoric and practice. But still, much of what we read in criminology and criminal justice journals seems wedded to analysis that, inadvertently at least, makes official responses to crime, from imprisonment to community release, 'cheaper, more efficient, and more effective in meeting its primary goal of separating criminals from society'.

Undoubtedly, there is some advantage to this. In North Carolina recently, two college women were murdered, allegedly by persons who were on probation at the time of these crimes. The *News & Observer*, a statewide newspaper based in Raleigh, ran a three-part investigation series, which found over 150 other instances of homicides committed since 2000 by persons on probation. A key aspect of this investigation was that probation officials were making inadequate use of admittedly poor computer technology available to them for the purpose of tracking probationers who were subsequently arrested for serious or violent offenses. In this series, the *News & Observer*, supported by a technical assistance report prepared for the state by the National Institute of Corrections, argued for the use of more sophisticated and up-to-date computer-based offender tracking technology.

But the bureaucratic and technocratic orientation of much criminal justice and criminological research obscures much of what might be called 'the larger picture'. Most notably, at least in this brief response to the articles collected in this volume, we need to consider the broader policy framework of criminal justice interventions, whether they are called restorative justice or rehabilitative programming.

This chapter has three purposes: the first is to briefly report some of the collective, although not necessarily cohesive, findings and perspectives of the essays and studies contained in the chapters of this volume. The second is to stress particular emphasis on the policy and practice implications of these contributors. And third, this chapter places these findings and implications within a larger policy context and, in the process, suggests some recommendations that can be derived, one way or another, from the results of the reported research. Overall, it is hoped that this chapter hints at the evolution – and future – of this policy context, because it is difficult to understand the feasibility of these findings and implications without a comprehensive, historical understanding of the larger policy context within which the research was conducted.

The plight of prisoners and practitioners

British criminologist Mike Hough suggests the core of current dilemmas concerning the quality and impact of offender programming, including those that assist prisoners reentering local communities and society in general, stating:

> Our knowledge about the impact of programs has improved some-what, but our knowledge about other dimensions of work with offenders has advanced more slowly. There are still problems about offender assessment. We still know little about how best to integrate and sequence programs of work with offenders. Government attempts to reform the organizational structure of 'offender management' are in considerable disarray. (Hough 2008)

Some while ago I wrote that women's prisons are overused, meaning that too many women are sent to prison (or jail for that matter). They are unnecessarily, and wastefully, incarcerated when there are multiple non-incarcerative options that would more effectively improve the lives – and active citizenship – of not only the women, but also the women's victims and communities involved with the criminal justice system (Immarigeon and Chesney-Lind 1992). I also believe that the same holds for men's prisons. They are full of men who would be healthier and more productive if imprisoned for less time, or kept out of prison in the first place through reliance on various community resources. But, contemporary criminal justice and corrections practices face important institutional and ideological obstacles centering on the primacy of incarceration over community-based interventions.

Consider the following: in a recent North Carolina newspaper article, reporter Jennifer Fernandez wrote that women are a growing proportion of the state's overall prison population, which is also expanding, and that the program 'services' provided them in prison do not reflect their needs. 'Prison remains a man's world,' she reported. 'Men make up more than 90 per cent of the inmates incarcerated in North Carolina, and classes intended to rehabilitate prisoners reflect that' (Fernandez 2009).

In truth, state prisons (and probation and parole agencies) across the United States are making progress integrating 'gender-specific program-ming' into their operations. But gender-specific programming, at least so far in its development, tends to connote female-specific programming, with males, who also have gender-specific needs, being left out of this mix. And both men and women facing or serving prison time are too infrequently assessed in terms of the appropriateness of incarceration versus community-based options. In fact, the failure to identify, or address, 'unnecessary incarceration' affects the lives of prison practi-tioners as well as prisoners themselves.

In a video presentation that accompanies her article, Fernandez inter-views Bernice McPhatter, a 52-year-old black female prisoner, and Benita Witherspoon, the black superintendent at the North Piedmont Correc-tional Center in Lexington, North Carolina where McPhatter is confined. The remarks of these two women – a prisoner and a prison superintend-ent – are suggestive of similar components that should come into play whenever one considers the plight of prisoners (or prison superintendents for that matter). They also imply weaknesses in the arguments that provide imprisonment its foundation as an acceptable societal response to criminal or illegal activity.

McPhatter, who appears apprehensive, cautious about saying some-thing 'wrong', or at least not officially sanctioned, sets things up:

> I guess if I could start out, I guess I want to make it clear that the purpose of this interview for me is to show how prison has changed me. So, I'm in here because I made a bad choice. I made a decision that was in violation of the state of North Carolina's laws. I'm here being rehabilitated from some choices that I made when I was on the outside. Unfortunately, it cost me five years away from my family, but in lieu of all that, who I am today I would not have been if I had not had this journey. Being 52 years old, 47 when I was sentenced, I had never been in trouble in my life before, I was actually a model citizen. For one to be sentenced to prison was a complete shock for me because I thought that the worst case scenario would be probation, but when that didn't happen for me, it didn't destroy who I was. I took this opportunity to focus on me.

Superintendent Witherspoon, sitting behind her desk, speaks about prison offender programming from an administrator's perspective:

> We make sure [prisoners] participate in these programs to address the problems for which they are incarcerated, whether it's alcohol or substance abuse or lack of education. I think women have different issues. I think we can improve all the way around and, you know, I'm one to say that people should be treated equally. But women have a different set of problems, different health concerns, different family concerns, from men. I think more effort should be focused on women's issues in the North Carolina Department of Corrections. Although [incarcerated women] are here, they're still mothers and sometimes one questions why you are concerned about your child now when you were committing the acts, the crimes, when you had the chance to be with your family. What we've noticed, once they are incarcerated, is that they have the time to sit down and think about the repercussions of their actions on others. It provides them outlets for them to do for others. We just concentrate on making women the best they can be, no matter if they are incarcerated or not.

Later, McPhatter, the prisoner, adds: 'I'm just looking forward to going back home. You know, every once in a while I get a little nervous. I realize the big test will come when I walk out the door. I'm certain that the remainder of my life will be spent giving back to people. I'm certain that I'll be more than I ever could have been accused of taking' (Fernandez 2009).

But apparent reforms such as gender-specific programming, as well as the constricted organizational context of program managers and participants, leave practitioners and prisoners alike in 'knots', as the British psychiatrist R. D. Laing once put it, where neither party is in full control of either their environmental setting or actions within their environment.

Policy context

In the 1970s, many advocates of prison reform, and more than a few correctional administrators or policy-makers, turned their attention from improving the quality of penal confinement to establishing 'alternatives to incarceration', community-based options that would keep those persons convicted of crimes out of prison while providing them with, or at least directing them towards, community-based programs to assist them in combating alcohol and drug abuse, economic instability, educational deficiencies, health or mental health issues, and other relevant social problems. Subsequently, emerging 'law and order' campaigns started to flood American jails and prisons with non-violent as well as violent offenders, many of whom were involved with either drug use or drug trafficking. In this context, prison overcrowding (or merely prison crowding as some called it) shifted criminal justice or corrections officials' attention from the front end of the criminal justice system, where alternatives to incarceration could serve preventive as well as diversionary purposes, to the back end of the system, where the construction of new, and more, jails or prisons seemed the only immediate solution.

Over the last three decades of the twentieth century, and now the first decade of the twenty-first century, incarcerated populations rose and rose and rose. They continue to rise, although there are geographical or jurisdictional spots where population decreases are occurring for one reason or another. Still, despite the prominence of a prison-industrial complex that has emerged over this period of time, with the heightened attention given to such matters as mandatory sentencing, 'three-strikes-and-you're-out' legislation, the threatened demise of probation and parole, and public–private partnerships, offender rehabilitation (or simply rehabilitation) remains significantly important. Other reform initiatives, especially those that are said to challenge mainstream practices, have not fared so well. Despite the many contributions of academic scholars and day-to-day activists and practitioners over the course of this time, restorative justice, for instance, is still a relatively marginal concept (for example, the main four purposes routinely given to the topic of criminal justice intervention are still old steadfast standards, namely incapacitation, rehabilitation, deterrence, and retribution).

Writing early in the year 2009, it is easy enough to acknowledge a range of criminal justice events or issues that establish a policy context for evaluating offender-oriented programming (and other interventions). At this point in time, the economy is endangered. Banks are faltering, employment levels are falling, people are fearful, and governments are scraping along, hoping one short, sharp fix or another will settle things down. Prisons, as they have been for many decades now, are often full or overcrowded, although it is important to note that this is not true for some states. In New York, for example, the prison population has fallen in recent years. However, a state governmental proposal to close some 'underutilized' juvenile and adult facilities has kicked up a maelstrom of local opposition. Opposition to prison closings has also occurred in Illinois and elsewhere. Still, pressed by a weakened economy, states (most recently New Hampshire) continue to freely propose prison closures, largely for the purpose of 'saving money'. Still, according to the opposition, closing prisons is shortsighted because it terminates good paying jobs that are scarce in the current economy. The opposition has also raised the specter of fewer local services provided through 'inmate' labor. In response, governments, not just in New York but also elsewhere, have backed off, keeping these facilities going, failing in the process to consider or develop alternative economic or criminal justice options.

193

Since the articles in this volume cover initiatives occurring in local communities as well as in various correctional facilities, I focus my attention on the interplay, or the tension between, community- and institution-based 'treatment' programs. In particular, I direct my observations of how the relative size of prison populations has been addressed and what our alternatives are for more effective interventions. More specifically, I argue from the perspective that we already incarcerate too many people and, on that basis alone, reductions in prison populations, and indeed prison closings, are justifiable, not only in terms of fiscal responsibility, but also because of social justice concerns.

Prisoners and the formerly incarcerated

A strong aspect of this collection is that nearly all of the contributors result from qualitative research conducted with either prisoners or formerly incarcerated persons (see in this volume Maruna *et al.*; Veysey *et al.*; Martinez; Presser and Kurth; Hughes; Owen; Morash; Harris; LeBel). Harris 2009; LeBel 2009. Christian *et al.* and Maruna *et al.* (Chapters 2 and 3) integrate prisoner or formerly incarcerated perspectives into their analytical and descriptive essays. The number of prisoners or formerly incarcerated persons involved with these qualitative studies ranges from one to 229; Owen (Chapter 7) also conducted fieldwork at a therapeutic community, where she interacted with women participating in a treatment program.

Overall, the research reported in this volume results from face-to-face interviews, focus group conversations, written statements, survey-derived data sets, and ethnographic observation. Among the various findings of this research are the following:

- Some form of external, third-party affirmation, or 'certification', might be necessary for offenders to 'maintain the difficult process of "recovery" and desistance' (Maruna *et al.*).

- One-size-fits-all interventions are illusionary; 'moments of transformation' appear in opposing forms – short-term change occurs when 'concrete action' follows altered perceptions and long-term change occurs when 'external events and factors [result] in the shedding of the stigmatized label' (Christian *et al.*).

- Offenders can suggest or set goals for responsible behavior for themselves (sobriety, for example), but this is only one step in a longer process, which must be strengthened through 'institutional and structural supports' (Owen).

- Advocacy-oriented activities transform restrictive 'convict' or 'ex-convict' identities from 'part of the problem' to 'part of the solution' (LeBel).

- Intervention may succeed at some levels of 'rehabilitation', crime reduction for example, but not at others, including substance abuse (Morash).

- Identity change is not simply a matter of 'insider' (offender) change, but also a matter of 'outsider' (staff, agency, institution) change (Hughes).

Through this focus on prisoner (ex-offender) perspectives and voices, chapters in this volume help transform the identity and character of criminological research, a shift that has been a long time coming.

Program implications

'Healing is a human process,' Christian *et al.* observe in Chapter 2. 'Treatment, on the other hand, seeks to identify the "problem" and fix it.'

Four of the contributions in this collection emerge from research conducted at particular program sites. Harris interviewed members of the Public Safety Initiative of LIFERS, Inc at the State Correctional Institution at Graterford, Pennsylvania; Martinez collected data for an evaluation he conducted at the Illinois Going Home Program at the Illinois Department of Corrections Westside Adult Transition Center in Chicago; Maruna *et al.* conducted focus group and one-on-one interviews with participants in an ex-prisoner oriented program, Father Young's Housing Industry and Treatment, outside of Albany, New York; and Owen observed and gathered data at a Phoenix House-like therapeutic community in California. Yet all of the articles, even the research of Presser and Kurth, whose chapter is based on one inmate's life, have sufficient basis for suggesting program implications.

Presser and Kurth challenge cognitive-behavioral programs that simply stress changing offender or prisoner thinking patterns. They argue that negative or 'bad' thinking may have positive purpose. They urge 'a rather thorough reconceptualization of resistance not as pathological, but rather as a show of strength, and defiance not as obstacle, but as an indicator of the will to independence'. Furthermore, they note that prisoners may not want to accept subjugation, even if it's presented as a barrier to change. 'To help ex-offenders with identity transformation,' they say, 'we must begin with *their* preferred identity, not those we prefer for them' (Presser and Kurth, emphasis in original).

Resistance to change arises elsewhere in this collection. In Owen's ethnographic study of a women's therapeutic community, she observes, 'While some women resist this process, others experience epiphanies and "see the light" about the possibilities of changing identity and, ultimately, changing their lives.'

Harris also addresses offender resistance to change, but states that change is possible, even among those persons least expected to change.

Harris' research focuses on a group of prisoners whose lives are, or ought to be, of significant concern not only to criminologists and students of personal and societal change, but also to public officials and citizens in general. Her study involves in-depth exploration of how and why men who report having been deeply immersed in a culture of crime and violence came to reject those values and now strive to live as upstanding citizens who also devote themselves to eradicating the beliefs that draw and retain others in the culture they now reject. Confined in a maximum-security prison, almost all serving life or other long-term sentences, these men may serve as a focal point for legislation and other policies focused on protecting the public from 'the worst of the worst'.

Yet Harris finds that these individuals have undergone – or more properly – have undertaken, dramatic changes for the better. So as 'bad men gone good', as she notes, they not only challenge conventional wisdom and common stereotypes, but also provide rich grist for the public policy mill.

In this context, LeBel's survey of over 200 participants in rehabilitation programs in New York City and upstate New York is notable because he finds that advocacy – for public policy as well as for program options – helps ex-prisoners adjust to community life upon reentry from prison. LeBel sees advocacy as a 'coping orientation', which brings benefits for communities and individuals. According to LeBel,

> Becoming involved in advocacy-oriented activities that contribute to pro-social changes may aid formerly incarcerated persons in shedding the negative connotations of the 'ex-convict' identity, while also giving their lives purpose and meaning. Therefore, becoming involved in advocacy appears to help transform formerly incarcerated persons from being part 'of the problem' into part 'of the solution' as they fight back to produce broad and fundamental changes in the criminal justice system to increase the likelihood that other soon-to-be released prisoners can 'make it' in a law-abiding way in society.

The role of ex-prisoners, or the formerly incarcerated, in public policy is an oft-neglected topic, and the inclusion of these perspectives about and concerning the formerly incarcerated is valuable. In March 2009, the Women's Prison Association's Institute on Women and Criminal Justice released a website-based report that profiles new organizations that feature advocacy efforts in seven states that are initiated, mobilized and/or managed by women who are, or have been, involved with the criminal justice system. According to the report, these groups are instrumental in identifying solutions as well as problems, bridging the gap between communities inside or outside of prison, speaking out on issues, supporting new leaders and developing leadership skills, and taking multiple routes to change (Villanueva *et al.* 2009)

Recommendations

For two years running, the Pew Center for the States has issued reports that identify three major problems – rising rates of incarceration, racial and gender disparities in the use of incarceration, and inequities in state spending on institution- and community-based corrections – that have confronted criminal justice and corrections practitioners and policy-makers for at least the past three decades (Pew Center on the States 2008, 2009).

In February 2008, the Pew Center on the States' Public Safety Performance Project reported, with widespread media coverage, that more than one in every 100 adults in the United States was in jail or prison and that this level of incarceration was seriously affecting state-level budgets without clear evidence of any significant return in terms of Americans' public safety. Moreover, the report found that this trend has disarming consequences for particular groups of Americans,

> While one in 30 men between the ages of 20 and 34 is behind bars, for black males in that age group the figure is one in nine. Gender adds another dimension to the picture. Men still are roughly 10 times more likely to be in jail or prison, but the female population is burgeoning at a far brisker pace. For black women in their mid- to late-30s, the incarceration rate also has hit the 1-in-100 mark. (Pew Center on the States 2008: 3)

A year later, in March 2009, the Pew Center on the States issued another highly publicized report stating that the United States now supervises 1.6 million more men and women through community corrections than it did a quarter of a century ago. In 2009, the report observed, one in 45 American adults is under community-based supervision. Moreover, a significant disparity in state funding exists between institution- and community-based corrections. According to the Pew Center's report:

> Probation and parole, the dominant community corrections programs, have had larger population growth than prisons, but far smaller budget growth. Looking at a handful of states that were able to provide long-term spending figures, eight times as many new dollars went to prisons as went to probation and parole. And while fewer than one out of three offenders is behind bars, almost nine out of 10 corrections dollars are spent on prisons. (Pew Center on the States 2009: 1)

The sheer size and expense of the American penal empire stifles the development of offender-oriented programming that is sufficient in terms of its quality of care and its impact on offenders, offenders' families, and offenders' communities. Moreover, the cost of incarceration consistently constricts the ability of states to provide for an adequate extent and range of programming necessary and useful for offenders who want to break their criminal patterns and for jurisdictions that want to become more reliant on community-based interventions.

The contributions in this volume suggest many policy changes that affect the nature and extent of offender programming, the quality and internal dynamics of such programming, and the larger context within which this programming reflects. However, three general recommendations seem paramount in terms of moving public policy discussions (and actions) about offender programming forward.

No more prisons

In the 1970s and 1980s, arguments for a moratorium on prison construction were complicated by the fact that conditions at many facilities were poor to dismal. The often unconstitutional conditions at many American jails or prisons were not simply the result of increased population pressures, or overcrowding. They reflected old architecture, poorly trained staff, and shoddy management, among other factors. In significant part, the legal challenges to the correctional conditions of this period, which were frequently driven by the American Civil Liberties Union's National Prison Project or other reform-oriented litigators, were eventually (partially) responsible for the enhanced professionalization of corrections. More 'pro-prison' groups such as the American Corrections Association and the American Jail Association also played an important role. So, over the past 40 years, prisons have been built with blinding speed, and a significant lobby, from those wanting to profit from new construction as well as those who wanted to improve the practice and management of prisons, has emerged to support continued development of prison facilities across the country. More than ever, the United States provides evidence of a 'prison-industrial complex'.

The original impetus for a 'prison moratorium' was fiscally conservative in nature. At one point in the 1960s, I was told while working at the National Council on Crime and Delinquency (NCCD), the federal prison system was starting to expand, and one mid-western legislator was concerned about the cost of this. In particular, he worried about the growth of such federal expenditures, which he felt should be kept to a minimum. In this context, he argued that new prisons should not be built unless there was evidence not only that were more 'needed', but also that all had been done, through other means, to forestall the need for such facilities. In short, he was asking whether all had been done to keep offenders out of prison and, if not, then we needed to do what we could do to keep offenders out of (the more expensive option of) prison before starting construction.

The 'prison moratorium' position was later placed in the body of an important federal report, and, later still, the NCCD and the Unitarian Universalist Service Committee (UUSC) established a national lobby group, the National Moratorium on Prison Construction (NMPC), to advocate for it. However, this effort was more successful at increasing public awareness than in affecting practice to reflect the caution projected through the original moratorium ideal. As a consequence, the United States now not only has a vastly expanded, and embedded, prison bureaucracy and infrastructure, but also has more than two million prisoners (a prison count that keeps rising).

More programs

In recent years, officials have started to recognize the flood of former prisoners returning to their communities. One result has been new and recent initiatives, including some of the research in this volume, on offender reentry. But while a focus on reentry has its inherent validity, reentry is not the only piece of the larger puzzle, especially when focusing on population pressures (and their expenses). Pre-trial and sentencing practices are as important as the reentry and release functions of the criminal justice system. Moreover, the fiscal folly of contemporary corrections is not just that too much money is spent on prisons, but also that, as research has shown, prisons are less effective (and probably more harmful) than non-incarcerative alternatives.

So, while criminologists and criminal justice researchers study both institution- and community-based programs, it is infrequent that we read of researchers assessing programs in terms of their settings. Moreover, we rarely see efforts to compare the relative merits (and demerits too) of these settings. More documentary, or case study, evidence is needed about the seemingly dysfunctional dominance of jails and prisons over community-based programming. If nothing else, how is it that funds are so frequently given over to one, rather than to the other?

A central problem is this: prison programming is more likely than community-based programming, but prison programming receives less attention than prison security. In each of these settings, the programming that exists tends to result as an afterthought, or as a luxury item. As a result, much needs to change, starting with the ability of prison managers to call for and push for programming. A small but important example: a decade or so ago, Michael Hennessey, who oversees the San Francisco County Jail, established himself as a leader who welcomed and nurtured staff who wanted to promote and develop innovative programming. In this environment, jail staff actually came up with ideas for programs. Moreover, these programs were often remarkable, if only because of the issues they tackled, either in the community or in prisons. In the 1980s, Hennessey hired a woman, Sunny Schwartz, to develop programs. One program she started was Resolve to Stop Violence Project (RSVP), which housed violent offenders in one dormitory (as opposed to distributing them throughout the facility). Violent men lived together, and met in groups together. Various outside speakers, including victim advocates, were brought in to share their perspectives, and inmates were given the time and space to talk among themselves (Schwartz and Boodell 2009). The importance of such rare efforts is that they manifest the ability of correctional staff to 'make a difference', although this is not likely to happen without the support of correctional leadership. As time goes by, researchers can helpfully conduct evaluations of innovative programs, or traditional programs for that matter, that guide correctional – and community-based – programs toward better practices. But useful research findings (the foundation of much 'What Works?' rhetoric) do not appear in a vacuum; indeed, program practices have to come first, even if they are guided by principles of effective correctional practice.

More community

Criminal identities and criminal thinking come out of communities, whether through local employment opportunities (or the lack thereof), or familial relationships, or drug distribution networks and the lack of treatment services, or poor schools. And criminal behavior continues in communities, especially when the necessary 'institutional and structural supports' that encourage or enable law-abiding behavior are missing. One of the disadvantages of relying on incarceration in response to crime is that it masks, or diverts attention from, the places where crime occurs. These places, and the issues that often fester within them, are often ignored, and consequently the conditions that 'cause' crime are left unattended. The neglect of communities does not make for safer communities. Accordingly, official attention, and discretion, must be directed toward improving communities, not just offenders, or even the victims of crime.

Martinez concludes the following:

Former prisoners do have risks, but focusing merely on decreasing those risks leaves a vacuum as to what actually should be done – such as using their skills to complete tasks, reinforcing positive cognitive shifts in their identity, and maneuvering through institutional and programmatic obstacles. If family members and others accept former prisoners' gestures of and requests for support, the exchange can lead to former prisoners pursuing transformative paths. If, however, the importance of these acts is minimized, as it so often is, former prisoners get the message that they are expected to pursue other avenues (such as getting a job or going to school), which do not, in and of themselves, alter the desire to engage in criminal pursuits.

Moreover, he adds that:

social workers and criminal justice practitioners can encourage family members to focus on former prisoners' strengths. In particular, when working with individuals released from prison, clinicians and criminal justice practitioners must focus on both former prisoners and family members in the treatment context. The idea that released prisoners should be the primary focus of interventions leads treatment providers, criminal justice agencies, and policy advocates down the wrong road because it excludes individuals who can contribute significantly to the transformation of former prisoners. Further, interventions should focus on what the families and former prisoners can offer, and build on the particular strengths of their relationships.

Community and governmental leaders should create opportunities to forge innovative agencies and interventions that can build on Martinez's insights. As Carol Shapiro (2009) suggests:

Existing workforces can implement a wealth of strength-based, family-focused strategies to achieve greater family well-being. For example, imagine a prison or jail that does not charge families triple or quadruple rates for collect phone calls to a loved one. In a system truly committed to assisting families and maintaining healthy relationships, we could provide inmates and their families with phone cards to help them stay connected instead of charging exorbitant amounts for collect calls. We could facilitate more frequent visitation by extending hours, providing transportation to distant institutions, hosting special events for families, and making the process of entering correctional institutions more welcoming and less humiliating. (Shapiro 2009: 300)

Imagine, too, what could be done if agencies and communities rallied resources of information, finances and staff, and programs to the task of building on the strengths and resources of communities and families.

Conclusion

Joan Petersilia recently observed:

Few graduate schools urge the same attention to the implications of one's research as to the research itself. This training gap manifests itself most in articles we publish, which typically include a small paragraph called 'policy implications' at the end of a frightfully long and detailed research article. Research matters, but we must help the policy maker answer why they should care about our conclusions, and if they do care, what they should do about them. It cannot be assumed that the policy maker will 'see' how interesting and useful the research actually is. The analyst must do that work for decision makers. (Petersilia 2008: 347)

In this chapter I have reported some of the empirical findings, theoretical insights, and program implications or policy recommendations suggested by the contributors to this volume. But I have argued, also, that criminologists and criminal justice researchers are too often too narrowly focused in the scope of their recommendations. I agree with Petersilia that criminologists and criminal justice researchers must do more not only to bring their research to the attention of policy-makers, but also to inform policy-makers in a manner that enables them to cogently understand the research and its implications. I also agree with her that criminologists and criminal justice researchers must 'do that work for decision makers'. That said, however, 'that work' is itself an often neglected topic of research and inquiry. Indeed, researchers would do well to examine the feasibility of integrating their empirical work with the efforts of citizen or reform groups pressuring legislators and others for policy change. Researchers, too, would do well, nationally for sure, but also on state-by-state levels, to align themselves with one another, especially since it is still uncommon to see criminologists or criminal justice practitioners addressing aspects of criminal justice policy, such as prison construction, expanding correc-tional budgets, sentencing practices, and even program development.

Petersilia's experience as an embedded criminologist in the California Department of Corrections and Rehabilitation is an important body of work. Paul Rock, the eminent British criminologist, has also produced significant, and sizeable, case studies of criminal justice agencies and initiatives in England (see Rock 2004 as one example). By and large, however, detailed and insightful observation and analysis of criminal justice policy-making and development is woefully neglected not only as a matter of graduate school or professional training in criminology and criminal justice, but also as a topic for dissertation or post-dissertation studies. Criminal justice agencies, too, inadequately reflect upon their own history, context, and prospective future.

Regardless of whether such work is undertaken in the future, it will be valuable to consider the implications of research findings for the growth, operations and comparative utility of institution-based versus commu-nity-based corrections. Prison growth, it seems easy and reasonable enough to suggest, is likely to continue, especially without a robust program of research-related work that explicitly informs policy-makers what can be done in terms of offender programming not only in prison, but also instead of prison. In this context, the contributions in this volume are undoubtedly helpful.

References

Fernandez, J. (2009) 'Women prisoners struggle in a man's world', *News & Record*. Available online at: *www.news-record.com/content/2009/02/14/article/women_prisoners_struggle_in_a_mans_world*.

Garman, J. C. (2005) *Detention Castles of Stone and Steel: Landscape, Labor, and the Urban Penitentiary*. Knoxville, TN: University of Tennessee Press.

Hough, M. (2008) *Reducing Reoffending: Getting off the Treadmill*, unpublished paper prepared for the National Audit Office. Available online at *www.kcl.ac.uk/depsta/law/research/icpr/publications/reducing_reoffending_final.pdf*.

Immarigeon, R. and Chesney-Lind, M. (1992) *Women's Prisons: Overcrowded and Overused*. San Francisco, CA: National Council on Crime and Delinquency.

Petersilia, J. (2008) 'Influencing public policy: An embedded criminologist reflects on California prison reform', *Journal of Experimental Criminology*, 4(4): 335–56.

Pew Center on the States (2008) *One in 100: Behind Bars in America 2008*. Washington, DC: The Pew Charitable Trusts.

Pew Center on the States (2009) *One in 31: The Long Reach of America Corrections*. Washington, DC: The Pew Charitable Trusts.

Rock, P. (2004) *Constructing Victims' Rights: The Home Office, New Labor, and Victims*. New York, NY: Oxford University Press.

Shapiro, C. (2009) 'Turning our attention to families: A natural resource for improving reentry outcomes', in E. R. Rhine and D. Evans (eds) *Research into Practice: Bridging the Gap in Community Corrections*. Lanham, MD: American Corrections Association.

Schwartz, S. and Boodell, D. (2009) *Dreams from the Monster Factory: A Tale of Prison, Redemption and One Woman's Fight to Restore Justice for All*. New York, NY: Scribner.

Villanueva, C., Nixon, C. and Pearson, B. (2009) *Women's Voices: Advocacy by Criminal Justice-Involved Women*. New York, NY: Women's Prison Association Institute on Women and Criminal Justice. Available online at *www.wpaonline*.

Index

age
  in accounts of change and resistance
    among women prisoners study
    106
  in advocacy/activism and
    reintegration of formerly
    incarcerated persons study 173,
    175, 176t, 178, 178t, 180, 181
  in moments of transformation study
    17, 17t, 18, 21t
agency
  and desistance from crime 84, 146
  in LIFERS, Inc. transformation model
    and identity change study 148,
    158, 159
  in parole supervision, change in self,
    and desistance from substance
    abuse study 135
  and resistance 73, 84–5
  see also autonomy; empowerment
aggression, in negotiating ex-convict
    identity with multiple
    co-conversationalists study 83
alcohol abuse 32, 35–6, 124, 125
  see also parole supervision, change in
    self, and desistance from
    substance abuse study
Alcoholics Anonymous (AA) 41, 125, 131
Alex, in prisoner education, learning
    identities and possibilities for
    change study 89
Ali, in prisoner education, learning
    identities and possibilities for
    change study 98
All of Us or None 167, 181, 183
alternative roles, and identity
    transformation 4
Anderson, E. 169
Andie, in accounts of change and
    resistance among women
    prisoners study 116
Anspach, R. R. 166, 167, 180, 182
anti-education attitudes 95–6, 97, 101
antisocial logic 147
Antwan, in LIFERS, Inc. transformation
    model and identity change study
    149
Arnold and family member support
    exchanges 61, 63–4
Arrigo, B. A. 75
attitudes

in advocacy/activism and
    reintegration of formerly
    incarcerated persons study 172,
    178t, 179, 182
in looking-glass identity
    transformation study 44, 45
in prisoner education, learning
    identities and possibilities for
    change study 95–6, 97, 101
August, in LIFERS, Inc. transformation
    model and identity change study
    156
autonomy 79, 81, 84
  see also agency; empowerment

bad self 76, 80–4
Barrie, in parole supervision, change in
    self, and desistance from
    substance abuse study 136
Barry, M. 159
Bazemore, G. 50
behavior see behavioral change; criminal
    behavior; negative behavior;
    non-criminal behavior;
    non-deviant behavior; pro-social
    norms and behaviors
behavioral change
  and desistance from crime concept 30
  in LIFERS, Inc. transformation model
    and identity change study 147,
    148, 149–50, 152, 154
  in therapeutic community (TC) 107–8,
    109, 110, 116–17, 118, 119, 120
Benita, in negotiating ex-convict identity
    with multiple co-
    conversationalists study 79–80
Berg, B. 105
Bernburg, J. G. 33
Bertrand, J. 105
beyond drug use, in parole supervision,
    change in self, and desistance
    from substance abuse study 128t,
    129, 130–4, 135
Bill, in prisoner education, learning
    identities and possibilities for
    change study 92–3
Bishop, in LIFERS, Inc. transformation
    model and identity change study
    149
black, non-Latino former prisoners 178,
    178t, 180